# Strategic Change

**Books in the series**

*Cross-cultural Management*
Terence Jackson

*Marketing Strategy*
Dale Littler and Dominic Wilson

*New Thinking in Organizational Behaviour*
Haridimos Tsoukas

*Strategic Change*
Colin A. Carnall

*Strategic Information Management*
R. D. Galliers and B. S. H. Baker

*Strategic Issues in Finance*
Keith Ward

# Strategic Change

Edited by Colin A. Carnall

Butterworth-Heinemann
Linacre House, Jordan Hill, Oxford OX2 8DP
A division of Reed Educational and Professional Publishing Ltd

ᴿ  A member of the Reed Elsevier plc group

OXFORD   BOSTON   JOHANNESBURG
MELBOURNE   NEW DELHI   SINGAPORE

First published 1997

**British Library Cataloguing in Publication Data**
A catalogue record for this book is
available from the British Library

ISBN 0 7506 1932 5

Typeset by RefineCatch Limited, Bungay, Suffolk
Printed in Great Britain by Biddles Ltd, Guildford and King's Lynn

# Contents

# Part One
# Managing Strategic Change

My first encounter with business schools was as a MBA course member who had entered the programme having worked as a professional engineer in the mechanical engineering industry. This was in 1971. I remember two things vividly. The organization behaviour course was very stimulating. I had seen that attempts to achieve significant change often ran into vested interests, whether of the management or of trade unions. The teaching reinforced this by focusing upon 'resistance to change' as *the* key aspect of change. I remember wondering why this would be so, given the emphasis given elsewhere in the teaching of motivation.

In the sessions on motivation we were taught the following:

● money does not motivate;
● at best money is a hygiene factor – i.e. satisfying people in financial terms does not positively motivate them;
● people are motivated by the scope of their jobs and by the discretion, challenge and autonomy within their work.

Frankly I suspected that the idea that money did not motivate was unrealistic (to be polite) but I was much more intrigued by the other ideas. If people were motivated by job challenge, discretion, autonomy, etc., why did they not welcome change? Surely change was likely to create the very conditions which they were supposed to find motivating?

Many offered an easy answer. Change was being driven by new technology. New technology destroyed jobs and, some said, diminished many of the jobs which remained. At the time some commentators obviously felt that there was a finite amount of work to do. If technology destroyed jobs then either there would be fewer jobs around or working weeks would need to be reduced, the retirement age reduced and other innovations such as job shares would be needed.

Without suggesting that the economic problems of the modern world had been 'solved' and taking account of the point that the structure of employment had changed dramatically (e.g. more part-time work for example) even a cursory glance at employment statistics in the western world suggests that much of this 'lump of work' or 'finite limits of work' argument is nonsense. Throughout the 1980s more people have entered employment despite the fact that technology and other changes have increased productivity, often quite quickly. Again I recall being impressed by talk of 3–4 per cent p.a. improvements in productivity in the 1960s. Now 6–8 per cent p.a. can be commonplace, particularly when recession or competition stimulates corporate restructuring. Moreover in case after case, improvements of 50 per cent or more are commonplace now. And yet this is not the only change since 1971. The power of 'vested' interests is now by no means as strong. Whether you believe that this is due to Thatcherism or to long-term social and economic changes is unimportant. It is nevertheless the case that collectivist ideas have given way to a focus on the individual. Indeed the moral challenge we now face is whether 'possessive' individualism is to be the order of the day (Macpherson, 1962).

Thus various changes have gone forward across much of the world. In particular public sector organizations have been privatized. Market mechanisms have been introduced. Large organizations have been broken up. Others have been 'flattened'. Decentralization has created corporate structures focused on 'strategic business units'. People talk about 'networked' organizations, 'federal' organizations and empowerment.

It is obvious that all of this has placed greater demands on the capabilities of managers. But these changes have also transformed the nature of what some call the 'psychological contract between the employing organization and the employee'. If 'jobs for life' cannot be guaranteed, then people have to apply for their 'own' jobs on re-organization, where flattened structures mean empowerment for some but redundancy for others. Where organizations use early retirement or voluntary retirement as an essential part of policy and where some organizations emphasize the benefits to the organization and the employee of subcontracting – maintaining a stable core of permanent employees and a periphery of subcontractors – they are reflecting a significant change.

Once upon a time managers and professionals and for that matter, other employees, particularly skilled employees, expected to stay in one career path and one organization throughout their careers. Now, people *expect* careers to include periods in more than one organization and expect to have more than one career in a working life.

It would defy common sense to suggest that social changes of this extent would have no impact on the nature of the relationship between employer and employee. One depiction of this change was published in the *Harvard Business Review* Global Management Survey, 1990. Every ten years HBR surveys chief executives throughout the developed world. Roughly 6500 CEOs responded in 1990. In Figure 1 we reproduce

|  | Well educated | Creative | Ambitious | Loyalty |
|---|---|---|---|---|
| Senior Managers |  |  |  |  |
| 1980 | 36 | 23 | 25 | 49 |
| 1990 | 66 | 48 | 58 | 37 |
| Others |  |  |  |  |
| 1980 | 22 | 18 | 16 | 48 |
| 1990 | 52 | 37 | 37 | 32 |

**Figure 1.** Global management survey. *Source: Harvard Business Review*, July–August, 1991

the results for one question in which CEOs were asked to describe managers, either senior or 'all others'.

From the figure we can see that chief executives at least view managers as better educated, more creative, more ambitious but less loyal. Indeed the survey suggests that this is true in each of the countries surveyed, even in Japan, although the relative position, particularly on loyalty, is different. I have discussed this figure with hundreds of management audiences throughout Europe. All agree that the change is real. All suggest that this change is a consequence of various social, economic and technological changes. But all also emphasize that loyalty is a two-way process and that organizations demonstrate less loyalty to their managers mainly as a consequence of de-layering and other major changes which have led to the 'redundant executive' capturing as much if not more of our attention than the redundant unskilled or semi-skilled worker.

All of this suggests that the statement so often articulated 'the most important resource of this business is its people' is increasingly meaningful not merely as rhetoric but also in practice. If we depend more and more on fewer people and if the loyalty of those people, particularly managers, can no longer be assumed, but rather must be earned and retained then clearly we need to be concerned about how we utilize them, develop them and resource them and about the opportunities for rewards, promotion and success which we provide. If changes depend upon the people who implement them then one must be concerned to ensure that those people possess the necessary skills. If those same people are motivated by challenge and opportunity then we must provide that as well. But if the latter will only follow if changes are successful then the introduction of changes which our people view as being credible, as likely to succeed, becomes a paramount issue.

Does this not then mean that the task of developing, implementing and managing major strategic changes becomes a key management challenge of the modern world? Some say that it must begin with the articulation of strategic vision. You need to be able to conceive of what the organization might become in three or five years' time. To do this managers must combine analysis and intuition, knowing and doing, thinking and feeling. Visualizing strategic change is not merely a matter of analysis, it requires the ability to think about, to conceptualize the future, the willingness to experiment and learn, to see what might happen, to estimate how the organization might respond, and much more.

But all of this relates to individual behaviour which will take place in teams, whether boards of directors, management teams, working parties or whatever. Thus we need a range of inputs into the discussion and debate on strategy if we are to understand the social, political, economic and technological friends with which we must deal; and so we need many inputs perhaps both from inside and outside the organization. However, if we are to bring these people together effectively then we must adopt managerial styles conducive to learning, to development, to creating and to articulating/communicating vision. In part it demands that we understand the processes of innovation, adaptation and change – what hinders change at individual, group, unit and corporate level and what can be done about these 'blockages'. Processes such as these are often referred to under the rubric 'culture change'.

Here we simply wish to make the point that successful strategic change seems to demand a combination of cognitive/analytical skills and knowledge alongside a range of behavioural or process skills and knowledge. In Figure 2 we set out a 'map' of the cognitive/analytical components which appear to be needed. Here we suggest that successful strategic change requires knowledge and techniques for corporate diagnosis, in the culture change area and in putting together programmes of change. All of this is not enough however without the necessary process skills needed to encourage learning and change.

In a world in which the ability to change is a key 'engine of success' the shift from strategy into capability demands leadership, action planning, the ability to cope with pressure and uncertainty and a willingness to learn. More analysis will help us in that it aids our understanding of where we are and how we came to get there – but analysis alone will not create the future.

Van der Erve reaches the same conclusion from a different starting point. In Chapter 1, he sets out to discuss culture only to conclude that culture is difficult to define and cannot be managed but must be understood as a dynamic process which can be destructive. Culture and change interconnect. No organization has a single culture. Organizations themselves operate within changing and diverse cultural conpartexts: out of complexity and a continual struggle between autonomy and control emerge new forms of organization as functional hierarchies evolved into multi-divisional structures, to matrix organizations, federal organizations and so on. These are not accidental shifts but new solutions to new challenges in the corporate environment. Are we now seeing the emergence of the 'virtual company' – the organization which trades on knowledge and which must therefore find ways of emitting knowledge bases and people (as inter-mediaries and interconnectors of knowledge to problems). In turn this argues the need to move from fragmentation to integration; from organizing ourselves into product structures towards presenting an integrated service to the customer. This requires power bases to be challenged and focuses attention away from the current organizational structure and toward the value chain.

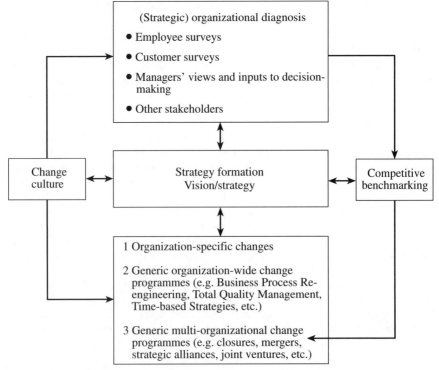

**Figure 2.** Strategic change

Chapter 2 is from Peter Senge's book *The Fifth Discipline*. In a powerful section on how to achieve the 'learning organization' he talks about 'shared vision'. The import-ance of the extract for me lies in two thoughts. The first is that we need shared vision to achieve change and shared vision emerges from personal vision. The second is that building shared vision is hard work. It is often unglamorous work because it demands endless talk with people throughout the organizations. As Senge argues, what we need in order to make progress is commitment. Clearly we want more than apathy or compli-ance. As Senge makes clear, we need something more than enrolment (a commitment contingent on other factors, i.e. I want to see that change in place but not if I have to run risks as part of its implementation).

Finally Chapter 3 by Hinterhuber and Popp focuses upon the individual manager. Are you a manager or a strategist is the question they pose. Winston Churchill was once heard to define great men not in terms of what they achieved in their life-time but more in terms of the impact their achievements have on successive generations. The chapter examines what it is that makes a strategist out of a manager. For them, and following the great Prussian General Moltke (the elder), there are two characteristics of the superior strategist, as follows:

- the ability to understand the significance of events without being influenced by current opinion, changing attitudes, or prejudices;
- the ability to make decisions quickly and to take the indicated action without being deterred by a perceived danger.

But do these characteristics distinguish good managers from superior strategists (or the truly 'great' or influential leaders)? In order to explore this question they offer a profile of strategic management competences – some of which are personal, some of which are organizational (e.g. Is the corporate culture in harmony with the strategies?). However, these authors argue the key importance of the individual behaviour of top management in creating the organizational conditions to which they refer. Ultimately the reading does not offer a means of clearly differentiating the strategist but they do raise some stimulating questions for us. In a more detailed report of the research on which the chapter is based they argue:

'At the end of the day, you can tell a strategist this way:
- What sort of vision he had at the beginning of each phase of his career or life;
- How he kept modifying his guiding ideas to suit changing conditions;
- The extent to which, and conditions under which, he put these ideas into action or had others do so.'

More importantly perhaps, they are people who put ideas into action.

## References

Macpherson, C. (1962) *The Political Theory of Possessive Individualism*, Clarendon Press, Oxford.

# 1 Evolution management

*M. Van der Erve*

## Achievement: through impulse or potential?

If managers cannot 'manage' culture, what *can* they do? If they are too dominant, they'll destroy the self-organizing capability of a social structure. If too
distant, they'll become its outcast observers.

## The force of direction

Colin Sharman, chairman of the management consultancy practices of the
KPMG federation in Europe, successfully turned around the culture of the
KPMG practice in the United Kingdom. Colin refers to project 2020 Vision
which he introduced in the United Kingdom inspired by Stanley Davis (1991).
When discussing the matter in more detail, it became apparent that the
replacement of an established functional structure with one which is more
client focused is what really did it. Colin Sharman led the development of a
new organizational purpose and eventually reincarnated the organization and
its culture with the establishment of customer focused units.

When Peter Weijland – a young head of research in the laboratories of the
PTT Telecom in the Netherlands – joined the company, he was thirty-two
years old, had a doctorate in mathematics and philosophy and a few years of
experience as president of a small research concern. In his new job, he faced an
established research department with highly educated scientists, often much
older than himself, who had been with the company for years. As incoming
manager, Peter first talked with all the people in his organization. Then, he
thoroughly prepared a week-long session in which he got all his people together
to establish a new mission. The resulting mission was strictly adhered to when
new organizational groups had to be formed in support of new research projects. In hindsight, Peter Weijland recognizes that one particular action was
pivotal during this process. He was forced to break up a recognized, and successful group in his organization because its existence did not support the
agreed mission. As result, the evolution of his organization as a whole is continuing because its culture was prevented from becoming inelastic by an

imbalanced influence from within. Rather than maintain and institutionalize an existing group as the main reference for potential success he chose to regroup. This caused the diffusion of people and their ideas while keeping the door open to new mutations.

When the disintegration of an organization seems imminent, managers can effectively produce an impulse – with the objective to reincarnate the culture – by 'spinning off' some of its elements. If its new CEO, Louis Gerstner, allows it to happen, IBM will choose for an evolutionary approach to cut costs in a structural way. In 1993, rather than closing four European plants and terminate approximately 4800 people, IBM plans to spin off each plant as an independent unit. The plants will be given a free hand to sell their products and expertise either within IBM or outside. Before the transition takes place, they will be given time to identify their own business purpose – their customers, products, services, competencies, capabilities, and skills. Restructuring for the sake of restructuring does not lead to performance improvements (Jack, 1991). By facilitating the update and agreement of the purpose of an organization, managers create an impulse which influences the evolution of their organization and, consequently, its culture. Such an impulse is complete, however, only when new subcultures, i.e. groups, are carved out and dedicated to supporting the overall purpose. In this process it is important that each of these groups is allowed to develop self-organizing characteristics. Klimecki and Probst (1992) conclude that to an observer 'culture works out to be a development process which leads to a normative model of order by the interplay of its elements.'

What organizations achieve is partly the result of management impulses and partly dependent on the intrinsic potential of the culture as a whole. The force which managers exert on culture as a process is a function of the characteristics of culture as a self-organizing phenomenon. Consequently, the 'force of direction' – as a series of impulses which produce new groups and subcultures – is a function of autonomy, interdependence (as equivalent of complexity; see the coming section), self-reference, and redundancy.

Force = F (autonomy, interdependence, self-reference, redundancy)

The characteristics of self-organizing systems are key process parameters in the evolution of culture. They represent the basic degrees of freedom or the initial conditions by which managers determine, negotiate, and reach agreement when developing an organization as a profit or non-profit concern.

## Parameters of cultural evolution

As creation catalysts, managers walk on the fine line between the interests of the overall culture and the cultures of the contributing elements. As Gurcharan

Das observes in his *Local Memoirs of a Global Manager* (1993): 'managers nourish each blade of grass but don't neglect the garden'. Cultures as conglomerates of subcultures are less homogeneous as we would expect them to be. Helmers (1991) refers to the views of Kathleen Gregory, who pictures organizations as 'multiple, cross-cutting cultural contexts changing through time, rather than as stable, bounded, homogeneous cultures'. This view comes close to the bootstrap philosophy of David Bohm and Geoffrey Chew. Diversity within a cultural texture is a requirement for long-term survival. It makes the spontaneous development of mutations more likely. On the other hand, cultures should not be too diverse within. Certain coherences or resonance situations are required to ensure the evolution of the overall culture toward more complex forms. Emphasis on the whole rather than its elements associates with the dynamic balance between autonomy and interdependence. This dynamic balance turns out to be a challenge for managers across our society. In his book *Head to Head*, the renowned economist Lester Thurow (1992) concludes:

> In the intense competitive atmosphere that will exist in the twenty-first century, all of the participants should remind themselves daily that they play in a competitive-cooperative game, not just a competitive game. Everyone wants to win, but cooperation is also necessary if the game is to be played at all.

In other words, in a purely competitive mode, 'autonomy' is overemphasized while cooperation requires that the 'interdependence' between companies is recognized. Interdependence or complexity is an essential characteristic of self-organizing systems. Probst and Lorange (1987) define complexity as: 'the nature of the relatedness between parts when putting together a highly interrelated network. It is the dynamics that grow with the interrelations and interactions that create complexity'. By simulating the evolution of earth's life forms on a computer, the biologist Thomas Ray demonstrated that only ecosystems – with creatures that were truly interdependent – can evolve. People and their views of order have grown from a tribal perspective to that of a city state, region, country, empire, and eventually the world, symbolized by the United Nations Organization. This may seem overambitious given the existing conflict on earth, but progress along the axis of interdependence is inevitable. Companies, too, have evolved from a regional to a national, multinational, and global scope. Possibly because of the inherent drive of self-organizing systems to create internal redundancy, the interdependence between elements in a culture extends to the interrelatedness with other cultures. In his essay *Organization Theory in the Postmodern Era* (1992), Kenneth Gergen concludes:

> For as organizations join with their surrounding cultures for purposes of mutual empowerment, and the circle of interdependence is ever widened, we may become aware of the world as a total system.

A broadening interdependence may accompany with the need for more autonomy. In *Rethinking Organization* (1992), Robert Cooper reminds us that the interdependence between colonies required relatively autonomous governing bodies. Great distances from the mother country made autonomy necessary to maintain the interdependences within the colonial web. Similarly, spacecraft sent out to distant planets need to be able to operate autonomously. Millions of miles make it impossible for an earth-based tracking station to detect and react fast enough. Conversely, when organizations devolve decision-making to decentralized units (making them more autonomous), measures are required to consolidate and control the results of the whole to maintain the interdependence between the units.

The groping relationship between autonomy and interdependence within the business world causes new organizational forms to emerge. Hierarchies evolve into matrix and project organizations where people, representing various departments, functions, and businesses, work together within a corporate framework. Matrix organizations evolve into network organizations which 'connect' people – with distinct capabilities and backgrounds – for a certain business purpose. The virtual company – also referred to as the relationship-enterprise – represents yet another wave in the evolution of organizations; the dynamic networking of people is expanded to the dynamic networking of companies. In evolution, each wave results in a more complex self-organizing whole which requires new and more refined ways of establishing autonomy and interdependence. The state of the art in technology plays an important role in the evolution of organizational life forms.

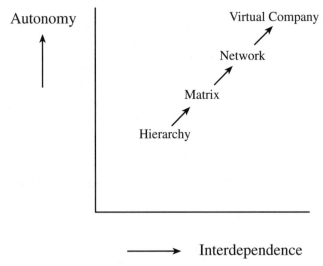

**Figure 1.** Toward self-organizing social structures or webs

Computer, telecommunication, and software advancements improve the way people 'connect' thus enabling their autonomous behavior as a whole. On the other hand, these advancements make it possible to improve the grip on the performance of the whole by controlling the interdependence between the organizational elements. Robert Cooper (1992), based on Zuboff's work, concludes:

> Information technology encapsulates a general function of all formal organization: the need to make transparent what is opaque, to make present what is remote, and to manipulate what is resistant. It is not just a question of information or symbolization but of technologies which enable us to represent information and symbols in a convenient form.

But technology in itself is not enough. The increasing complexity of a more dynamic world also requires improved, more refined self-referencing processes with new procedures, languages, and models.

## Values: cause or consequence?

Values do not easily change and if they do it may take years for any change to permeate a social structure (Hofstede, 1980). But, do we have to wait for a generation or more, perhaps, to see the values in societies and companies change? Does it make sense even to try changing the values? Values, however, are not only the overarching criteria which eventually determine our actions. They are also the overarching *consequences* of our visions, of our actions, and, therefore, of the rules we set. For example, when the environment and the rules of the game change, the interactions between the elements in the culture system may cause the reappearance of *latent* values which start to influence what we do and how we do it. An example: in many countries, civilians would face imprisonment when they kill the criminal who has assaulted their family. After all, 'thou shalt not kill'. The day war breaks out, however, civilians who kill the attacking enemy are seen as saviors. Apparently, values shift and may even 'flip-flop' when 'the unseen meaning between the lines in the rulebook' have truly changed. In light of the above, the following account of my experience in Digital Equipment reveals that:

- Value shifts show the contours of two *extreme* stages in the evolution of social structures, those of *fragmentation* and *integration*.
- Value shifts are company specific and do not necessarily apply to the entire industry.
- When the necessary change of values is slowed down by the inertia of an organization, corporate reincarnation is the means to survival.

## From craftsmanship to process

In 1988, between Christmas and New Year, I sat down to summarize my conclusions based on my first year at Digital's European headquarters.

After years of overwhelming success and revenue growth, Digital seemed to be stuck in a dead-end. Its fragmented structure was in the way of a badly needed integration of operational processes. In the fifties, Digital began as a company of engineers making electronic components. Not until it put these components together and turned them into the first minicomputer did Digital become a rising star. Its engineering capability, fostered by Kenneth Olsen, in the role of founder and president of the company, focused on the development of product after product to satisfy an endlessly growing demand. The increasing amount of product shipments in turn led to the development of a formidable manufacturing capability which established its power in a growing empire. At the same time, with the expanding population of computers in the field, the need for after-sales services grew dramatically. The success of the services organization became increasingly more dependent on its capability to move computer parts around the world. In 1987, the European logistics organization for computer parts was expanded to incorporate the entire customer order processing activity including the administration of both product orders and service contracts. The new administration and logistics division became a potent powerhouse consisting of literally thousands of employees across Europe. The objectives of this merger were to streamline the logistics processes by cutting out redundancies, improving operational efficiencies, and consolidating unnecessarily dispersed, geographical units. The achievement of these goals would also help Digital to improve the quality of its logistics and administration services to its customers. The inevitable trend in technology was one of the key factors which had fuelled the decision to reorganize. Technological progress made workstations and personal computers become more powerful at increasingly lower prices. Consequently, year after year more units had to be shipped just to make the same revenue as the year before. For Digital and others in the industry, the technological rules of the game were being reset. Computers changed from capital equipment into 'commodities' forcing the operations of sales, logistics, manufacturing, and engineering to keep up with the trend – often in a panic mode.

The relationship between the new logistics organization and manufacturing became a critical focus point when management realized that business processes could only be redesigned effectively if the design covered the entire supply chain, that is from suppliers to customers. This task – which would cut deeply into the historically established processes of both logistics and manufacturing – could only be done if the top managers of both camps and their people were totally and truly committed. For over a year, meetings and workshops were organized between representatives from every level in the respective organizations to get the process of operational clean-up and integration going. Managers seemed willing to cooperate. However, the potential loss of power and the pressures from the 'home base' caused managers to distort the logical and process oriented objectives.

The blueprints of Digital's organization were essentially focused on the supply of capital equipment and did not foresee in a high volume product-flow capability. Although the trends in technology were recognized, Digital failed to accept them. This caused the underlying organizational principles to remain unchanged. 'Institutions', such as sales, logistics, manufacturing, and engineering – already working in a relatively independent mode – became even more internally focused when they had to grapple with the inevitable operational challenges of a changing business. The impact of product managers – within Digital's matrix organization – was negligible. Product managers were only indirectly responsible for the activities of contributing functions and could not effectively mobilize for support. In the rush to generate revenue, the coherence between organizational elements further diminished. As 'societies of craftsmen' functions and subfunctions resembled the guilds in the European middle ages which had been organized essentially to protect their own interests. The developing fragmentation blossomed in spite of Digital's strong sense of culture.

On first sight, the unifying aspects of Digital's culture seemed to be in conflict with the fragmentation I observed. Later on, I realized that Digital's dominant, and rigid culture actually encouraged the dogmatic, and self-centered behavior of the various functions and subfunctions. The cornerstone of my conclusions was the necessary shift in values which Digital would experience should it decide to improve its competitiveness in the current business arena. Alternatively, Digital had the option to change its business. The values had to shift from craftsmanship to process or, in other words, from fragmentation to integration. In Figure 2 the necessary transitions of values and norms for Digital move from left to right. Although my conclusions incorporated a comprehensive set of recommendations, techniques, and communication material, the 'value shift' is what caught the eye of Pier-Carlo Falotti – president of Digital in Europe at that time. Pier-Carlo used the value shift as keynote in speeches to customers, employees, the European management board, and the board of directors at corporate headquarters. On December 5, 1991 – three years after the conception of the value shift – he sent me an electronic mail message to confirm that he had finally achieved corporate acceptance, 'I just wanted you to know that your transition from fragmentation to integration will

| *Fragmentation* ⟷ | *Integration* |
|---|---|
| My goal, your goal | Our goal, your contribution |
| Distinct organizational borders | Distinct organizational links |
| Functional performance | Cross-functional performance |
| More visions, one culture | One vision, more cultures |
| Management by control | Management by resolution |
| Functional management | Process management |
| Functional pride and identity | Process identity |
| Skills framework | Process framework |
| Hierarchical structures | Goal-driven networks |
| Reward for functional success | Reward for process success |
| Measure all the time | Measure to resolve or improve |
| Measure activity performance | Guaranteed activity performance |
| Connect by reporting | Connect by design |
| Policies and procedures | Process standardization |
| *Craftsmanship* ⟷ | *Process* |

**Figure 2.** Balancing between fragmentation and integration

be used as a key tool in training and development at corporate level'. As I shall explain at several stages in this book, Pier-Carlo Falotti's thoughtful message was not to be interpreted as 'mission completed'.

## The value shift from fragmentation to integration

The value shift – from fragmentation to integration – is a culmination of insight after 5 years with Digital and one year at its European headquarters. Value trends, like these, have not passed unnoticed. Many companies – including Digital's rival IBM – are facing similar challenges although not all as explicit. Experts in the field of management and corporate engineering have come to similar conclusions. Two partners at McKinsey & Company, Jon Katzenbach and Douglas Smith (1993), redeveloped the team concept and formulated a similar shift in values and norms when they compared 'working groups' with 'teams'. The craze of business re-engineering (Lorenz, 1993), based on the work of Michael Hammer and James Champy, also 'involves transforming an organization from one based on separate functions (or specialist departments) to one based on the processes which span most or all of these activities and disciplines'. These trends are spurred by the growing sophistication of computer systems (Cooper, 1992) which allows companies 'to make transparent what is opaque, to make present what is remote, and to manipulate what is resistant'.

The 'transitions' in Figure 2 seemed like 'overarching criteria which eventually determine our actions' (Etzioni, 1988). This is why they were considered to be transitions of 'values'.

The following summaries explain in more detail the envisaged value transitions *for Digital* at the time. The value transitions differ sometimes only in a subtle way; the objective was to create a sense of atmosphere, so people would get the idea and start to relate to it.

*My goal, your goal – Our goal, your contribution.* Functions were used to commit to their functional goals and leave it at that. In principle, this is not bad but it lacks something. Each function, in an extreme situation, could blame the other for not having achieved its goal sometimes to hide its own short-coming. The achievement of the overall goal in this hassle would be at risk. The idea here is to agree on a common goal and then to explore what each function might have to contribute. The focus, thereby, is shifted away from functional goals toward the achievement of the common goal.

*Distinct organizational borders – Distinct organizational links.* In extreme situations, functions were eager to pinpoint where their territory starts and where the other one's ends. This situation can cause unnecessary territorial wars. The idea here is to focus on 'linking' while discouraging 'borders'.

*Functional performance – Cross-functional performance.* The overall performance of a process may be at risk when one link in the chain under- or even over-performs. The idea here is to broaden the view of management across contributing organizations to the performance of the whole. This is to ensure that contributors evaluate how their over- or under-performance may affect the overall performance.

*More visions, one culture – One vision, more cultures.* A rigid, introvert culture eventually fosters dogmatic and introvert thinking in functions and subfunctions. As a result, functions may develop their own interpretation of the corporate vision which could replace the official one especially when the latter is not clearly defined. The idea here is to create a new, and unifying vision for the corporation which identifies the corporation's goals, what it really wants to be, and which freedoms it desires. A strong corporate vision would open the mind's eye for other cultures, for example, those of customers, suppliers, and business partners. In fact, other cultures may think of new and better ways to accomplish the corporate vision.

*Management by control – Management by resolution.* In extreme situations, managers become the outcast observers of the organizations they 'manage', until, that is, something goes wrong. Then, they change into tyrants who deny the self-organizing characteristics of their organization. The idea is to turn managers into facilitators who continuously seek to resolve structural problems through the adjustment of the business architecture while utilizing the self-organizing capabilities within their organization.

*Functional management – Process management.* The idea here is to replace functional management with competency management. Competency managers should ensure that corporate competencies become and remain a leading edge. Business managers, as process managers, should focus on the integration of competencies in support of overall process goals.

*Functional pride and identity – Process identity.* The 'we-they' mentality in functional organizations often hinders even the most basic forms of collaboration. The idea here was to strip off the 'they' from the 'we-they' mentality.

*Skills framework – Process framework.* In functions, as in guilds, skills can be used to build up and maintain power. The idea is not to deny the necessity of skills but to emphasize the importance of the interactions between skills. In an increasingly more dynamic world, most of the work requires the fruitful interaction between various skills.

*Hierarchical structures – Goal-driven networks.* A matrix organization – for which Digital was renowned – does not prevent the build-up of hierarchical 'institutions'. The idea here is to remind people that organizations are created to achieve corporate goals and not for the purpose of sustaining their own existence. People should ideally be 'networked' into self-organizing wholes to achieve certain well-defined goals.

*Reward for functional success – Reward for process success.* In order to create the right sort of behavior, rewards be based less on functional performance. Almost intuitively, people should base their sense of success on the degree to which their efforts have contributed to the success of the overall process.

*Measure all the time – Measure to resolve or improve.* Measurements are a necessary evil. Companies, such as Wal-Mart, have shown that they can speed up processes, reduce cost, and prevent stock-outs in their stores while minimizing the number of measurements. The idea is to instill the thought that measurements, if used, must lead to achievement. As a result, people become more directly attached to core business processes which will boost their self-esteem and contributions.

*Measure activity performance – Guaranteed activity performance.* In a world with increasingly more integrated material- and information-flows, the guaranteed performance of contributing activities speeds up the flow, reduces cost, and improves flexibility. Toyota, for example, works intensively with its suppliers to ensure the quality level of the parts and subassemblies they deliver.

*Connect by reporting – Connect by design.* The effective integration of efforts across contributing functions can only be achieved by the design and implementation of integrated business processes, not by reporting.

*Policies and Procedures – Process standardization*. Over time, policies and procedures were used to allow for exceptions. Exceptions cause unnecessary interruptions and complications in business processes. The idea was to focus people on the process flow design rather than on the exceptions.

## Value shift as evolutionary phenomenon

Digital, as evidenced in its identified value transitions, needed to *unlearn* ways of thinking and acting which had settled in after repeated business successes. The internally perceived reputation of success caused Digital's culture to become less flexible and, therefore, less sensitive to external influences. Reduced sensitivity to influences from outside at the same time causes organizational elements to become less sensitive to influences from other elements. Effectively by boundaries of its own making, Digital's interdependence seemed to fade away eventually diminishing its self-organizing capabilities.

*Note:*
A value shift is not a cultural shift, as others often presume. Culture *is* the self-organizing social system as a whole. Values are part of the 'culture system' (see the section *The Culture System*).

To summarize, Digital seemed to arrive at a turning point in its life cycle and needed a re-conception. In spite of all the other identified value transitions created to ensure their cognition, Digital's evolutionary state was essentially characterized by:

- Fragmentation.
- An inflexible and dominant culture.
- The lack of a clear corporate vision.
- Diminishing organizational responsiveness and interdependence.

*Note:*
Evolution is not a prerogative of companies. Political systems face similar situations. Without too much imagination, one can see how closely the break-up of the Soviet Union resembles the situation in Digital – and also that in IBM. The fragmentation of the Soviet Union is still on-going. Its rigid culture embodied by the ruling apparatus imposed an often unwritten code of conduct. The utopian vision of progress in the vivid minds of revolutionaries vanished long ago. The responsiveness of the population and the self-organizing characteristics of the whole have significantly diminished.

Not all companies need to move from fragmentation to integration, some move the other way. In 1990, two large Dutch banks teamed up to form the ABN-AMRO concern. The vision of becoming a major player in the international banking world was clear and, in fact, the basis for the merger. In order to make the merger a success, strong functions – such as trading and private banking – needed to be developed effectively to establish its presence as a key international player. The offices of the two banks would have to be consolidated and

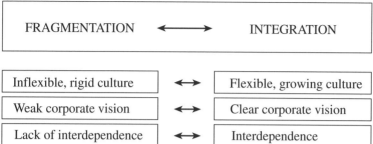

**Figure 3.** The contours of two extreme stages in evolution

the implementation of a common code of conduct was to ensure a reliable and respected banking climate. A new culture was required to provide a distinctive identity to both clients and employees. In other words, culture, acting as a 'glue' would ensure coherence between employees and at the same time provide 'nest warmth'. Eventually, the new culture could be relaxed to allow new and innovative subcultures to emerge. In a presentation to representatives of the directorate of personnel, it became apparent that the company would more than likely move from right to left, i.e. from integration to fragmentation.

Asea Brown Boveri is driven by the strong vision of Percy Barnevik, its president and CEO. Barnevik travels around the globe and 'seems to be everywhere at once, leading seminars with his managers, prodding, questioning, inspiring, and being a missionary' (Handy, 1992). In a federation of geographical operations, a high degree of autonomy is balanced by a centralized reporting system which keeps track of the performance of 50 business areas. Worldwide centers of excellence are developed across the globe to ensure ABB's technological leadership. 'Our managers need well-defined sets of responsibilities, clear accountability, and maximum degrees of freedom to execute'.

The situation in Asea Brown Boveri resembles that of the ABN-AMRO bank, although, ABB has had an earlier start. Both companies are driven by a strong vision and both have decided measures which will cause their cultures to become more distinct. The responsiveness is pursued in ABB by the intensive communication efforts of Percy Barnevik and, in the case of the ABN-AMRO bank, by the emphasis of management on creating nest warmth. Although the value transitions for these two companies are likely to show differences, their evolutionary state is essentially characterized by:

● Integration
● A flexible, growing culture.
● A clear corporate vision.
● Growing organizational responsiveness and interdependence.

Unlike Digital, which faces the nineties at a turning point, ABB and the ABN-AMRO concern seem to have passed their turning points. ABB, for example, grew a new identity from several mergers and acquisitions. Others, such as the local telephone business of AT&T in 1984, decided (or were forced) to break up into various companies. Digital is in a critical stage of its evolution: one of fragmentation and hopefully reincarnation. The dynamics at play eventually make companies move between the fragmentation and integration stages. No company can prevent itself from eventually reaching one of these stages. The path which companies follow and their capability to steer away from extreme situations depends on the choices their people make. We can try to improve the quality of these choices. The unknown influences from within and without, however, make it difficult to predict the outcome of the 'process of evolution' which we call 'culture'. Which company eventually survives and in what form is up for grabs.

## Good morning or good mourning that is the question

It may have been pure coincidence that in the autumn of 1992 Bob Palmer became president of Digital Equipment. Although Bob Palmer was hired from within the company, he effectively was a newcomer originally attracted to streamline Digital's manufacturing division. Not long before he became Digital's president, his team started to look into the improvement of the supply chain. The idea was to rationalize and integrate all operational processes in the company, i.e. from suppliers to customers. Although the latter is often badly needed, an advanced state of decay also requires a more fundamental approach: the reincarnation of the company. Reincarnation starts with the development of a clear corporate vision, i.e. including the *purpose of the business*. To summarize, a lasting corporate turnaround requires the following steps:

- Immediate process simplifications and rationalizations.
- Development of the purpose of the business; a clear corporate vision.
- De-construction and construction of the organization; clustering.
- Gene-hopping; getting people from outside to 'infect' an organization.
- Definition and communication of key strategies; the rules of the game.
- Assessment of emerging values and lifecycles; cognition.

As soon as the above steps have been completed, the cycle should be restarted never to be interrupted again. The model of the culture system can be used to guide the de-construction and construction of the organization. In the chapter *Breakthrough in Business*, however, the process of identifying organizational clusters will be discussed. The time-based division of power should ensure that waves of competency improvements pulsate through an organization without creating power-bloated, stagnating institutions. The evolutionary process can further be enriched by, what I call, 'gene-hopping'. Recent research has revealed that genes can jump from one species to another. This discovery in itself seriously alters established evolutionary theories. In short, 'bacteria have borrowed genes from plants, animals and fungi; bacterial genes have found their way into animals and plants; animals and plants have passed genes to each other'. Gene-hopping in organizations concerns the transplantation of 'cultural genes', i.e. people and the rules they bring, from other corporate cultures. Gene-hopping may be used to stimulate the process of differentiation and to prevent an organization from becoming self-centered. Ideally when the business purpose and the organizational clusters have been defined, people should be attracted from carefully selected companies to grow specific organizational characteristics. In the following chapters, ways to determine the necessary characteristics – as 'the conditions for the evolutionary selection of rules' (Amitai Etzioni, 1988) – will be explored further.

To conclude, the values which eventually emerge are the consequences as much as the causes of an unfolding evolutionary process. Once values become visible, their influence may last for years. In Digital, the *Economist* observes, 'the towering genius of Ken Olsen – its founder and ousted president – still casts a long, proprietary shadow over the way Digital thinks'. The focus of management, therefore, should be on the inception of values.

# References

Cooper, Robert. 1992. *Formal Organization as Representation: Remote Control, Displacement and Abbreviation.* In: *Rethinking Organization.* London: Sage Publications.
Das, Gurcharan. March–April 1993. *Local Memoires of a Global Manager. Harvard Business Review.*
Davis, Stanley, and Davidson, Bill. 1991. *2020 Vision.* New York: Simon & Schuster.
Etzioni, Amitai. 1988. *The Moral Dimension.* New York: The Free Press.
Gergen, Kenneth. 1992. *Organization Theory in the Postmodern Era.* In: *Rethinking Organization.* London: Sage Publications.
Handy, Charles. Nov–Dec 1992. *Balancing Corporate Power. Harvard Business Review.*
Helmer, Sabine. Spring 1991. *Anthropological Contributions to Organizational Culture.* SCOS Network Newsletter of the Standing Conference on Organizational Symbolism. Volume 10. No. 1.
Hofstede, Geert. 1980. *Culture's Consequences.* Newbury Park: Sage Publications.
Jack, Andrew. 1991. *Benefits of an Open Company. Financial Times.*
Katzenbach, Jon, and Smith, Douglas. March–April 1993. *The Discipline of Teams. Harvard Business Review.
Lorenz, Christopher. April 2, 1993. *The Side-Effects of a 'Cure-All' Approach. Financial Times.*
Probst, Gilbert. 1987. *Selbst-Organisation.* Berlin: Verlag Paul Parey.
Thurow, Lester. 1992. *Head to Head.* New York: William Morrow and Company.

Reproduced from Van der Erve, E. (1994) *Evolution Management.* Butterworth-Heinemann, Oxford. Reprinted with permission.

# 2 The learning organization

*P. Senge*

## The discipline of building shared vision

### Encouraging personal vision

Shared visions emerge from personal visions. This is how they derive their energy and how they foster commitment. As Bill O'Brien of Hanover Insurance observes, 'My vision is not what's important to you. The only vision that motivates you is your vision.' It is not that people care only about their personal self-interest – in fact, people's personal visions usually include dimensions that concern family, organization, community, and even the world. Rather, O'Brien is stressing that caring is *personal*. It is rooted in an individual's own set of values, concerns, and aspirations. This is why genuine caring about a shared vision is rooted in personal visions. This simple truth is lost on many leaders, who decide that their organization must develop a vision by tomorrow!

Organizations intent on building shared visions continually encourage members to develop their personal visions. If people don't have their own vision, all they can do is 'sign up' for someone else's. The result is compliance, never commitment. On the other hand, people with a strong sense of personal direction can join together to create a powerful synergy toward what I/we truly want.

Personal mastery is the bedrock for developing shared visions. This means not only personal vision, but commitment to the truth and creative tension – the hallmarks of personal mastery. Shared vision can generate levels of creative tension that go far beyond individuals' 'comfort levels'. Those who will contribute the most toward realizing a lofty vision will be those who can 'hold' this creative tension: remain clear on the vision and continue to inquire into current reality. They will be the ones who believe deeply in their ability to create their future, because that is what they experience personally.

In encouraging personal vision, organizations must be careful not to infringe on individual freedoms. No one can give another 'his vision,' nor even force him to develop a vision. However, there are positive actions that can be taken to create a climate that encourages personal vision. The most direct is for leaders who have a sense of vision to communicate that in such a way that others are encouraged to share their visions. This is the art of visionary leadership – how shared visions are built from personal visions.

## From personal visions to shared visions

How do individual visions join to create shared visions? A useful metaphor is the hologram, the three-dimensional image created by interacting light sources.

If you cut a photograph in half, each part shows only part of the whole image. But if you divide a hologram, each part shows the whole image intact. Similarly, as you continue to divide up the hologram, no matter how small the divisions, each piece still shows the whole image. Likewise, when a group of people come to share a vision for an organization, each person sees his own picture of the organization at its best. Each shares responsibility for the whole, not just for his piece. But the component 'pieces' of the hologram are not identical. Each represents the whole image from a different point of view. It's as if you were to look through holes poked in a window shade; each hole would offer a unique angle for viewing the whole image. So, too, is each individual's vision of the whole unique. We each have our own way of seeing the larger vision.

When you add up the pieces of a hologram, the image of the whole does not change fundamentally. After all, it was there in each piece. Rather the image becomes more intense, more lifelike. When more people come to share a common vision, the vision may not change fundamentally. But it becomes more alive, more real in the sense of a mental reality that people can truly imagine achieving. They now have partners, 'co-creators'; the vision no longer rests on their shoulders alone. Early on, when they are nurturing an individual vision, people may say it is 'my vision'. But as the shared vision develops, it becomes both 'my vision' and 'our vision'.

The first step in mastering the discipline of building shared visions is to give up traditional notions that visions are always announced from 'on high' or come from an organization's institutionalized planning processes.

In the traditional hierarchial organization, no one questioned that the vision emanated from the top. Often, the big picture guiding the firm wasn't even shared – all people needed to know were their 'marching orders,' so that they could carry out their tasks in support of the larger vision. Ed Simon of Herman Miller says, 'If I was the president of a traditional authoritarian organization and I had a new vision, the task would be much simpler than we face today. Most people in the organization wouldn't need to understand the vision. People would simply need to know what was expected of them.'

That traditional 'top-down' vision is not much different from a process that has become popular in recent years. Top management goes off to write its 'vision statement,' often with the help of consultants. This may be done to solve the problem of low morale or lack of strategic direction. Sometimes the process is primarily reflective. Sometimes it incorporates extensive analysis of a firm's competitors, market setting, and organizational strengths and weaknesses. Regardless, the results are often disappointing for several reasons.

First, such a vision is often a 'one-shot' vision, a single effort at providing overarching direction and meaning to the firm's strategy. Once it's written, management assumes that they have now discharged their visionary duties. Recently, one of my Innovation Associates colleagues was explaining to two managers how our group works with vision. Before he could get far, one of the managers interrupted. 'We've done that,' he said. 'We've already written our vision statement.' 'That's very interesting,' my colleague responded. 'What did you come up with?' The one manager turned to the other and asked, 'Joe, where is that vision statement anyhow?' Writing a vision statement can be a first step in building shared vision but, alone, it rarely makes a vision 'come alive' within an organization.

The second problem with top management going off to write their vision statement is that the resulting vision does not build on people's personal visions. Often, personal visions are ignored altogether in the search for a 'strategic vision.' Or the 'official vision' reflects only the personal vision of one or two people. There is little opportunity for inquiry and testing at every level so that people feel they understand and own the vision. As a result, the new official vision also fails to foster energy and commitment. It simply does not inspire people. In fact, sometimes, it even generates little passion among the top management team who created it.

Lastly, vision is not a 'solution to a problem.' If it is seen in that light, when the 'problem' of low morale or unclear strategic direction goes away, the energy behind the vision will go away also. Building shared vision must be seen as a central element of the daily work of leaders. It is ongoing and never-ending. It is actually part of a larger leadership activity: designing and nurturing what Hanover's Bill O'Brien calls the 'governing ideas' of the enterprise – not only its vision per se, but its purpose and core values as well. As O'Brien says, 'The governing ideas are far more important and enduring than the reporting chart and the divisional structure that so often preoccupy CEOs.'

Sometimes, managers expect shared visions to emerge from a firm's strategic planning process. But for all the same reasons that most 'top-down' visioning processes fail, most strategic planning also fails to nurture genuine vision. According to Hamel and Prahalad:

> Creative strategies seldom emerge from the annual planning ritual. The starting point for next year's strategy is almost always this year's strategy. Improvements are incremental. The company sticks to the segments and territories it knows, even though the real opportunities may be elsewhere. The impetus for Canon's pioneering entry into the personal copier business came from an overseas sales subsidiary – not from planners in Japan.[1]

This is not to say that visions cannot emanate from the top. Often, they do. But sometimes they emanate from personal visions of individuals who are not in positions of authority. Sometimes they just 'bubble up' from people interacting at many levels. The origin of the vision is much less important than the process whereby it comes to be shared. It is not truly a 'shared vision' until it connects with the personal visions of people throughout the organization.

For those in leadership positions, what is most important is to remember that their visions are still personal visions. Just because they occupy a position of leadership does not mean that their personal visions are *automatically* 'the organization's vision.' When I hear leaders say 'our vision' and I know they are really describing 'my vision,' I recall Mark Twain's words that the official 'we' should be reserved for 'kings and people with tapeworm.'

Ultimately, leaders intent on building shared visions must be willing to continually share their personal visions. They must also be prepared to ask, 'Will you follow me?' This can be difficult. For a person who has been setting goals all through his career and simply announcing them, asking for support can make him feel very vulnerable.

John Kryster was the president of a large division of a leading home products company who had a vision that his division should be preeminent in its industry. This vision required not only excellent products but that the company supply the product to their 'customer' (retail grocers), in a more efficient and effective manner than anyone else. He envisioned a unique worldwide distribution system that would get product to the customer in half the time and with a fraction of the cost in wastage and reshipments. He began to talk with other managers, with production workers, with distribution people, with grocers. Everyone seemed enthusiastic, but pointed up that many of his ideas could not be achieved because they contradicted so many traditional policies of the corporate parent.

In particular, Kryster needed the support of the head of product distribution, Harriet Sullivan, who – while technically Kryster's peer in the firm's matrix organization – had fifteen years more experience. Kryster prepared an elaborate presentation for Sullivan to show her the merits of his new distribution ideas. But for every piece of supporting data he offered, Sullivan had a countering criticism. Kryster left the meeting thinking that the doubters were probably right.

Then he conceived of a way to test the new system out in only one geographic market. The risk would be less, and he could gain the support of the local grocery chain which had been especially enthusiastic about the concept. But what should he do about Harriet Sullivan? His instincts were just not to tell her. After all, he had the authority to undertake the experiment himself, using his own distribution people. Yet, he also valued Sullivan's experience and judgment.

After a week of mulling it over, Kryster went back to ask for Sullivan's support. This time, though, he left his charts and data at home. He just told her why he believed in the idea, how it could forge a new partnership with customers, and how its merits could be tested with low risk. To his surprise, the crusty distribution chief started to offer help in designing the experiment. 'When you came to me last week,' she said, 'you were trying to convince me. Now, you're willing to test your idea. I still think it's wrongheaded, but I can see you care a great deal. So, who knows, maybe we'll learn something.'

That was five years ago. Today, John Kryster's innovative distribution system is used worldwide by almost all the corporation's divisions. It has significantly reduced costs and been part of broad strategic alliances the corporation is learning to forge with retail chains.

When visions start in the middle of an organization the process of sharing and listening is essentially the same as when they originate at the top. But it may take longer, especially if the vision has implications for the entire organization.

Bart Bolton was a middle manager in IS (Information Systems) at Digital Equipment Corporation when, back in 1981, he and a small group of colleagues began to form an idea of Digital as an interconnected organization. 'A group of us had been together at a workshop, and when we came back we just started talking about how we were going to turn around IS. The fundamental problem as we all saw it was that there simply was no IS vision. Everyone argued about the "how to's" but no one knew the "what." Yet, we felt we could see an end result that was really worth going for. We didn't know exactly what it would look like, but the idea of tying the organization together electronically just felt "right." Given our products and technology we could become one of the first, if not the first large corporation that was totally and completely electronically interconnected.' The idea was so exciting that he couldn't sleep much for several days as he thought about the implications.

But in 1981, no one had any idea how this could be done. 'It was simply beyond the realm of what was possible at that time. We could transfer files between computers, but we couldn't network. There was some networking software under development but there were lots of problems with it. Perhaps, if we worked really hard at it we could interconnect ten or twenty machines, but no one even dreamed of interconnecting a hundred machines, let alone thousands. Looking back, it was like they say about Kennedy when he announced the "Man on the Moon" vision – we knew about 15 percent of what we needed to know to get there. But we knew it was right.'

Bolton and his compatriots had no 'authority' to pursue the idea, but they couldn't stop thinking about it. In November 1981, he wrote a short paper which he read to all the senior IS people at a staff meeting. In it he said that the organization of the future would involve new IS technologies, would see 'data as a resource just like the organization of the past saw capital and people as resources,' and that 'networks would tie together all the functions.' 'When I finished, no one spoke. It was like being in church. I really thought I'd blown it. My boss, Al Crawford, the head of IS, suggested a ten-minute break. When people came back, all they wanted to know was, "How do we promote it? How can we make it happen?" My only response was, "This has got to be your vision not mine, or it will never happen." '

'I knew the guys at the top had to be "enrolled", and my job was to help them lead. By enrolling others, they too would become messengers.' An IS group prepared a 35-mm slide show to be used by Crawford throughout the organization. He came up with the image of 'wiring up the corporation.' 'It became incredibly exciting,' says Bolton, 'to watch the vision build, each person adding something new, refining it and making it come alive. We literally began talking about the "copper wires running around the world." '

Crawford presented the slide show to all Digital's major functional staffs in 1982. The idea, 'the what,' started to take hold. Then the IS organization created five overlapping programs to tackle the 'how to's': a network program, a data program, an office automation program, a facilities program, and an applications program. By 1985 the first network was in place. By 1987, over 10,000 computers were on line. Today, Digital has over 600 facilities in over 50 countries and they are all interconnected. There are over 43,000 computers interconnected. Digital is now seen by experts as one of the pioneer 'networked organizations.' Moreover, the 'networked organization' is a dominant theme in Digital's marketing strategy and advertising.

Organizational consultant Charlie Kiefer says that, 'Despite the excitement that a vision generates, the process of building shared vision is not always glamorous. Managers who are skilled at building shared visions talk about the process in ordinary terms. "Talking about our vision" just gets woven into day-to-day life. Most artists don't get very excited about the *process* of creating art. They get excited about the results.' Or, as Bill O'Brien puts it, 'Being a visionary leader is not about giving speeches and inspiring the troops. How I spend my day is pretty much the same as how any executive spends his day. Being a visionary leader is about solving day-to-day problems with my vision in mind.'

Visions that are truly shared take time to emerge. They grow as a by-product of interactions of individual visions. Experience suggests that visions that are genuinely shared require ongoing conversation where individuals not only feel free to express their dreams, but learn how to listen to each others' dreams. Out of this listening, new insights into what is possible gradually emerge.

Listening is often more difficult than talking, especially for strong-willed managers with definite ideas of what is needed. It requires extraordinary openness and willingness to entertain a diversity of ideas. This does not imply that we must sacrifice our vision 'for the larger cause.' Rather, we must allow multiple visions to coexist, listening for the right course of action that transcends and unifies all our individual visions. As one highly successful CEO expressed it: 'My job, fundamentally, is listening to what the organization is trying to say, and them making sure that it is forcefully articulated.'

## Spreading visions: enrollment, commitment, and compliance[2]

Few subjects are closer to the heart of contemporary managers than commitment. Prodded by studies showing that most American workers acknowledge low levels of commitment[3] and by tales of foreign competitors' committed work forces, managers have turned to 'management by commitment,' 'high commitment work systems,' and other approaches. Yet, real commitment is still rare in today's organizations. It is our experience that, 90 percent of the time, what passes for commitment is compliance.

Today, it is common to hear managers talk of getting people to 'buy into' the vision. For many, I fear, this suggests a sales process, where I sell and you buy. Yet, there is a world of difference between 'selling' and 'enrolling.' 'Selling' generally means getting someone to do something that he might not do if they were in full possession of all the facts. 'Enrolling,' by contrast, literally means 'placing one's name on the roll.' Enrollment implies free choice, while 'being sold' often does not.

'Enrollment is the process,' in Kiefer's words, 'of becoming part of something by choice.' 'Committed' describes a state of being not only enrolled but feeling fully responsible for making the vision happen. I can be thoroughly enrolled in your vision. I can genuinely want it to occur. Yet, it is still your vision. I will take actions as need arises, but I do not spend my waking hours looking for what to do next.

For example, people are often enrolled in social causes out of genuine desire, for example, to see particular inequities righted. Once a year they might make a donation to help in a fund-raising campaign. But when they are committed, the 'cause' can count on them. They will do whatever it takes to make the vision real. The vision is pulling them to action. Some use the term 'being source' to describe the unique energy that committed people bring toward creating a vision.

In most contemporary organizations, there are relatively few people enrolled – and even fewer committed. The great majority of people are in a state of 'compliance.' 'Compliant' followers go along with a vision. They do what is expected of them. They support the vision, to some degree. But, they are not truly enrolled or committed.

Compliance is often confused with enrollment and commitment. In part, this occurs because compliance has prevailed for so long in most organizations, we don't know how to recognize real commitment. It is also because there are several levels of compliance, some of which lead to behavior that looks a great deal like enrollment and commitment:

---

**Possible attitudes toward a vision**

*Commitment:* Wants it. Will make it happen. Creates whatever 'laws' (structures) are needed.

*Enrollment:* Wants it. Will do whatever can be done within the 'spirit of the law.'

---

*Genuine compliance:* Sees the benefits of the vision. Does everything expected and more. Follows the 'letter of the law.' 'Good soldiers.'

*Formal compliance:* On the whole, sees the benefits of the vision. Does what's expected and no more. 'Pretty good soldier.'

*Grudging compliance:* Does not see the benefits of the vision. But, also, does not want to lose job. Does enough of what's expected because he has to, but also lets it be known that he is not really on board.

*Noncompliance:* Does not see benefits of vision and will not do what's expected. 'I won't do it; you can't make me.'

*Apathy:* Neither for nor against vision. No interest. No energy. 'Is it five o'clock yet?'

---

The speed limit is fifty-five in most states in the United States today. A person who was genuinely compliant would never drive more than fifty-five. A person formally compliant could drive sixty to sixty-five because in most states you will not get a ticket so long as you are below sixty-five. Someone grudgingly compliant would stay below sixty-five and complain continually about it. A noncompliant driver would 'floor it' and do everything possible to evade troopers. On the other hand, a person who was genuinely committed to a fifty-five mph speed limit would drive that speed even if it were not the legal limit.

In most organizations, most people are in states of formal or genuine compliance with respect to the organization's goals and ground rules. They go along with 'the program,' sincerely trying to contribute. On the other hand, people in noncompliance or grudging compliance usually stand out. They are opposed to the goals or ground rules and let their opposition be known, either through inaction or (if they are grudgingly compliant) through 'malicious obedience' – 'I'll do it just to prove that it won't work.' They may not speak out publicly against the organization's goals, but their views are known nonetheless. (They often reserve their truest sentiments for the rest room or the cocktail lounge.)

Differences between the varying states of compliance can be subtle. Most problematic is the state of genuine compliance, which is often mistaken for enrollment or commitment. The prototypical 'good soldier' of genuine compliance will do whatever is expected of him, willingly. 'I believe in the people behind the vision; I'll do whatever is needed, and more, to the fullest of my ability.' In his own mind, the person operating in genuine compliance often thinks of himself as committed. He is, in fact, committed, but only to being 'part of the team.'

In fact, from his *behavior* on the job, it is often very difficult to distinguish someone who is genuinely compliant from someone who is enrolled or committed. An organization made up of genuinely compliant people would be light-years ahead of most organizations in productivity and cost effectiveness. People would not have to be told what to do more than once. They would be responsive. They would be upbeat and positive in their attitude and manner. They might also be a bit 'drone-like,' but not necessarily. If what was expected of high performers was to 'take initiative' and be 'proactive,' they would exhibit those behaviors as well. In short, people in genuine compliance would do whatever they could to play by the 'rules of the game,' both the formal and subtle rules.

Yet, there *is* a world of difference between compliance and commitment. The committed person brings an energy, passion, and excitement that cannot be generated if you are only compliant, even genuinely compliant. The committed person doesn't play by the 'rules of the game.' He is responsible for the game. If the rules of the game stand in the way of achieving the vision, he will find ways to change the rules. A group of people truly committed to a common vision is an awesome force. They can accomplish the seemingly impossible.

Tracy Kidder, in his Pulitzer-prize-winning book *The Soul of a New Machine*, tells the story of a product development team at Data General, brought together by a talented team leader to create an ambitious new computer. Against a business atmosphere of urgency bordering on crisis, the team turned out a ground-breaking computer in remarkable time. Visiting with the team manager Tom West in the book, and team members several years later, I learned just how remarkable their feat was. They told me of a stage in their project where certain critical software was several months behind schedule. The three engineers responsible came into the office one evening and left the next morning. By all accounts they accomplished two to three months of work that evening – and no one could explain how. These are not the feats of compliance.

What then is the difference between being genuinely compliant and enrolled and committed? The answer is deceptively simple. People who are enrolled or committed truly *want* the vision. Genuinely compliant people accept the vision. They may want it in order to get something else – for example, to keep their job, or to make their boss happy, or to get a promotion. But they do not truly want the vision in and of itself. It is not their own vision (or, at least, they do not know that it is their own vision).

Highly desired, shared commitment to a vision can be an elusive goal. One executive VP at a consumer goods company deeply desired to turn the very traditional organization into a world-class competitor by developing shared commitment to a new business vision. But after a year's effort, people continued to follow orders and do what they were told.

At this point he began to see the depth of the problem. People in his organization had *never been asked to commit to anything in their careers*. All they had ever been asked to do was be compliant. That was all they knew how to do. That was their only mental model. No matter what he said about developing a real vision, about being truly committed, it didn't matter because they heard it within their model of compliance.

Once he grasped this, he shifted tactics. He asked, 'What might people be able to commit to?' He initiated a 'wellness program,' reasoning if there was anything to which people might become committed, it would be their own health. Over time, some did. They began to see that true commitment was possible in the workplace, and a near 'ear' for the vision was opened.

Traditional organizations did not care about enrollment and commitment. The command and control hierarchy required only compliance. Still, today, many managers are justifiably wary of whether the energy released through commitment can be controlled and directed. So, we settle for compliance and content ourselves with moving people up the compliance ladder.

## Guidelines for enrollment and commitment

Enrollment is a natural process that springs from your genuine enthusiasm for a vision and your willingness to let others come to their own choice.

- *Be enrolled yourself.* There is no point attempting to encourage another to be enrolled when you are not. That is 'selling,' not enrolling and will, at best, produce a form of superficial agreement and compliance. Worse, it will sow the seeds for future resentment.
- *Be on the level.* Don't inflate benefits or sweep problems under the rug. Describe the vision as simply and honestly as you can.
- *Let the other person choose.* You don't have to 'convince' another of the benefits of a vision. In fact, efforts you might make to persuade him to 'become enrolled' will be seen as manipulative and actually preclude enrollment. The more willing you are for him to make a free choice, the freer he will feel. This can be especially difficult with subordinates, who are often conditioned to feel as though they must go along. But you can still help by creating the time and safety for them to develop their own sense of vision.

There are many times when managers need compliance. They may want enrollment or commitment, but cannot accept anything below formal compliance. If that is the case, I recommend that you be on the level about it: 'I know you may not agree wholeheartedly with the new direction, but at this juncture it is where the management team is committed to heading. I need your support to help it happen.' Being open about the need for compliance removes hypocrisy. It also makes it easier for people to come to their choices, which may, over time, include enrollment.

The hardest lesson for many managers to face is that, ultimately, *there is nothing you can do to get another person to enroll or commit*. Enrollment and commitment require freedom of choice. The guidelines above simply establish conditions most favorable to enrollment, but they do not *cause* enrollment. Commitment likewise is very personal; efforts to force it will, at best, foster compliance.

## Anchoring vision in a set of governing ideas

Building shared vision is actually only one piece of a larger activity: developing the 'governing ideas' for the enterprise, its vision, purpose or mission, and core values. A vision not consistent with values that people live by day by day will not only fail to inspire genuine enthusiasm, it will often foster outright cynicism.

These governing ideas answer three critical questions: 'What?' 'Why?' and 'How?'

- Vision is the 'What?' – the picture of the future we seek to create.
- Purpose (or 'mission') is the 'Why?' the organization's answer to the question, 'Why do we exist?' Great organizations have a larger sense of purpose that transcends providing for the needs of shareholders and employees. They seek to contribute to the world in some unique way, to add a distinctive source of value.
- Core values answer the question 'How do we want to act, consistent with our mission, along the path toward achieving our vision?' A company's values might include integrity, openness, honesty, freedom, equal opportunity, leanness, merit, or loyalty. They describe how the company wants life to be on a day-to-day basis, while pursuing the vision.

Taken as a unit, all three governing ideas answer the question, 'What do we believe in?' When Matsushita employees recite the company creed: 'To recognize our responsibilities as industrialists, to foster progress, to promote the general welfare of society, and to devote ourselves to the further development of world culture,' they're describing the company *purpose*. When they sing the company song, about 'sending our goods to the people of the world, endlessly and continuously, like water gushing from a fountain,' they're proclaiming the corporate *vision*. And when they go to in-house training programs that cover such topics as 'fairness,' 'harmony and cooperation,' 'struggle for betterment,' 'courtesy and humility,' and 'gratitude,' the employees are learning the company's deliberately constructed *values*. (Matsushita, in fact, calls them its 'spiritual values.')[4]

At Hanover Insurance, articulating all three of these 'governing ideas' made an enormous difference in the firm's revival from near bankruptcy to a leader in the property and liability industry. Hanover's experience also illustrates the interdependencies among vision, values, and purpose.

'Early on,' says O'Brien, 'we recognized that there is a burning need for people to feel part of an ennobling mission. If it is absent many will seek fulfillment only in outside interests instead of in their work.

'But we also discovered that stating a mission or purpose in words was not enough. It ends up sounding like "apple pie and motherhood." People need visions to make the purpose more concrete and tangible. We had to learn to "paint pictures" of the type of organization we wanted to be. My simple vision for the company is "unquestioned superiority." This simple term has great meaning for me. It leads me to envision an organization that serves the customer in unique ways, maintains a reputation for quality and responsibility, and creates a unique environment for its employees.

'Core values are necessary to help people with day-to-day decision making. Purpose is very abstract. Vision is long term. People need "guiding stars" to navigate and make decisions day to day. But core values are only helpful if they can be translated into concrete behaviors. For example, one of our core values is "openness," which we worked long and hard to understand – finally recognizing that it requires the skills of reflection and inquiry within an overall context of trusting and supporting one another.'

## Positive versus negative vision

'What do we want?' is different from 'What do we want to avoid?' This seems obvious, but in fact negative visions are probably more common than positive visions. Many organizations truly pull together only when their survival is threatened. They focus on avoiding what people don't want – being taken over, going bankrupt, losing jobs, not losing market share, having no downturns in earnings, or 'not letting our competitors beat us to market with our next new product.' Negative visions are, if anything, even more common in public leadership, where societies are continually bombarded with visions of 'anti-drugs,' 'anti-smoking,' 'anti-war,' or 'anti-nuclear energy.'

Negative visions are limiting for three reasons. First, energy that could build something new is diverted to 'preventing' something we don't want to happen. Second, negative visions carry a subtle yet unmistakable message of powerlessness: our people really don't care. They can pull together only when there is sufficient threat. Lastly, negative visions are inevitably short term. The organization is motivated so long as the threat persists. Once it leaves, so does the organization's vision and energy.

There are two fundamental sources of energy that can motivate organizations: fear and aspiration. The power of fear underlies negative visions. The power of aspiration drives positive visions. Fear can produce extraordinary changes in short periods, but aspiration endures as a continuing source of learning and growth.

## Creative tension and commitment to the truth

I have argued that personal vision, by itself, is not the key to more effective creativity. The key is 'creative tension,' the tension between vision and reality. The most effective people are those who can 'hold' their vision while remaining committed to seeing current reality clearly.

This principle is no less true for organizations. The hallmark of a learning organization is not lovely visions floating in space, but a relentless willingness to examine 'what is' in light of our vision.

IBM in the early 1960s, for example, carried out an extraordinary series of experiments in pursuit of a daring vision, a single family of computers that would make virtually all its previous machines obsolete. In the words of a *Fortune* writer, IBM staked 'its treasure, its reputation, and its position of leadership in the computer field' on a radical new concept: a series of compatible machines serving the broadest possible range of applications, from the most sophisticated scientific applications to the relatively small business needs.[5]

Jay Forrester once remarked that the hallmark of a great organization is 'how quickly bad news travels upward.' IBM's capacity to recognize and learn from its mistakes proved pivotal during this period. One of the most discouraging was an early attempt at a high-end machine called 'Stretch,' introduced in 1960. IBM CEO Tom Watson, Jr., effectively killed the project in May 1961, after only a few had been sold. (Watson cut Stretch's hefty $13.5 million price tag almost in half, thereby making it uneconomical to produce.) To him, there was little choice: the machine did not satisfy its customers, never achieving more than 70 percent of its promised specifications. A few days later, Watson spoke candidly to an industry group. 'Our greatest mistake in Stretch,' he said, 'is that we walked up to the plate and pointed at the center field stands. When we swung, it was not a homer but a hard line drive to the outfield. We're going to be a good deal more careful about what we promise in the future.'

Indeed they were. Under the direction of many of the same men who had learned from Stretch, IBM introduced the System 360 three years later, which proved to be the platform for its extraordinary growth over the next ten years.

# Shared vision and the fifth discipline

## Why visions die prematurely

Many visions never take root and spread – despite having intrinsic merit. Several 'limits to growth' structures can come into play to arrest the building of momentum behind a new vision. Understanding these structures can help considerably in sustaining the 'visioning process.'

Visions spread because of a reinforcing process of increasing clarity, enthusiasm, communication and commitment. As people talk, the vision grows clearer. As it gets clearer, enthusiasm for its benefits builds.

And soon, the vision starts to spread in a reinforcing spiral of communication and excitement. Enthusiasm can also be reinforced by early successes in pursuing the vision (another potential reinforcing process, not shown on this diagram).

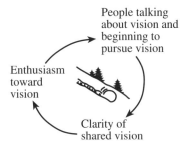

If the reinforcing process operated unfettered, it would lead to continuing growth in clarity and shared commitment toward the vision, among increasing numbers of people. But any of a variety of limiting factors can come into play to slow down this virtuous cycle.

The visioning process can wither if, as more people get involved, the diversity of views dissipates focus and generates unmanageable conflicts. People see different ideal futures. Must those who do not agree immediately with the emerging shared vision change their views? Do they conclude that the vision is 'set in stone' and no longer influenceable? Do they feel that their own visions even matter? If the answer to any of these questions is 'yes,' the enrolling process can grind to a halt with a wave of increasing polarization.

This is a classic 'limits to growth' structure, where the reinforcing process of growing enthusiasm for the vision interacts with a 'balancing process' that limits the spread of the visions, due to increasing diversity and polarization:

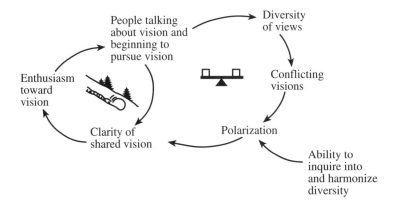

Reading clockwise around the balancing circle, from the top: as enthusiasm builds, more people are talking about the vision, the diversity of views increases, leading to people expressing potentially conflicting visions. If other people are unable to allow this diversity to be expressed, polarization increases, reducing the clarity of the shared visions, and limiting the growth of enthusiasm.

In limits to growth structures, leverage usually lies in understanding in the 'limiting factor,' the implicit goal or norm that drives the balancing feedback process. In this case, that limiting factor is the ability (or inability) to inquire into diverse visions in such a way that deeper, common visions emerge. Diversity of visions will grow until it exceeds the organization's capacity to 'harmonize' diversity.

The most important skills to circumvent this limit are the 'reflection and inquiry' skills. In effect, the visioning process is a special type of inquiry process. It is an inquiry into the future we truly seek to create. If it becomes a pure advocacy process, it will result in compliance, at best, not commitment.

Approaching the visioning as an inquiry process does not mean that I have to give up my view. On the contrary, visions need strong advocates. But advocates who can also inquire into others' visions open the possibility for the vision to evolve, to become 'larger' than our individual visions. *That* is the principle of the hologram.

Visions can also die because people become discouraged by the apparent difficulty in bringing the vision into reality. As clarity about the nature of the vision increases so does awareness of the gap between the vision and current reality. People become disheartened, uncertain, or even cynical, leading to a decline in enthusiasm. The limits to growth structure for 'organizational discouragement' looks like this:

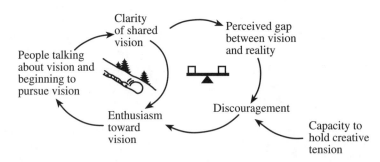

In this structure, the limiting factor is the capacity of people in the organization to 'hold' creative tension, the central principle of personal mastery. This is why we say that personal mastery is the 'bedrock' for developing shared vision – organizations that do not encourage personal mastery find it very difficult to foster sustained commitment to a lofty vision.

Emerging visions can also die because people get overwhelmed by the demands of current reality and lose their focus on the vision. The limiting factor becomes the time and energy to focus on a vision:

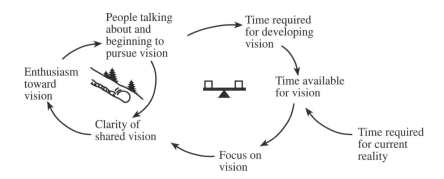

In this case, the leverage must lie in either in finding ways to focus less time and effort on fighting crises and managing current reality, or to break off those pursuing the new vision from those responsible for handling 'current reality.' In many ways, this is the strategy of 'skunk works,' small groups that quietly pursue new ideas out of the organizational mainstream. While this approach is often necessary, it is difficult to avoid fostering two polar extreme 'camps' that no longer can support one another. For example, the group that developed the Macintosh computer in the early 1980s broke off almost completely from the rest of Apple, most of whom were focused on the more mundane Apple II. While the separation resulted in a significant breakthrough product, it also created a significant organizational rift which took considerable time to heal and led John Sculley to reorganize Apple into a more conventionally functional hierarchy.[6]

Lastly, a vision can die if people forget their connection to one another. This is one of the reasons that approaching visioning as a joint inquiry is so important. Once people stop asking 'What do we really want to create?' and begin proselytizing the 'official vision,' the quality of ongoing conversation, and the quality of relationships nourished through that conversation, erodes. One of the deepest desires underlying shared vision is the desire to be connected, to a larger purpose *and* to one another. The spirit of connection is fragile. It is undermined whenever we lose our respect for one another and for each other's views. We then split into insiders and outsiders – those who are 'true believers' in the vision and those who are not. When this happens, the 'visioning' conversations no longer build genuine enthusiasms toward the vision:

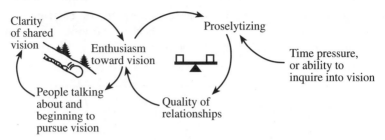

The limiting factor when people begin proselytizing and lose their sense of relationship can be time or skills. If there is great urgency to 'sign up' for the new vision, people may just not perceive that there is time to really talk and listen to one another. This will be especially likely if people are also unskilled in how to have such a conversation, how to share their vision in such a way that they are not proselytizing, but are encouraging others to reflect on their own visions.

# References

1   G. Hamel and C.K. Prahalad, 'Strategic Intent'.
2   The ideas expressed in this section come from many hours of discussion with my colleagues at Innovation Associates, notably Charles Kiefer, Alain Gauthier, Charlotte Roberts, Rick Ross, and Bryan Smith.
3   For example the Daniel Yankelovich and John Immerwahr study in 1983, which found that only 25 percent of U.S. workers said they were working as hard as they could be. 'Are U.S. workers lazy?' by Joani Nelson-Horchler, *Industry Week*, June 10, 1985, 47.
4   M. Moskowitz, The Global Marketplace (New York: Macmillan Publishing Company), 1987.
5   'IBM's $5,000,000,000 Gamble', *Fortune*, September 1966, and 'The Rocky Road to the Marketplace', *Fortune*, October 1966 (two-part article).
6   Sculley with Byrne, *Odyssey*.

Reproduced from Senge, P. (1990) *The Fifth Discipline*. Random House, London/Doubleday, New York. Reprinted with permission.

# 3 Are you a strategist or just a manager?

*H. H. Hinterhuber and W. Popp*

Perhaps the greatest strategist of all time was not a business executive or an entrepreneur but a general. Helmuth von Moltke, chief of the Prussian and German general staffs from 1858 to 1888, engineered the strategy behind the military victories that allowed Otto von Bismarck to assemble a loose league of German states into a powerful empire. A prolific writer and acute thinker, Moltke possessed two important characteristics that made him a superior strategist:

- The ability to understand the significance of events without being influenced by current opinion, changing attitudes, or his own prejudices.
- The ability to make decisions quickly and to take the indicated action without being deterred by a perceived danger.

The two characteristics support each other – and apply to managers and entrepreneurs as much as generals and national leaders. For example, General Electric's CEO Jack Welch has said, 'Strategy follows people; the right person leads to the right strategy.' But what makes a strategist out of a manager? How does a CEO gauge the strategic capabilities of managers rising in the organization? How can managers consciously work on themselves to develop their own strategic abilities?

There is no test that can precisely evaluate an individual's strategic management competence. But there are key questions whose answers can indicate the level of that competence. Managers who answer these questions in the form of a self-administered test can draw practical conclusions about their strategic abilities. Such a questionnaire makes the process of selecting good managers more objective, clear, and simple. At the same time, this method can provide individual managers with an instrument for developing their own management personalities.

# Strategy can't be taught

Helmuth von Moltke's superior strategies won the Austrian-Prussian War in 1866 and the French-Prussian War in 1871. A man of action, Moltke was also humane and cultured – and very reserved. One colleague said he could be 'silent in seven languages.' Instead of giving specific orders, Moltke issued 'directives' – guidelines for autonomous decision making. In the past, Prussian officers were discouraged from acting on their own; military commanders controlled most actions from the top. But Moltke turned such tradition on its head by expecting his officers to show individual initiative.

According to Moltke, strategy is applied common sense and cannot be taught. Moltke's general conception of strategy – viewing all obvious factors in the right perspective – cannot be learned in any school because every school essentially aims at mediocrity. Just as the monastery schools of the Middle Ages produced merely average monks and never saints, present-day business schools rarely turn out the equivalent of a Moltke or a Bismarck.

The actual educational purpose of any school is to achieve the highest possible average level; students learn and share values based on a common culture, which enables them to build on their own natural capabilities. The best a business school can do is to offer prospective managers ways to develop themselves – and refrain from creating obstacles or leading students down false paths. Differences in real life result much less from knowledge learned than from the individual's essential character. Ultimately, the ability to strategize is linked with the personality of successful entrepreneurs and managers.

So, what does it actually take to be a strategist? What factors determine the level of strategic management competence? Our questionnaire summarizes the criteria we use to identify good strategists. When entrepreneurs and managers take this test, they ask themselves or others ten questions. The answers then yield a profile that indicates an individual's ability to strategize.

*Question 1: 'Do I have an entrepreneurial vision?'*

The two Steves – Jobs and Wozniak, founders of Apple Computer – envisioned the 'democratization of the computer.' Gottlieb Duttweiler started Migros Cooperative, now the largest Swiss supermarket chain, in 1925 with five Ford Model-T trucks loaded with sugar, coffee, rice, macaroni, shortening, and soap – and a vision of scrapping traditional distribution structures to help society's poorer classes. Enrico Mattei, founder of ENI (Ente Nazionale Idrocarburi), the Italian state-owned petroleum company, envisioned making Italy relatively self-sufficient in oil and natural gas. The president of a Swiss technological institute wanted to create conditions that would enable a member of his faculty to win the Nobel Prize. And Stephen Davison Bechtel, founder of the biggest construction company in the world, regarded the entire planet as a construction site and always stuck to his guiding principle 'We'll build anything, anywhere, any time.'

As these and countless other examples demonstrate, there is always a vision at the beginning of any entrepreneurial activity, any major company restructuring program, any new phase in a person's life. Such visions are guides comparable to the North Star. The leader of a caravan in the desert, where sandstorms constantly change the landscape, looks to the patterns of the stars in the sky to stay on course. The stars are not the destination, but they do provide dependable guides for the journey to the next oasis, no matter which direction the caravan comes from, how well it is equipped for the trip, or how rough the terrain may be. Of course, the stars may point the way, but any Bedouin who hopes to reach the oasis safely knows to keep one eye on the ground to avoid quicksand – and to trust his caravan leader's sense of orientation.

Like the North Star, a manager's vision is not a goal. Rather, it is an orientation point that guides a company's movement in a specific direction. If the vision is realistic and appeals both to the emotions and the intelligence of employees, it can integrate and direct a company. Every entrepreneur who claims to possess strategic management competence should be able to state his or her vision clearly, in just a few sentences.

Of course, a vision may be more or less important to different companies and managers. A successful company intent upon steering its present course may need the ability to focus more than the ability to create a vision.

*Question 2: 'Do I have a corporate philosophy?'*

When a vision is put into concrete terms, it becomes a corporate philosophy: the ideological creed of both entrepreneurs and their top managers. A good corporate philosophy is like a good battle cry – and, as George Bernard Shaw pointed out, a good battle cry is half the battle. Frank Stronach, the entrepreneur who founded Magna International, an automobile parts company headquartered in Markham, Ontario in Canada, bases his vision on the idea of a 'fair economy.' The main principles of his corporate philosophy are:

- 10% of profit before taxes goes to employees – 3% as cash bonuses and 7% as shares.
- 6% of profit before taxes goes to management as cash bonuses.
- 2% of profit before taxes goes to charities, political institutions, and educational and cultural organizations.
- 7% of profit before taxes is spent for research and development.
- 20% of profit after taxes is paid out as dividends to shareholders.
- The rest is reinvested.

According to Stronach's corporate philosophy, the top management team at Magna also must be 'reformed' if these managers cannot generate profits over any given three-year period.

A family-owned company in Austria follows a different set of guiding principles. The company should grow, but no faster than it can finance growth with internal resources. Decisions of the advisory board become binding only if they are unanimous. Family members are not allowed to engage in private business activity. The company enters into no cooperation agreements with other companies. But at Olivetti, CEO Carlo De Benedetti has taken a completely different tack: his corporate philosophy emphasizes cooperation agreements, joint ventures, alliances, and the incorporation of his companies in strategic networks.

The corporate philosophy of a company is like the worldview of an individual – that combination of the most essential elements in a person's character. Of course, it is important for a landlady sizing up a potential lodger to know something about his income; but it is also important for her to judge his character and basic ideology. Similarly, an entrepreneur locked in cut-throat competition with a competitor should learn something about the competitor's products and resources; however, it is even more important for the entrepreneur to know the opponent's corporate philosophy.

Entrepreneurs and top managers who lose battles or even wars to competitors have probably failed in assessing the long-term intentions of those competitors. These managers may not even know enough about their own intentions. For example, the German automotive industry would do well to consider the philosophy of their Japanese competitors rather than assuming they don't have to worry because Japanese cars lack European design. The Japanese today exemplify the motto, 'Challengers change; our philosophy remains the same,' a view that often enables upstarts to become dominant.

*Question 3: 'Do I have competitive advantages?'*

Moltke noted that strategy is 'the evolution of the original guiding idea according to continually changing circumstances.' In business, the guiding idea is to assume a unique position in the market segment in which the company operates, based on permanently maintainable competitive advantages. In other words, one tries to become number one or number two – or at least to belong to the small group of leading competitors in any market segment.

But a company can capture a leading market position only if it offers customers a better product or a better solution to a problem at a favorable price. The central element of any strategy consists of creating permanent competitive advantages that, in the ideal case, establish a virtual monopoly in the market. Examples of competitive advantages are the company's price-performance ratio, unique product design, consistent or reliable service, and ability to deliver – in other words, the factors that motivate the buyer to choose one product over another comparable product.

The guiding idea of Franz Voelkl, a successful German ski manufacturer and former upstart, is 'the one who builds his skis slowest builds the fastest skis.' When racers wearing Voelkl's skis won gold medals during the Alpine World Championships at Lake Placid and Vail, sales boomed, confirming his guiding idea and competitive advantage. Customers who want success also want to use a successful product. Unlike his competitors, Voelkl's company produces all of the ski components in-house, including the wooden core, edges, and boot soles. This sort of manufacturing depth has produced a technically superior product – and a leap from fifteenth place to one of the top positions in the world ski market within ten years.

Artur Doppelmayr, an Austrian manufacturer of aerial transport systems, believes his main competitive advantage – in addition to innovative equipment design – is his service system. This allows Doppelmayr's company to come to the assistance of users within 24 hours anywhere in the world. Doppelmayr provides total quality management, standardization and reduction of components, a worldwide system of warehouses, and skilled personnel prepared to move immediately in emergency cases.

Both of these examples demonstrate strategies that have indirect effects. In the case of a direct strategy, such as taking the offensive in a price war, material and financial resources determine success rather than psychological factors or new-product development time. But when a company adopts an indirect strategy, such as a marketing plan that focuses on a product's overall benefits to customers – or excluding competitors with a clever policy of alliances – material and financial resources fade into the background.

Because of the acceleration of change and the increasing complexity of all human institutions, managers must learn to use indirect strategies. These are usually more effective and a better guarantee of lasting success than a direct strategy, although even indirect strategies require financial and material resources.

*Question 4: 'Do my employees use their ability to act freely in the interest of the company?'*

In theory, the strategically managed company is a confederation of entrepreneurs, with management responsibility vested in strategic business units. These microenterprises are centers for integrated action, backed by the whole corporation's resources, and headed by entrepreneurial-minded managers. Following Helmuth von Moltke's example, corporate management should issue directives to the managers responsible for these strategic business units – but not detailed instructions. Directives are guidelines for decisions reached autonomously and usually have a stimulating effect. Effective directives combine the strategic intention of top management with the initiative and creativity of the individual manager.

For example, top management could issue the following directive to a production manager as part of an offensive strategy: 'Achieve higher flexibility through the use of increased automation, and accomplish this within a specified time schedule and cost budget.' The manager's task then is to be creative in figuring out the best way to meet this directive.

The success of a company essentially depends on the extent to which managers use their ability to act freely in the company's interest. Bismarck once remarked that 'courage on the battlefield is common among us. But you will frequently find very respectable people lacking in civil courage.' He was talking about the courage to stand up for one's convictions; presumably, this also means the courage not to act on directives from top management – if this helps to implement strategic intentions better than passive obedience. Consequently, top management must allow directives to be modified and offer latitude for interpretation.

In everyday management practice, business-unit managers must be familiar with the overall corporate vision, philosophy, and strategic intentions in order to act in accordance with them – even if the particular competitive situation forces managers to deviate from an agreement struck with corporate management. This principle, which is as much Helmuth von Moltke's as Jack Welch's, represents the highest level of modern management and clearly promotes the greatest degree of entrepreneurial initiative. From it, we can ask a related question for evaluating the level of strategic management competence: Are all managers capable of expressing in just a few words the corporate vision, the corporate philosophy, and the strategic goal of the unit for which they are responsible?

If managers are not able to do this, the blame lies less with them than with their superiors, who probably also lack strategic management competence. No business-unit manager can be expected to act independently and take initiative in the interest of his or her company without knowing the corporate vision, philosophy, and directives.

*Question 5: 'Have I built an organization that implements my vision?'*

Entrepreneurs and top managers who feel they can improve matters by meddling at lower levels are usually mistaken. When they try, they assume functions normally carried out by other people, make the performance of those people superfluous, and add to their own management duties so much that they can no longer get everything done. These observations, which were made by Moltke, raise two useful questions in assessing strategic management competence: Are all management positions filled with people who think and act entrepreneurially? Are their duties, authority, and responsibilities such that they can formulate and implement strategies autonomously in the interest of the company?

The answer to both questions will be no if managers unable to meet strategic demands remain in their positions – and if the organization does not permit employees to take entrepreneurial initiative along strategic lines. Whenever that is the case, the level of strategic management competence certainly leaves something to be desired.

Of course, there is always a discrepancy between how the actual organization operates and how it is formally described on paper. Within limits, in fact, such a discrepancy is desirable. Capable top managers rely on elasticity and uncertainty in the organizational system in order to offer outstanding employees the possibility of taking action autonomously. Therefore, the extent to which top management has erected an organization that promotes creative behavior and permits effective implementation of strategies reflects the general level of strategic management competence.

*Question 6: 'Are the line managers involved in strategic planning?'*

Strategic planning is the job of those line managers who are responsible for implementing a strategy. For that reason, the key to successful execution of strategy is the early involvement of line managers in the strategic-planning process. This raises three questions: How do line managers temporarily become farsighted planners? How does top management use planning staff effectively? How should managers monitor the execution of strategies?

Successful companies familiarize line managers with strategic instruments in training courses and make sure they know the strategic intentions of their superiors; top management also alters planning-staff functions. In this case, the function of the planning staff is no longer strategic planning. Rather, it is strategic analysis of critical sectors and business areas that are or may become important for the company. Both functions support line managers – and both line managers and planning staff monitor progress in the execution of strategies.

If line managers are not involved in the process of strategic planning, top management certainly cannot claim a high level of strategic management competence. The same is true if strategic control is not carried out effectively or is used as a means of 'political' maneuvering. For example, in an Italian textile company, line managers are supposed to be free to plan and execute strategies; however, top managers use a strategic controller to quash the views of those who disagree with their personal expectations or priorities.

*Question 7: 'Is the corporate culture in harmony with the strategies?'*

The more business strategies and corporate culture are in true harmony, the higher the level of strategic management competence. Companies can only create an atmosphere of maximum creativity, for example, if they reduce hierarchial elements to a minimum. Outstanding companies are usually products of excellent entrepreneurs and managers who have crated a corporate culture in which their vision, company philosophy, and strategies can be implemented by employees who think independently and take initiative. When evaluating the general level of strategic management competence in a company, managers should ask, 'Does our corporate culture and corporate identity – our public image and the company's most tangible component – match the strategies?'

A company can be a management school or a school of life; theoretically, it can be both, but in reality this rarely happens. It is a management school if top managers set out to ground the corporate philosophy and strategies at all levels of responsibility in scientific principles. Among other large and midsize

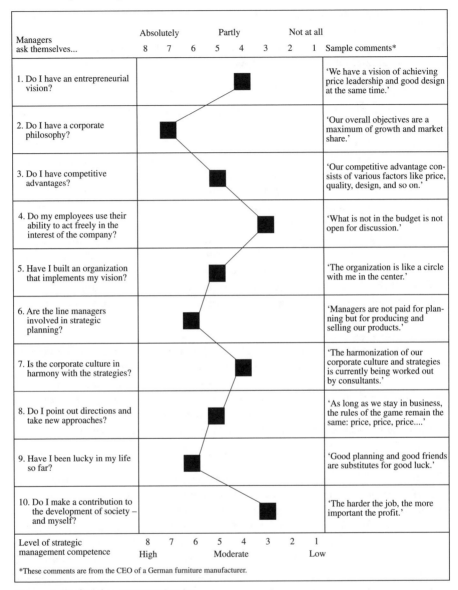

**Figure 1.** Profile of an average manager

corporations, Siemens, IBM, Unilever, Saint-Gobain, and Montedison have exemplified this 'management school' approach.

The company is a school of life if the vision and charisma of managers – and the company's size and that of its units – permit management on a face-to-face basis. Thus the company becomes a microcosm of the world rather than just a goal-oriented, single-purpose organization. This little world is not only well-organized but is also an institution that teaches living per se – the cultivation of tolerance, confidence, culture, aesthetics, taste, and humor within the framework of a common corporate philosophy and strategy.

Such institutions make the individual's work meaningful and fulfill expectations that are hard to measure. Employees of 'school of life' companies tend to project an active and involved work style. Of course, these kinds of companies are few and far between. And, unfortunately, their numbers will probably decrease. Given the economic demands of doing business in postindustrial society, an individual's personal development is often divorced from his or her development on the job.

*Question 8: 'Do I point out directions and take new approaches?'*

The value of great entrepreneurs or managers seems to come more from the fact that they lived than from what they accomplished. This is a counterintuitive conclusion; yet, sooner or later, all great business accomplishments are surpassed. What, therefore, is permanent about competent strategic management? Some possibilities include:

- The directions great entrepreneurs and managers take, not the limits they set.
- The projects, programs, and directions they initiate, not what they finish.
- The questions they raise, not the answers they find or already know.
- The paths they take, not the objectives they actually attain.
- The employees they select to carry on their vision, not the buildings they erect.

What is permanent about entrepreneurial capabilities and performance lies more in spontaneity than in education, more in originality and intuition than in learning, more in personal greatness than in specific, narrow capabilities.

A fable from India illustrates the difference between knowing and being. A man went to a mountain and said, 'What a fool you are, O mountain! You don't know how big you are, how high you are, or how you are shaped. But I, a mere man, know everything about you!' The mountain thought and then replied, 'You are right that I don't know these things. But *I* am the mountain!' Knowledge of facts is not important. What matters most is a person's understanding of who he or she really is.

In evaluating whether managers are good strategists, we ask: Are these entrepreneurs or managers capable of pointing directions, raising questions, initiating actions, choosing paths, and attracting employees in a way that has lasting effects? Are they capable of bringing about long-term improvement of the company's growth and profitability? Whatever an entrepreneur launches with a vision can have effects that last for decades – but what he or she has to offer in terms of solutions to individual problems often passes into oblivion

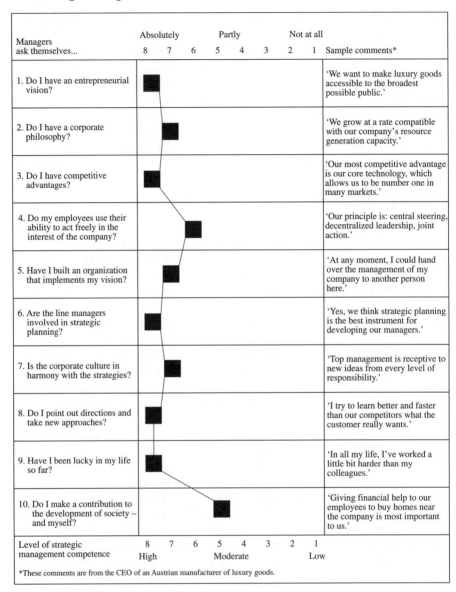

**Figure 2.** Profile of a good strategist

quickly. Good strategists also have the ability to make employees and the out-side world understand and embrace their visions.

Helmuth von Moltke is the best example of a man who knew the secret of always being armed with a 'system of assistants' and transmitted the authority of his personality to his underlings. Hermann Keyserling – a German philosopher and founder of the 'School of Wisdom' popular in Europe in the 1920s – noted that having integrity means being totally honest with oneself and others, never pretending to be what one is not, and acting in accordance with one's essential personality. Ultimately, a manager who is a good strategist must have such integrity.

*Question 9: 'Have I been lucky in my life so far?'*

As Moltke observed, the good strategist also needs good luck. Put another way, strategic management competence includes the ability to place oneself in a position that favors being lucky. Many successful entrepreneurs and managers actually accomplished very little on their own. Their success required numerous other events to converge with their professional choices, which produced the 'luck' they needed.

To tackle a tough challenge with good prospects for success, managers either need to feel deep down that they are up to the task – or else to trust luck to help them get the job done. However, luck in this connection does not mean mere chance; rather, it means that the serendipitous difficulties inherent in such challenges tend to stimulate and strengthen precisely those character traits necessary to succeed.

So, if we assume that human beings force their destiny by virtue of their essential character, it follows that the luckier a person has been, the higher his or her level of strategic management competence. Conversely, it is possible to rate the level of strategic management competence by the number of external setbacks and blows of fate a manager has been able to absorb without being deterred.

*Question 10: 'Do I make a contribution to the development of society – and myself?'*

Entrepreneurs and managers who possess a high level of strategic management competence may make individual mistakes, but they do not allow themselves to be deterred from the vision, corporate philosophy, or continued development of their guiding idea. They comprehend the big picture intuitively, remaining above mundane matters and deliberately avoiding identification with them. They experience relationships both inside and outside the company, as well as strategy formulation and implementation, within an overall context. They also are affected more consciously and directly by the big picture than by isolated events.

This highest level of strategic management competence is achieved only through a lifetime of work and training. It is absolutely unthinkable for entrepreneurs or managers worthy of the name to feel they have ever reached the final goal, have a perfect solution to a problem, or have spoken the last word on any subject.

This 'something' at which managers should aim over and above professional fulfillment of their managerial duties is described beautifully by Robert Louis Stevenson: 'You've had success in life if you have lived decently, laughed frequently, and loved a lot; won the respect of clever men and the love of children; filled out your place and accomplished your tasks; if you have left the world a better place than you found it, perhaps in the form of an improved strain of poppy, a perfect poem, or a saved soul; if you always appreciated the beauty of nature and also said so; if you saw the best in other people and always did your best.'

Managers and entrepreneurs should ask themselves a final, key question: 'What have we done to leave the world a better place than we found it?'

## The strategist as student, teacher, and symbol

How can we tell the difference between a visionary strategist and an unrealistic dreamer? The answer must be based on a reconstruction of the person's life: what he or she has accomplished or set in motion to date. In the end, strategists can be identified by measuring:

●  The nature of the vision they had at the beginning of each phase of their career or life.
●  The way in which they kept modifying their guiding ideas to suit changing conditions.
●  The extent to which – and under what conditions – they put those ideas into action or led others to do so.

Our evaluation procedure can help top management distinguish between average managers and good strategists. (See the sample profiles on the previous pages.) Using our questionnaire, company management can evaluate managers being considered for an open position or a promotion by drawing up their profiles. This procedure is not intended to replace other analyses of the performance potential and intellectual horizon of an individual, but it can supplement them. Clearly, our questionnaire and the evaluation profiles are merely tools for evaluating and comparing many different criteria. As with any questionnaire, the qualitative individual findings are more important than point scores.

Managers being evaluated complete the questionnaires first. Then top management may want to discuss these questionnaires with them. The process, however, is not only self-evaluative. When top managers look at the questionnaires, they can learn something about the initiative and self-confidence of those who took the test. This can help them in improving the company's managerial effectiveness. In fact, if the self-evaluation of managers is carried out realistically, the company average indicates overall strategic management competence.

As a final step in the process, top managers can also complete questionnaires in order to determine their own strategic abilities. The test may provide insight into their personal strengths and weaknesses. Obviously, all answers should be supported by facts and examples. In general, the questionnaire can be used as part of a company's formal evaluation and planning process.

Napoleon often said that he had to be present personally if his armies were to win; but the battlefields on which his soldiers fought became so large he couldn't be everywhere at once. Consequently, the strategist in either military or business situations must be not only a student but also a teacher. He or she needs employees who are thoroughly schooled in the organization's values and strategies; only then will directives be understood and carried out even in difficult situations where the strategist cannot take personal action.

In this sense, top strategists are symbols rather than examples, because employees have the right to run their own lives. But when employees have been trained in strategic thought and action on the job – and management agrees about certain basic values such as the importance of individual initiative and creativity – a company legitimately becomes a confederation of entrepreneurs.

# Part Two
# Organization Change in a Changing World

The only constant is change. This is often said by academics and managers alike. Increasingly people are questioning traditional cyclical models of change. These view change as discrete stages (e.g. from problem recognition, diagnosis, decision, implementation and review) but also as a cycle moving from stability through change to a new stability (freezing – moving – re-freezing in a typically influential formulation of Kurt Lewin). The period and process of changing is seen as a time of instability, of uncertainty and anxiety. Critics point out the difficulty of utilizing such a model where change follows change. But now there is some evidence to suggest that relative instability and uncertainty has become the norm. Beset by a myriad of rapid and dramatic changes, people demand leadership. On this view a period of change may bring the prospects of success. A period of change may therefore be a period of acceptance, of relative stability, motivation and hope. Here our purpose is not to formulate new change theory but only to suggest that there are various changes going on now which are changing organizations in fundamental ways. New demands are placed on managers at earlier points in life/career cycles. To fully understand change we need to understand the changing organizational context.

## Strategy and structure

There have been various formulations of the factors giving rise to various organizational structures. Many argue that there is a definite link between strategy and structure. Chandler's (1962) classic argument is that to be successful organizational structure has to be consistent with strategy. It is certainly widely accepted that a number of factors will have an important impact upon success, including the following:

1 The degree of uncertainty in the environment within which the organization operates.
2 The extent of diversity in products and markets, with larger firms operating in many markets often operating a divisional structure, based on products, or geographic regions, or even combinations of both.
3 Size, larger firms tending to adopt professional management approaches, more formalized procedures, etc. (but see below).
4 Technology, in the broad sense of both the physical infrastructure (machines,

computers, factories, offices, etc.) and the 'soft-ware' (e.g. the organization of work, product knowledge, information flows, work flows, etc.).

5 Culture, in that there seems to be national differences in appropriate forms of work organization and management style: in some countries team-work seems to be more strongly emphasized whereas in others managers rely less (or more) on formal authority. Quite a lot of research has been undertaken in this area since the landmark study by Hofstede. Some argue that you can identify regional influences (e.g. 'European managers', 'Asia-Pacific' managers whilst others suggest that either diversity within regions – even within countries – is too great for this to be meaningful, whilst others suggest that the advent of global corporations, information technology, integrated management training and development is creating some convergence. Be that as it may there are differences which, at the least, must be understood.

There are many research studies of the above (see below). A classic study on the growth of organizations (Greiner, 1972) suggests that organizations experience periods of evolution and revolution. Both size and age (or organizations) are important variables – the former can lead to size creating problems of co-ordination and control the latter to inflexibility as attitudes become fixed over time. The main message here is that as each period of revolutionary change creates a new form of organization then new management styles, control systems, reward systems and structures are introduced.

Classical changes in organizational structure include the emergence of the multi-divisional structure. Large corporations diversified into a variety of markets often geographically widely dispersed. Problems of control and co-ordination, the need to achieve focus of management effort, allocation of R&D spend, etc., lead firms to create divisions which then operated relatively autonomously (although in reality the true extent of the autonomy was often questionable and in many firms seemed to vary with the economic cycle – the centre tightening control in the down-swing of the cycle).

Of course there are many other factors to take into account. For example divisionalized organizations may find it difficult to capitalize on efficiencies which may be derived from sharing certain resources (e.g. manufacturing capacity, R&D, sales and distribution outlets/resources, etc.). In addition many organizations face rapidly changing markets and customers wishing to buy changing configurations of products or services. Sometimes it is difficult to sell where a product from various divisions is required. In some cases (e.g. a classic case are computer companies such as Bull in France) some products compete. In any event the purchaser may wish to complete a single deal through a single point of contact. Divisionalized organizations can find this difficult to achieve. One solution to these problems was the strategic business unit concept (Barnett and Wilstead, 1988). Here the focus was on product-market with a strategic business unit making sense where you could define a clear set of customers, a distinct set of competitors, for which it was possible to create a separate functioning business with an identifiable strategy and in which financial performance could be measured.

In recent times however, rapidly changing market, technological and other pressures have led firms to create more adaptability and also to seek to focus on core competences in which they are likely to achieve excellence. This has led to dramatic changes. Firms are 'de-layering'. For example at a recent conference the author attended, a senior executive from the North American computer industry claimed that large organizations had removed between 1 and 1.5 layers of management *on average* in the last five years. In consequence there are, in those organizations, many fewer managers, carrying more responsibility and more demanding jobs than formerly. Information technology, through making access to data easier, is supporting team-based approaches to management. The need to respond quickly to market pressures is leading many organizations to push responsibility down the organization, whether under slogans such as 'empowerment' or through customer service or total quality programmes. For these and other reasons connected with shareholder value many large businesses have 'demerged'. In many countries the public service is being reformed along similar lines. Public sector organizations which were once very hierarchical have either been privatized or have been taken out of the public service as independent agencies. We can see developments like this in North America, the UK, New Zealand and elsewhere. Healthcare reform in Thailand is proceeding apace on the basis of pushing responsibility down to providers (local hospitals and clinics) rather than managing them directly from the centre (in the capital city).

Over and above all of this companies out-source, engage in joint ventures, strategic alliances in order that each element of the 'value chain' (see Porter, 1985) is delivered in a high value-added way. This development is having a powerful impact creating what some call the 'networked' organization and others are now calling the 'virtual' organization.

Let us look at this trend in rather more detail (the discussion here derives from various sources, including Hastings, 1993 and recent work by a colleague Professor Bill Weinstein of Henley), Basically there has been a shift from a belief in the advantages of size to the advantages of adaptability. Thirty years ago many organizations set out to achieve integration from raw materials to final customer service, owning and controlling all functions in the value chain with only marginal sub-contracting. That way you could control costs, create certainty of delivery, project innovation and limit transaction costs (here we refer to the avoidance of the costs associated with, for example, having to purchase supplies in the open market as opposed to simply ordering from your own wholly owned supplier).

Increasingly some top managers are asking whether these larger groups are 'manageable'. The risks and problems of inertia are greater. Product development becomes a major problem. 'Time to market' grows with size. I well remember hearing an IBM Europe senior executive (in the late 1980s) complain that any new product proposal had to have seven different senior executives sign it off before it could proceed, including people located locally at Paris HQ and elsewhere. The possibility for delay is all too obvious. There is a growing literature on this time-to-market issue (see, for example Clark and Fujimoto, 1991 and Stalk and Hout, 1990) and no-one is suggesting that size is the only problem but the latter study shows that you can reduce time-to-market significantly if you move from a hierarchical to an 'entrepreneurial' structure, and even further if you adopt a 'time-based management' approach.

Thus we can see countless organizations focusing on their core competences (Prahalad and Hamel, 1990), dealing with 'preferred' suppliers with whom they develop strong links, de-layering, down-sizing, and focusing upon 'invisible assets' like product-market knowledge, competitor intelligence and the like as a source of added value (see Itami, 1987). The arguments presented above have been set out from a transactional cost perspective by Reve (1990). The practical consequences of these trends are that organizations are now much more likely to be engaged in strategic alliances, joint ventures, outsourcing, networking, joint development projects and so on. This implies a new context for managers.

In the new organization the manager is much more concerned with managing across boundaries (often as well as across borders). There is more dependence on 'outsiders' and less reliance on 'insiders'. Any part of the organization can be 'outsourced'. In the public sector the process is 'market-testing'. It creates new pressures. It also means that achieving added-value is more a matter of external networking and possessing relevant knowledge about the outside world than formerly. Increasingly managers find that rather than utilizing hierarchy and command and control they are managing exchange relations. Co-operation and negotiation are more relevant. Effective communication becomes vital. But this places greater emphasis on the need to develop your internal managerial and technological skills. Without doing so the organization risks being excluded because it brings no added value.

All of this implies that empathy, the ability to seek gains for all partners, flexibility and learning all become vital skills in the new organization. As we shall see they are also vital skills for those managing major change. Hastings (1993) talks about organizational networking in terms of the need to break down organizational boundaries, create successful partnerships, connect computers and connect people (see Figure 1). This implies a new set of priorities for management in this new organization. New management roles he thinks may be emerging include that of mentor (long talked about, increasingly practised), broker (connection people, ideas and resources) and what he calls the counterpart. This he describes as a vital role for the success of joint ventures and strategic alliances but it can be extended into project teams and other internal networks. The role is about providing explicit liaison between links (e.g. joint venture partners) over and above the informal linkages. Looking at cultural change at BP he reported the company view of the old and the new culture (the latter being one intended to encourage networking) as follows:

Old culture

- Hierarchies
- Boundaries
- Internal focus

- Paternalistic
- Second guessing
- Controlling

- Analysis
- Risk aversion

New culture

- Teams
- Connections
- External focus

- Empowerment
- Trusting
- Supportive

- Action
- Calculated risk-taking or innovation

**Figure 1.** Developed from Hastings (1993)

Not least of the characteristics of effective people in the new culture is that of *personal impact* – influencing others through example and recognition of their needs. But to conclude, the new thinking about organizations emphasizes the need for new thinking about careers and career development as well as moves to develop what has been called 'the self-reliant' manager (Bones, 1994).

The other source of pressure for change to which we have briefly referred is that of internationalization. Doz and Prahalad (1991) identify characteristics of the diversified internationally operating company as follows:

1 Organizational solutions based simply on either centralization or decentralization will not meet the complexity of the modern environment.
2 Processes and structure need to allow differentiation to meet the needs of various products, functions and countries.
3 Integrative processes are needed if diverse interests are to be balanced – i.e. we must work at maintaining interfaces, networks, etc.
4 Effective information flows throughout the business are a vital source of added value.
5 Flexibility is structure and process and the capability of including external partners is important.
6 There needs to be stability and consistency of purpose – a leadership task.

So once again the demands arising out of internationalization lead to the need to create and operate networks – see Bartlett and Ghoshal (1990) for an analysis of NV Philips as an international network.

It is important to realize that the issues we have referred to are not simply personal issues for which the solutions lie within the 'people' skills area. They are business issues demanding business skills – indeed the management skills required combine business and personal skills. Gould and Campbell (1987) articulate this idea through identifying three corporate styles which you can observe in large, diversified groups, as follows:

1 Strategic planning style – strong central management involvement in strategy development through an extensive planning review process and powerful initiatives to secure development of the business arising from the centre. Focus on creating shared vision leads to flexibility in performance targets with performance being viewed in the context of longer-term objectives.
2 Strategic control – emphasis on planning at the business unit level with the centre concerned primarily with the exercise of tight controls.
3 Financial control – the annual budget becomes the key control mechanism focusing attention on short-term targets.

Here we simply wish to make the point that successful strategic change seems to demand a combination of cognitive/analytical skills and knowledge alongside a range of behavioural or process skills and knowledge. In Figure 2 on page 4 we set out a 'map' of the cognitive/analytical components which appear to be needed. Here we suggest that successful strategic change requires knowledge and techniques for corporate diagnosis, in the culture change area and in putting together programmes of change. All of this is not enough however without the necessary process skills needed to encourage learning and change.

In a world in which the ability to change is a key 'engine of success' the shift from strategy into capability demands leadership, action planning, the ability to cope with pressure and uncertainty and a willingness to learn. More analysis will help us in that it aids our understanding of where we are and how we came to get there – but analysis alone will not create the future.

Charles Handy sees paradox as an inevitable consequence of the complex and changing world in which we live. He lists nine as paradoxes of the mature economies, arguing that they will inevitably emerge in Southeast Asia and Africa. They are the paradoxes of intelligence, work, productivity, time, riches, organization, age, the individual and of justice. My purpose is not to summarize his discussion of these paradoxes (you should read his book for that) but rather to introduce the extract I have chosen from his discussion of how to find the balance, how to find pathways through paradox.

Chapter 5 deals with the paradox of change. All too often in the past people accept the need for change only when they meet disaster in the face. Then it is too late. The time to change is when we are still successful enough to generate the income streams necessary to pay for change. For Handy we must always engage in 'second curve' thinking. We must always assume that our present success will be short-lived ('we are only as good as our last success!'). In turn this suggests that we should always seek relative instability, discomfort, uncertainty. Too much stability encourages complacency and much worse. We could go beyond this and argue that instability is now inevitable, the only question is can we embrace it?

# References

Bartlett, C. A. and Ghoshal, S. (1989) *Managing Across Borders: The transnational solution*, Harvard Business School Press, Boston, MA.
Bones, C. (1994) *The Self Reliant Manager*, Routledge, Henley-on-Thames.
Barnett, J. H. and Wilstead, W. D. (1988) *Management: Concept and Cases*, PWS-Kent.
Chandler, A. (1962) *Strategy and Structure: Chapters in the history of the American industrial enterprise*, MIT Press, Cambridge, MA.
Clark, K. B. and Fujimoto, T. (1991) *Product Development Performance*, Harvard Business School Press, Boston, MA.
Doz, Y. L. and Prahalad, C. K. (1991) *Managing DMNCs: A search for a new paradigm, Strategic Management Journal*, **12**, 4.
Gould, M. and Campbell, A. (1987) *Strategies and Styles: The role of the centre in managing diversified corporations*, Blackwell, Oxford.
Greiner, L. (1972) Evolution and revolution as organizations grow, *Harvard Business Review*, July–August.
Hastings, C. (1993) *The New Organization*, McGraw-Hill, London.
Itami, H., (1987) *Mobilizing Invisible Assets*, Harvard University Press, Cambridge, MA.
Porter, M. (1985) *Competitive Advantage*, Free Press, New York.
Prahalad, C. K. and Hamel, G., (1990) The core competence of the corporation, *Harvard Business Review*, **68**(3), 79–91.
Reve, T. (1990) Personal communication.
Stalk, G. and Hout, T. (1990). *Competing Against Time: How Time-Based Competition is Reshaping Global Markets*, The Free Press.

# 4 The intelligent enterprise

## J. B. Quinn

## Obtaining both customization and lowest cost

At the outset, we need to set aside some widely accepted strategic dogmas about 'generic strategies'. These pose an inherent – and in the case of services, false – conflict between obtaining 'lowest cost' and offering highest 'differentiation' (through flexibility and customization) within the same strategy.[1] Many well-run service companies *do both;* they optimize flexibility at the customer contact point *and* maximize the 'production efficiencies' that flow from repeatability, experience curve effects, and integrated cost and quality control. They accomplish this by (1) seeking the smallest possible core unit at which activity or output can be 'replicated' or repeated, (2) developing micro measures to manage processes and functions at this level, and (3) mixing these micro units in a variety of combinations to match localized or individual customers' needs. This approach has been the touchstone of some of the most successful service strategies. With properly implemented systems, many outstanding service companies – including Bankers Trust, AT&T, Toys 'R' Us, Domino's Pizza, ServiceMaster, Wal-Mart, Federal Express, American Express, McKesson, and American Airlines – have achieved both maximum flexibility and lowest cost in their market segments.

What do these 'smallest replicable units' look like? 'Replicable' simply means 'repeatable with a small variation' in response to local conditions. The nature of the particular unit that will be most useful, of course, varies by industry and by strategy.

● For Mary Kay Cosmetics or Tupperware, the elements of a sales presentation provide such repeatable core units. For accountants, audit check procedures, inventory control processes, unique problem solutions, or tax preparation subroutines may be critical. For hotels, it is information about customers' preferences, past service selections, special personal needs, travel patterns, and so on. For lawyers, prepackaged documents, paragraphs, phrases, court opinions, or case briefings may be the leverageable units. In financial services, elements of individual 'transactions' (buy/sell

information about names, units traded, prices, times received and trans-
acted, customer codes, opposite parties' positions, and their relationships
to total market movements) are the core units. For information retrieval
businesses, it is the 'category' or 'key word'; for communications, it is the
'packet' or even the 'bit'; and so on.

## Seeking the smallest replicable unit

Early in the life cycle of many service industries, the smallest truly replicable
unit seemed to be an individual office, store, or franchise location. Later, as
volume increased, it often became possible for the headquarters to develop
and replicate greater efficiencies within locations by managing and measuring
critical performance variables at individual departmental, sales counter, activity, or stock-keeping unit (SKU) levels.[2] Then the successful reduction of key
activities to their most refined elements allowed McDonald's, Federal
Express, Wal-Mart, Citicorp, Mrs Fields, Pizza Hut, and even the New York
Stock Exchange (NYSE) to push the repeatability unit to even smaller 'micro
management' levels. Replicating precisely measured activity cycles, delivery
times, customer query sequences, personal selling approaches, customer
data, inventory control patterns, ingredients, freshness and cooking cycles,
counter display techniques, cleanliness and maintenance procedures, and so
on, in detail became keys to service and financial success. Lapses led to
difficulties.

The concept of seeking the 'minimum replicable level' of information for
more flexible and precise management now goes even further in many industries – like transportation, banking, communications, structural design, or
medical research – where it has become possible to disaggregate the critical
units of service production to the level of data blocks, packets, or 'bytes' of
information. Accessing and combining such units on a large scale are emerging
as the core activities in achieving flexibility, quality and cost control, and economies of scale on a level never before envisioned. So precise are many large
enterprises' (AT&T, Fed Ex) and many nationwide chains' (Mrs Fields, General Mills Restaurants Group) measurement and feedback systems that their
headquarters can tell within minutes – or even seconds – when something goes
wrong in the system, at a client contact point, or in a decentralized unit, and
often precisely what the problem is. Broadcast, power utility, or transmission
networks, of course, must know of problems within split seconds and have on-
line electronic monitoring devices for the purpose. CNN, for example, has
found that a pause of more than five seconds is a complete disaster, causing
massive audience tune-outs, and all employees and systems are keyed to preventing such catastrophes. In these cases, on-line monitors signal the problem
immediately; people throughout the system are trained to anticipate possible
sources of interruption and are empowered to move instantly to take whatever
action is necessary to avoid or correct an aberration. Most problems end up

being fixed before the customer ever knows there is an issue – the ultimate goal of quality control in services.

How does disaggregation of data and control at the appropriate minimum replicable level work in practice? Most of the successful large service systems in our study (many named earlier) first analyzed their processes into the smallest measurable details. Then, through careful work design and iterative learning processes, they both reengineered their processes to use this knowledge and developed the databases and feedback systems to capture and update needed information at the micro levels desired. Only then did they automate repeated or difficult processes – usually in sequence to avoid unnecessary risks and disruptions – within an overall system design that maintained compatibility and interface control among the subsystems. The best systems were flexibly designed with a five-to-ten-year time frame in mind, allowing new modules and data comparisons to be added as needed in the future.

Wherever possible, automated processes were interlinked to market-based feedback systems that provided up-to-date or continuous quality measurements and allowed mixing and matching of data in new ways to create greater value-added for customers. Unfortunately, insufficient attention to the feedback loop between customers and the company's own information/control systems has led to the failure of many strategies. When systems were automated properly – as in the cases of AT&T, McKesson, ADP Services, Mrs Fields, Federal Express, and so on – the systems and their associated organization concepts became the core of the institution's strategy.

● For example, in the early 1970s the New York Stock Exchange (NYSE) recognized that its hand-entry trading procedures would soon constrain its growth and threaten its capacity to maintain its status as the world's premier securities trading institution. To automate properly, NYSE had to understand clearly the many different values its customers expected it to produce. It undertook extensive customer interviews with all its stakeholders to secure this understanding. In addition to merely handling 'transactions,' NYSE found its systems had to (1) be seen as 'fair and objective' by buyers and sellers, (2) maintain detailed control over each party's interest in a transaction, (3) generate the data all parties need to analyze the total market as well as individual securities, (4) connect individual buyers and sellers with common interests at remote points, (5) report transactions accurately to all interested public and private groups as required by law, (6) be absolutely reliable despite totally unforeseeable shifts in volume, new products, and external contingencies, and yet (7) meet all the needs of their NYSE owners and brokers for business information.[3]

NYSE ultimately was able to break each transaction down into the microscopic pieces of information that were common to each transaction yet when aggregated could meet all those other needs. Individual pieces of the system, like data input devices, were extensively pretested with their users. To ensure adequate capacity, NYSE built the system to handle fifty times the volume of transactions it anticipated, which saved the system on Black Monday in 1987. Yet despite its complexity, the system was brought up to complete operational levels over one weekend to ensure the market never closed – meeting a most important criterion for the customer: reliability. Its advanced automation system allowed NYSE not only to survive the vicissitudes of the 1980s but to lead the world in permitting the new trading practices that reshaped financial services in the 1980s.

Service management was not always based on minimum replicable concepts. In the past large transportation companies (airlines or railroads), utilities (AT&T and electric power grids), and large department stores (Macy's and Gimbels) relied more on traditional economies from large-scale facilities and purchasing power. In pioneering micro techniques, however, railroads were among the leaders. They installed completely automated switching and safety feedback systems that used micro measures to locate and control entire trains and individual boxcars. Airlines soon found they could not realize the benefits of their large-scale equipment investments – especially filling all the seats in a fixed-cost flight network – without learning to manage customer relationships at the micro level. Once identified and structured in detail, these micro units permitted the individualized routing, pricing, seating, baggage handling, special services, frequent flyer incentives, minute-by-minute scheduling, massive operations coordination, and interconnected reservations, billing, and payment systems that are now the key to competitiveness. In fact, many credit SABRE, the leading automated system, with moving American from being one of the weakest airlines in 1978 to its 1980s preeminence, while other previously prominent airlines – notably TWA, Pan Am, Braniff, and Eastern – fell into oblivion during deregulation.

## Managing customization at the micro level

Ted Levitt, in a classic article, long ago recognized the mass production analogy in some service operations.[4] The ultimate purpose of focusing on the smallest replicable unit of operations, however, is not just the mass production benefits that standardization allows. There are much more interesting strategic benefits. Effectively combining these micro units permits one to achieve the highest possible degree of segmentation, strategic fine-tuning, value-added, and customer satisfaction in the marketplace. Interestingly, the larger the organization, the more refined these replicability units may practically be – and the higher their leverage for creating value-added gains. Greater volume allows the larger company to (1) collect more detail about its individual operating and market segments, (2) efficiently analyze these data at more disaggregated levels, and (3) experiment with these detailed segmentations in ways smaller concerns cannot. For example:

● American Express (AmEx) is the only major credit card company with a large travel service. By capturing in the most disaggregated possible form – essentially data bytes – the details of transactions that its 22 million traveler, shopper, retailer, lodging, and transportation company customers put through its credit card and travel systems, AmEx can mix and match the patterns and capabilities of each group to add value for them in ways its competitors cannot. It can identify life-style changes (like marriage or moving) or match forthcoming travel plans with its customers' specific buying habits to notify them of special promotions, product offerings, or services AmEx's retailers may be presenting in their local or planned travel areas. From its larger information base AmEx also has the potential to provide more detailed information services to its 2 million retailer or transportation customers – like demographic and comparative analyses of their customer bases or individual customers' needs for wheelchair, pickup, or other convenience services. These can provide unique added value for both its consumer and commercial customers (see 'Vignette: American Express' at the end of this chapter).

The key to high-profit micro management is to break down both operations and markets into such compatible detail that managers can discern, by properly cross-matrixing their data, how a slight change in one arena can affect some critical aspect of performance in another. The ability to micro manage, target, and customize operations in this fashion, using the knowledge base that size permits, is fast becoming the most important scale economy available in services today. For example:

● In its now classic strategy, Benetton was able to develop such detail in its information base that it could fine-tune the offerings of each individual store to the specific demographics of the customers in its immediate shopping area. Thus colors, styles, and sizes could be adjusted to the specific characteristics of customers for stores only a few blocks apart, allowing Benetton a much denser store location strategy and offering customers greater selection of those garments they most desired.

Critical to effective system design is conceptualizing the smallest replicable unit and its potential use in strategy as early as possible in the design process. Summing disaggregated data later, if one so desires, is much easier than moving from a more aggregated system to a greater refinement of detail. Further, highly disaggregated data often capture unexpected experience patterns that more summary data would obscure. Much of the later power and flexibility of

American's SABRE, McKesson's ECONOMOST, and National Rental Car's EXPRESSWAY systems derived from making this choice correctly, while less successful competitors' systems did not. The latter usually chose a larger replicability unit in order to save initial installation costs. In the process they lost crucial detailed experience and segmentation data that could have become the core of their later strategies. An unfortunate example was in car rentals, where Hertz, despite its larger size, allowed Avis and National to steal the early march with their more detailed and flexible Wizard and Expressway systems.

## Motivating and empowering the point person

One may easily see how the micro unit approach addresses issues of efficiency and potential flexibility. But what about the necessity to motivate and empower service people? Do such systems empower employees to be able and activated to perform their jobs better? Or does the opposite happen? If they feel denigrated or frustrated by the company's control systems, contact people will tend to abuse, rather than assist, customers. So much of a service's perceived value is created at the moment and point of contact that it is crucial to the entire enterprise's success that such people handle the customer interface with both diligence and flair. This point is especially critical in retail or consumer sales, but it affects many other service activities as well. IBM, for example, found that the way the receptionist answered the phone predetermined much of its customers' reactions to the company even after they had reached the person they were seeking. Many other studies have found that 'pleasure' in buying – especially interactions with the contact person in consumer sales – is at least as important to customers as price, efficiency, or other aspects of quality.[5]

Companies as diverse as Steuben Glass and Honda have also found that the salesperson's handling of a customer carries over to the later perceived quality of the product. Consequently, both place elaborate emphasis on dealership selection and personal training of contact people. Quality hotels set up their communication systems to call customers by name and to track their preferences and perceptions of service to treat them better on the next visit. Portman Hotel, for example, says that its most valuable asset is its capacity to manage such information to individualize and optimize its service presentation to clients. Such hotels also teach their employees to develop eye contact, to use customers' names, and to smile when delivering services – and to prevent the buildup of queues like the plague. Such simple acts, easy to check and costing little once other elements are built into the software system, are often as important to quality perceptions as are elaborate building or facilities investments. One need only note the long, customer-satisfying survival of old eastern US and European spas with out-moded facilities but finely developed personal services.

## Style, personalization, and efficiency

In commercial markets, a company's style can also be a major influence on purchases of more technical services. EDS, the leader in the huge independent network management business, is admittedly technically competent and a very low-cost operator. But, *The Economist* notes, EDS

> . . . badly needs a change of image. Electronic Data Systems may be number one in the $30–40 billion market for information-technology services, but its hard driving, starched-shirt style makes even rival IBM cuddly. That, despite its daunting competence, is costing EDS business it needs if it is to escape the influence of its major shareholder and main customer, General Motors.
>
> EDS does one thing for its more than 7,000 customers, big or small: it runs their computer networks on contract more cheaply than they can. EDS makes its money by achieving economies of scale (in both buying equipment and running systems, and in keeping up with technical advances) that are beyond the scope of most individual customers. The ever-falling cost of computer power means ever-widening margins on its fixed-price contracts. . .
>
> Just how much the firm needed to change was brought home when [EDS] lost – to IBM – the highly publicized battle to take over Eastman Kodak's data processing. . .
>
> Under its new boss, Les Aberthal, a 47-year-old whose school-masterly manner wins friends in Detroit, EDS responded by reorganizing its top management into customer groups, and set about trying to look more friendly. The changes aimed to flatten the hierarchy, to keep the company hard driving and entrepreneurial. . . The company's biggest challenge in managing its rapid growth is people. When it takes over a firm's data processing, EDS also takes over its staff, not all of EDS's own choosing. [Smaller firms especially] have to feel comfortable that EDS understands their businesses, as they will necessarily rely on [EDS] for the development of software applications as well as bulk data processing.[6]

Properly designed service systems will simultaneously deliver both a personalized feeling and efficiency.

- Federal Express's DADS computer system for automated pickup and delivery allowed sophisticated real-time truck routing, eliminated input errors, provided a basis for monitoring service cycles, and freed the contact person to interact with customers on a more personal basis, a key to the FedEx strategy. It is fascinating to see the pride and confidence the hand-held scanner/computer (tied to the DADS and COSMOS systems) gives to a relatively untrained individual operating at the customer contact point for FedEx. It allows the point person to feel and behave essentially as an individual agent taking time to personalize the service, yet be linked to a huge network whose goal is to deliver 'absolutely, positively on time' with a strategy of personalized customer contact. (See 'Vignette: Federal Express Co.,' at the end of this chapter for further details.)
- Domino's Pizza, perhaps the fastest-growing food chain in history, encourages its local store managers to regard themselves as individual entrepreneurs. First, for each of its 4,500 highly decentralized outlets, industrial engineering and food research automated the making of a pizza

to as near a science as possible, eliminating much of the drudgery in such tasks, yet ensuring higher quality and uniformity. Then, finding that its store managers were still spending fifteen to twenty hours a week on paperwork, Domino's introduced NCR 'mini-tower' systems at its stores to handle all of the ordering, payroll, marketing, cash flow, inventory, and work control functions. This freed store executives to perform more valuable supervisory, follow-up, menu experimentation, public relations, or customer service activities – expanding and elevating their management roles and focusing them even more on founder Tom Monahan's goals of (1) making them independent entrepreneurs and (2) supporting the company's strongly held customer service philosophies.

Some strategies, of course, call for more education, motivation, or empowerment; some for more standardization of activity. Some specific service situations even require that technologies be used primarily to obtain uniformity rather than flexibility. In such services – e.g., bank accounting, letter sorting, film processing, systems programming, or aircraft maintenance – one may actively discourage too much independence. Repeated exactness and tight tolerances, not creativity, are required. Great service successes, however, generally exhibit a unique blend of (1) a distinctly structured technology system and (2) a carefully developed management style and motivation system to support it. The subtle development and timing of the balance between the two can lead to quite different strategic postures in the same industry. Amplifying the FedEx example above and contrasting it with another well-known company, UPS, will make the point quickly. The rest of this chapter will develop in detail how new organization forms can support specific empowerment strategies.

● Federal Express (FedEx) has historically emphasized the use of a friendly, people-oriented, entrepreneurial management style in conjunction with 'state of the art' technology systems as the basis of its competitive edge. Its DADS (digitally assisted dispatch) and COSMOS II (automated tracking) systems give FedEx maximum capability to be responsive, while its training programs, colorful advertising, decentralized operating style, and incentive systems emphasize the need to 'go to the limit' personally in responding to customer needs and ensuring reliable on-time delivery. By contrast, UPS long utilized old-style trucks, hand sorting, detailed time and motion studies, and tight controls for its drivers. A hard-headed cost control system gave it a lower-cost – but considerably less customer responsive – market position. Both companies have been successful, FedEx by emphasizing 'highest reliability and customer service' and UPS by emphasizing 'the most efficient ship in the shipping business.'

Neither approach is right in the abstract, or for all parties. But with better technological capabilities, customers' demands for more flexibility and responsiveness are driving more and more companies toward decentralization and empowerment at the contact level.

## New organization forms for both efficiency and flexibility

In their efforts to harness these two principal service drivers – maximum technological efficiency and flexibility at the micro level along with personal empowerment for customer contact personnel – some service companies have developed strikingly new, and much more effective, organizational models for all businesses. In this respect, service company managements have often moved well ahead of their manufacturing counterparts. Some of the basic concepts are also appearing in service activities within manufacturing companies, where they often prove to be remarkably easy to apply. Although some suggest that all organizations are moving – or should move – toward some predetermined new form,[7] we found a rich new variety of organizational strategies available. Each seems most suitable in certain circumstances, and not others. But all seem to embrace similar themes and to call for somewhat comparable technology and management support. First, what are some of the more important new organizational forms and where can they best be used? Later we shall develop their common themes.

## 'Infinitely flat' organizations

When technology is creatively implemented in service activities, there appears to be virtually no limit to the potential reporting span – the number of people reporting to one supervisor or center – that a service organization can make effective. While spans of 20–25 have become relatively common, spans of hundreds exist in some service organizations. Even the term 'span of control' seems an anachronism. Perhaps a better term would be 'span of communication' or 'span of coordination.' In most of these 'very flat' organizations, few orders are given by the line organization to those below. Instead, the central authority becomes an information source, a communications coordinator, or a reference desk for unusual inquiries. Lower organizational levels more often connect into it to obtain information for the purpose of performing better rather than for instructions or specific guidance from above.

Many examples exist. It is common for twenty to forty fast food operations to be connected to a single logistics support or order coordinating center. Domino's Pizza is moving toward two hundred connections per center. A single conductor often coordinates a hundred or more people in a symphony orchestra.[8] And two, or even more, symphony orchestras in different locations could easily play together simultaneously, if linked by fiber optics. A single communications and satellite tracking system can coordinate and direct innumerable aircraft or container ships worldwide. And so on. In other fields:

- Shearson American Express's 310 and Merrill Lynch's 480 domestic brokerage offices each connect directly into their parents' central information offices for routine needs, yet can bypass the electronic system for personal access to individual experts in headquarters. Merrill Lynch has a PC-based workstation for each of its 'financial consultants' (brokers) linked through LANS and SNA to its central mainframe computers. Although regional marketing structures exist, business is conducted as if each of Merrill Lynch's 17,000 branch office contact people reported directly to headquarters, with their only personal oversight being at the local level. Computers extend Merrill Lynch's system capabilities to the level of individual customers, printing 400 million pages of output a year, largely customer reports captured directly from on-line transaction data. In effect, technology permits the company to compete in a coordinated fashion with the full power and scale economies of a major financial enterprise, yet local brokers can manage their own small units and accounts as independently as if they alone provided the total service on a local basis. From an operations viewpoint, the organization is absolutely flat; 17,000 brokers connect directly into headquarters for all their needs.
- Federal Express, with 42,000 employees in more than three hundred cities worldwide, has a maximum of only five organizational layers between its nonmanagement employees and its COO or CEO. Typical operating spans of control are 15–20 employees per manager, with only 2.1 staff employees per $ million in sales – about one-fifth the industry average. As many as fifty couriers are under the line control of a single dispatching center. FedEx's DADS and COSMOS II computer-communications capabilities allow it to coordinate its 21,000 vans nationwide to make an average of 720,000 'on call' stops per day within a few hours' time. Because of its leading-edge flight operations technologies and avionics controls, as many as two hundred FedEx aircraft can be in the air simultaneously, but under the control of a single authority, should it become necessary to override flight plans because of weather or special emergencies.[9]

## Destroying hierarchies

There is no inherent reason that organizations cannot be made 'infinitely flat' – i.e., with innumerable outposts guided by one central 'rules-based' or 'computer controlled inquiry' system. As the above examples suggest, these need not be simple repetitive activities. Functions as various as personal sales, brokering, piloting aircraft, captaining ships, running railroads, playing music, reporting news, and performing research also qualify.

Nevertheless, most executives immediately think of harnessing routinized activities like those of fast food operations into the 'infinitely flat' form. This should also quickly suggest its applicability to many equally routine manufacturing operations, where spans of control are often still tragically held to the seven-to-nine-person level, dictated by concepts that date back to Frederick Taylor. Once production jobs have been adequately analyzed, and real-time electronic measurement systems have been put in place, manufacturing can be an ideal place for 20–100-person spans of coordination. In fact, GM's Nummi joint venture with Toyota operates with an average span of twenty now.

By routinizing and automating operating parameters at their finest replicable level, both manufacturing and services companies can also develop the detailed cost and quality controls they need for system coordination and productivity at each of their many highly decentralized operating nodes. Under proper circumstances, the scheduling, order-giving, and information feed-back functions normally provided by hierarchical structures can be completely automated. And if retained the hierarchy itself becomes a costly artifact. General Mills Restaurant Group found that as it automated more of its restaurant operations, it could double its spans of control, eliminate whole layers of management, and save tens of millions in administrative costs alone. Union Pacific removed six layers of its organization after it automated operations and delegated responsibility for on-time performance to small front-line teams.

Technology naturally supports several of the major trends that lead to empowerment and flatter organizations. New technologies permit today's burgeoning number of less-trained employees to perform to much higher quality and output standards than they otherwise possibly could as beginners.[10] Then they encourage these new workers to learn further skills and with these to take over many of the traditional functions of middle managers.[11]

● High school trained typists or accounting clerks – given word processors, spell-checks, and spreadsheet software – can quickly achieve better output volumes and finished work quality than all but a few executive secretaries or senior accountants used to attain. Then they begin to tinker with their computers, seeking more interesting things to do, expanding their skills and range of services into areas their supervisors used to handle.

As the software system takes over most of the quality checks middle managers used to perform, it becomes natural to extend the latter's spans of control. Since front-line people can do most of the work actually needed (and cost less), this leads naturally to the elimination of intermediate management and the 'delayering and flattening of organizations' so widely observed today. In the past, the lowest ranks were the most vulnerable persons in an economic downturn. In the 1991–92 recession it has been the middle managers made redundant by the empowerment of lower levels.[12] Repeatedly, our respondents noted that re-engineering of contact jobs – followed by automation and reorganization of tasks to empower the point person – had led to the elimination of two to six layers of administrative management.

# References

1  M. Porter, 'Generic Competitive Strategies', in Michael Porter, *Competitive Advantage* (New York: Free Press, 1985).
2  This was the secret to McKesson's, SuperValu's, and Toys 'R' Us's success.
3  C. Keith and A. Grody, 'Electronic Automation of the New York Stock Exchange', in *Managing Innovation: Case Studies from the Services Industries* (Washington, DC: National Academy Press, 1988).
4  T. Levitt, 'Industrialization of Service', *Harvard Business Review*, September–October 1976.
5  V. Zeithaml, A. Parasuraman, and L. Berry, *Delivering Quality Service* (New York: Free Press, 1990).
6  'Lots of Respect, Little Love', *The Economist*, July 27, 1991.
7  T. Peters, 'Get Innovative or Get Dead', *California Management Review*; Fall 1990; D.Q. Mills, *Rebirth of the Corporation* (New York: J. Wiley & Sons, 1991).
8  P. Drucker, 'The Coming of the New Organization', *Harvard Business Review*, January–February 1988.
9  'Federal Express Corporation' (case), in H. Mintzberg and J. Quinn, *The Strategy Process*, 2nd ed. (Englewood Cliffs, NJ: Prentice Hall, 1991).
10  J. Bright, *Automation and Management* (Boston, MA: Division of Research, Graduate School of Business Administration, Harvard University, 1958).
11  C. Handy, *The Age of Unreason* (Boston: Harvard Business School Press, 1990).
12  Mills, *Rebirth of the Corporation*.

# 5  The empty raincoat

## C. Handy

## The discipline of the second curve

The concept of the Sigmoid Curve has, I find, helped many people and many institutions to understand their current confusions. The question which they always ask, however, is 'How do we know where we are on the first curve?' One way of answering that is to ask them to make their own private and personal assessment of their position, or that of their organisation, to draw the first curve as they see it, and to mark an X on it to show where they are now. Almost invariably, when they reveal their perceptions of the curve, there is a consensus that they are farther along the curve that any of them would previously have admitted. They are nearer to point **B** than to point **A**.

Like the story of the road to Davy's Bar, you will only know for sure where you are on the curve when you look back. It is easier, too, to see where others are on their curves than to see yourself. We must therefore proceed by guess and assumption. There is no science for this sort of thing.

The discipline of the second curve requires that you always assume that you are near the peak of the first curve, at point **A**, and should therefore be starting to prepare a second curve. Organisations should assume that their present strategies will need to be replaced within two or three years and that their product life-cycles are shorter than they were. Richard Foster of McKinsey studied 208 companies over 18 years in order to discover those who were consistently successful. There were only three who lasted the course for the whole 18 years. Fifty-three per cent could not maintain their record for more than two years. Individuals should also work on the assumption that life will not continue as it has for ever and that a new direction will be needed in two or three years.

It may well be that the assumption turns out to be wrong, that the present trends can be prolonged much longer, and that the first curve was really only in its infancy. Nothing has been lost. Only the exploratory phase of the second curve has been done. No major commitments will have been undertaken until the second curve overtakes the first, which will never happen as long as the first curve is still on the rise. Keeping the two curves going will become a habit.

The discipline of devising that second curve will, however, have had its effect. It will have forced one to challenge the assumptions underlying the first curve and to devise some possible alternatives. It is tempting to think that the world has always been arranged the way it is and to delude ourselves that nothing will ever change. The discipline of the second curve keeps one sceptical, curious and inventive – attitudes essential in a time of change, and the best way of coping with the contradictions which accompany such a time.

The discipline of the second curve follows the traditional four-stage cycle of discovery. Questions start it off. The questions spark off ideas, possibilities, hypotheses. The best of these must then be tested out, tentatively and experimentally. Finally, the results of the experiments are reviewed. The first two stages cost nothing except the time for imagination. They can be very stimulating, particularly if they start from the greenfield hypothesis – 'If we did not exist would we reinvent ourselves and, if so, what would we look like?' Or, in a more personal example of second-curve thinking, 'If we did not live here, or do what we are doing, what would we be doing, where and how would we be living if we had the chance to start again?' The discipline of the second curve requires that you do not reinvent the same life, because that would merely perpetuate the first curve. The second curve is always different, although it builds on the first and grows out of it.

In *The Paradox of Success*, his book on the personal renewal of leaders, John O'Neil uses the model of the second curve to describe how leaders do, or do not, move on in life. He points out that one essential is to let go of your past. If one is too emotionally attached to what has gone before, it is difficult to be different in any way. One can then cling on until it is too late. He quotes Odysseus as an example of a young warrior chief who was so committed to roaming and raiding, at which he once excelled, that he spent 20 years coming back from the war in Troy to his kingdom of Ithaca, reluctant to assume the responsibilities of government. By the time he did get home he was a failed commander, in rags, with his kingdom in a mess. It is the story of the man who did not want to grow up.

If success comes early, it can be particularly hard to turn one's back on it when one's star begins to wane. It was sad to watch Bjorn Borg return to the tennis courts in an attempt to recapture past glories, long after his talents had faded. It is often easier to move on from disasters than from successes. I have always, therefore, been impressed by people like Leonard Cheshire, the distinguished and heroic British fighter pilot who, after the war was over, left all that behind and set out to create a network of homes for the elderly and disabled. I am impressed by the family business in France which, at just the right time, turned its back on the textile industry in which it had made its name, and launched a chain of supermarkets. 'Where did you find the courage to do something so completely different?' I asked. 'It would have required more courage to do nothing,' the head of the family replied. 'We had the responsibility to provide a future for the family, and the past, distinguished though it was, could not have been that future.'

# Curvilinear logic

Moving on requires a belief in what Schumacher used to call curvilinear logic, the conviction that the world and everything in it really is a Sigmoid Curve, that everything has its ups and then its downs, and that nothing lasts for ever or was there for ever. Just-In-Time Manufacturing was developed in Japan, and later copied everywhere. The idea of a constant stream of deliveries to your factory door, as and when you needed them, was blindingly obvious when you thought about it. Cut out the warehouse and all those storage costs. Let the suppliers carry the inventory costs instead, or rather, eliminate them completely, provided always that you can guarantee that the lorries with the bits will arrive 'just-in-time'. Unfortunately, the idea became too popular. They tell me that the delivery vehicles now jam all the freeways around Tokyo, meaning that just-in-time often gives way to just-too-late. The costs of the traffic jams are beginning to outweigh the costs of the original warehouses, to say nothing of all the environmental damage caused by those idling exhausts. You can have too much of a good thing, or, curvilinear logic strikes again.

Curvilinear logic is not intuitively obvious if you are still ascending the first curve. Business history is littered with the stories of founding fathers who thought that their way was the only way. The French textile business mentioned above is a notable rarity among family businesses. The paradox of success, that what got you where you are won't keep you where you are, is a hard lesson to learn. Curvilinear logic means starting life over again, something which gets harder as one gets older. It is better, therefore, in organisations, to entrust the curvilinear thinking to the next generation. They can see more clearly where the first curve is heading and what the next curve might look like. It is the job of their elders to give them permission to be different, and then, when the next curve is established, to get out of the way. For that to happen, there has to be a new curve for them, outside.

'My father brought me back from America to run the business here in Treviso,' his daughter said. 'But he still comes into the office every day, even Sundays. He wants me to run the business as if I was him, and I'm not. And the business has to change, if he would only let it. It's very frustrating.' Her story was not unusual. The father had nothing else he wanted to do. The business had been his life, and now he had no other. 'Wet leaves, we call them in Japan,' said the Japanese lady, describing the reaction of Japan's women to their retired executive husbands. 'You know how it is with wet leaves, they just stick around!' For curvilinear logic to work in the organisation there has to be a life beyond the organisation for the heroes of the first curve.

The Coca-Cola Company is, on the face of it, the great exception to the concept of the second curve. For 104 years they have sold the same product in the same packaging with much the same advertising. The only time they changed the formula they were forced by their customers to reverse the decision. Their secret may lie, however, in the motto which is inscribed in their central offices and in the minds of all its officers – 'The world belongs to the discontented'. It was the favourite saying of their early and long-time chairman, Robert Woodruff. He was warning against complacency and advocating a perpetual curiosity – the itch of the second curve. Coca-Cola's Japanese company, I was told, test-markets a new soft-drink variety or other product every month. Even if most of them fail most of the time, it keeps the questing spirit alive. When and if Coca-Cola's 104-year curve turns down, they hope that they will be prepared.

The Japanese, of course, have their own word for it – *kaizen*, or continuous improvement. The assumption behind *kaizen* is the assumption behind this book – that there is no perfect answer in a changing world. We must therefore be forever searching. Anita Roddick, of the Body Shop, puts it more succinctly: 'What is so wonderful about the Body Shop is that we still don't know the rules.' As long as they think that way, so long will they thrive. Complacency is the enemy of curiosity.

Reproduced from Handy, C. (1994) *The Empty Raincoat*. Random House, London. Reprinted with permission.

# Part Three
# Strategic Diagnosis

In Figure 2 on page 4 we identify the diagnostic components of a 'map of major change'. We reproduce these components below as Figure 1.

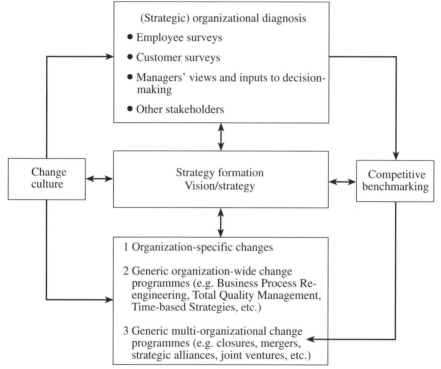

**Figure 1.** Strategic change

From this we see that strategic diagnosis is driven by and/or formed by ideas formulated about the future of the organization leading to a 'vision of the future' which in turn are influenced by and give rise to the need for surveys, employee surveys, customer surveys and benchmarking. There are techniques available for vision/strategy formulation, but it is important to focus initially on what we are doing in the diagnosis process. We are not merely attempting to collect symptomatic evidence but to *understand* what has happened. Thus falling sales or increasing costs are problems which demand some form of change but it is impossible to say what without understanding *why*. So much is obvious enough but rarely do we really attempt to understand what has happened as part of a preparatory diagnosis of what and how to change an organization.

In Chapter 6 Danny Miller provides us with an impressive treatment of the dynamics of corporate success, decline and renewal. This is important because it both extends the ideas of how the seeds of both success and failure can be understood and because it provides us with a better understanding of the corporate dynamics within which we are enmeshed and which we both attempt to transform and within which we might attempt to introduce changes. In turn this is vital simply because much treatment of change is too narrowly focused.

What does this mean? Basically most studies of change are narrowly focused on what is being changed and are treated in rather a static way. Thus we see that an organization is deemed to need improved quality and the discussion focuses upon the implementation of a total quality management programme and the associated culture changes needed for it to be successful. Rarely is any attempt made to carry out a longitudinal study (there are a few rare exceptions to this) but even less often is there any real attempt to examine the dynamics which created the need for a total quality management programme in the first place. Thus it is that we often cannot judge whether or not the programme will succeed.

The extract we re-print from *The Icarus Paradox* is one attempt to examine these dynamics. However before we proceed to examine Miller's ideas it is worth looking briefly at two other attempts to deal with these dynamics.

Why is it that people are often managed inappropriately in a period of change? There are two main reasons. Managers managing change are under pressure. This pressure undermines their own performance. Also, organizations often do not possess managers who are sufficiently skilful in handling change. Kotter (1988), for example, suggests one 'syndrome' associated with inadequate leadership, which we might similarly associate with inadequate change management. In summary, the argument is that successful organizations can carry the seeds of their own later decline, unless managers learn to be both successful and adaptable. The syndrome is set out in Figure 2. The tensions created by declining performance create performance.

Thus the argument combines the success of a few key people, a period of easy success and growing organizational complexity followed by declining performance creating pressures towards short-termism and an inward focus. All of this can lead to a lack of credibility amongst top management combined with a 'fear of failure' throughout the organization.

Particularly interesting is the point about 'fear of failure'; the pressures are dual in nature. On the one hand the short-term approach combined with a functional or departmental orientation, centralization and autocratic management styles creates a powerful tendency to limit risk-taking. On the other, managers moving rapidly through careers and not having to face up to their mistakes do not learn the interpersonal skills needed to do so. They find facing up to performance issues difficult. Therefore, when forced to do so by those same short-term pressures, they often do so inadequately and in a volatile, even primitive, fashion. This further reduces risk-taking, over time creating an organization within which the 'fear of failure' is very high indeed.

Kotter (1988) identifies a number of the 'characteristics needed, to provide effective leadership', overcoming the problems identified in the syndrome outlined above. To be effective, leaders need a range of knowledge of industry, business functions and the firm.

---

**Stage 1**: The firm is in a strong position, with little competition. It develops systems, management practices and a culture which depend on a few capable leaders. The management style is a combination of autocratic, directive and paternalistic.

**Stage 2**: The firm grows and becomes more complex. Competition increases and new technology emerges. The firm now needs strong and capable leadership but does not have enough people with these skills. Many people with good leadership potential left because of the frustrations created in Stage 1. However, the firm's performance does not deteriorate dramatically. It remains well-placed in its established markets. It 'lives' off its reputation.

**Stage 3**: Declining performance leads to a focus on short-term results. Internal tensions lead to conflict which cannot be handled constructively. Senior managers seem incapable of facing these tensions. Functional rather than corporate policies prevail. The firm lacks a co-ordinated strategy. This, in turn, undermines efforts to improve the quality of management.

---

**Figure 2.** Syndrome of ineffective leadership and change management (modified from Kotter, 1988)

Also needed are a broad range of contacts and good working relationships in the firm and the industry. Linked to this will be good track record in a relatively broad set of activities. Kotter also refers to 'keen minds' (whatever that means), strong interpersonal skills, high integrity, seeing value in people, and a strong desire to lead.

All of this points us toward the new strategy paradigm proposed by Hamel and Prahalad (1994). For them competing for the future means lifting our sights. Re-engineering internal processes is not enough, we must regenerate strategies. Transforming the organization is essential but the winners transform their industry (such as CNN). Having strategic plans focuses attention internally; what is needed is a new strategic architecture. The essential point is that it may be necessary to re-engineer our processes to reduce cost and improve service but that is insufficient to gain competitive advantage because our competitors can do the same. To be successful we must create new strategies aimed at transforming our industry – whether it is food, medicine, education, entertainment or whatever. In the modern world renewal demands that we do more than identify how to do more, better and for less. We must also regenerate what we do.

We include the first chapter of *The Icarus Paradox* in which Miller describes his key ideas and identifies a number of trajectories that can lead to failure. Ultimately the purpose of the book is to understand those trajectories and how to mange them for corporate renewal. For that you must read Miller's book but suffice it for us to think in terms of 'avoidable failure'.

The second of these we find in a study published recently by John Kay (Kay, 1993). This study attempts to identify the origins of corporate success from distinctive structures of relationships between the corporation and employees, customers and suppliers. Continuity and stability in these relationships allows for a flexible and co-operative response to change. At the core of his analysis lies the concept of added value. This he argues, derives from the architecture of the firm (basically the structure of relationships referred to above), and the application of distinctive capabilities in particular markets. Continuity and stability provide for the development of organizational knowledge (of its identity, vision, distinctive capabilities and invisible assets (Itami, 1987), the free exchange of information, and a readiness to respond quickly and flexibly to changes in the world.

In turn the distinctive capabilities which provide the basis of competitive advantage are architecture, innovation, reputation and strategic assets. Architecture is both internal (the corporate structure and management processes) and external (networks of relationships with suppliers and other organizations – joint ventures, strategic alliances, etc.). Strategic assets are the inherent advantages a company may possess (e.g. licences, access to scarce factors) which cannot easily be copied.

Chapter 7 comes from Gregory Watson's *Strategic Benchmarking*. This adds an important idea to the concept of diagnosis. The vital point is to compare your own organization to the world's best. Thus we identify where we are, the causes of our present situation *and* (through benchmarking) we identify the potential for improvement and ideas for change. Benchmarking as a technique has evolved (at least in principle and concept) from first generation benchmarking in which the focus would be on bench-marking a particular product or system, through competitive benchmarking, process benchmarking, strategic benchmarking to 'global benchmarking'. Thus the ambi-tions of its proponents are nothing short of being to achieve global excellence.

Most importantly benchmarking represents a learning technique. Essentially cogni-tive in orientation it applies rational analysis based on comparisons to the process of diagnosis. It is also (like all diagnosis) an intervention in the system and must be under-stood as such. In the chapter Watson looks at how to develop benchmarking capability.

Chapter 8 deals with business process re-engineering. Admittedly more than a tech-nique for diagnosing what needs to be changed it nevertheless incorporates techniques for diagnosis. Most importantly proponents of this approach conceive it as a technology for breakthrough or 'discontinuous leaps in performance'. The focus is upon the 'busi-ness architecture' – locations, structure, technology and skills. Alongside the analysis of the business architecture conceived in terms of value added is risk assessment looking at change and organizational issues. Our contention is that in techniques such as bench-marking and business process re-engineering we see a combination of the soft organiza-tional development approaches of the 1970s (e.g. French and Bell, 1984) and the socio-technical systems school but now operationalized because of the opportunities provided by new information infrastructures. Thus diagnosis has become more thorough and broader in scope.

Finally in Chapter 9 some of the techniques for corporate diagnosis are reviewed briefly. The main message is that diagnosis of readiness for change is as important as diagnosis of what changes are needed. Implementation is the key issue in change and to achieve effective implementation we must often change the 'mind-set' of the organiza-tion. Thus we must seek ways of 'transforming' the organization, an issue picked up in the next chapter.

## References

French, W. and Bell, D. (1984) *Organization Development*, Addison-Wesley, New York.

Hamel, G. and Prahalad, C. K. (1994) *Competing for the Future*, Harvard Business School Press, Boston, MA.

Kay, J. (1993) *Foundations of Corporate Success*, Oxford University Press, Oxford.

Kotter, P. (1988) *The Leadership Factor*, Free Press, New York.

Itami, H., (1987) *Mobilizing Invisible Assets*, Harvard University Press, Cambridge, MA.

# 6  The Icarus paradox

## D. Miller

The fabled Icarus of Greek mythology is said to have flown so high, so close to the sun, that his artificial wax wings melted and he plunged to his death in the Aegean Sea. The power of Icarus' wings gave rise to the abandon that so doomed him. The paradox, of course, is that his greatest asset led to his demise. And that same paradox applies to many outstanding companies today: their victories and their strengths often seduce them into the excesses that cause their downfall. Success leads to specialization and exaggeration, to confidence and complacency, to dogma and ritual. This general tendency, its causes, and how to control it, are what this book is all about.

It is ironic that many of the most dramatically successful organizations are so prone to failure. The histories of outstanding companies demonstrate this time and time again. In fact, it appears that when taken to excess the very factors that drive success – focused tried-and-true strategies, confident leadership, galvanized corporate cultures, and especially the interplay among all these things – can also cause decline. Robust, superior organizations evolve into flawed purebreds; they move from rich character to exaggerated caricature as all subtlety, all nuance, is gradually lost. That, in a nutshell, is the book's thesis.

Many outstanding organizations have followed such paths of deadly momentum – time-bomb trajectories of attitudes, policies, and events that lead to falling sales, plummeting profits, even bankruptcy. These companies extend and amplify the strategies to which they credit their success. Productive attention to detail, for instance, turns into an obsession with minutia; rewarding innovation escalates into gratuitous invention; and measured growth becomes unbridled expansion. In contrast, activities that were merely deemphasized – that were not viewed as integral to the recipe for success – are virtually extinguished. Modest marketing deteriorates into lackluster promotion and inadequate distribution; tolerable engineering becomes shoddy design. The result: strategies become less balanced. They center more and more upon a single, core strength that is amplified unduly, while other aspects are forgotten almost entirely.

Such changes are not limited to strategy. The heroes who shaped the winning formula of a company gain adulation and absolute authority, while others drop to third-class citizenship. An increasingly monolithic culture impels firms to focus on an even smaller set of considerations and to rally around a narrowing path to victory. Roles, programs decision-making processes – even target markets – come to reflect the central strategy and nothing else. And avidly embraced ideologies convert company policies into rigid laws and rituals. By then, organizational learning has ceased, tunnel vision rules, and flexibility is lost.

This riches-to-rags scenario seduces some of our most acclaimed corporations: our research on over one hundred such outstanding companies has turned up four variations on the theme, four very common 'trajectories' of decline (see Table 1).[1]

**Table 1**   The four trajectories

| | Focusing | |
|---|---|---|
| | *Craftsman* ⟶ | *Tinkerer* |
| *Strategy* | Quality leadership | Technical tinkering |
| *Goals* | Quality | Perfection |
| *Culture* | Engineering | Technocratic |
| *Structure* | Orderly | Rigid |
| | **Venturing** | |
| | *Builder* ⟶ | *Imperialist* |
| *Strategy* | Building | Overexpansion |
| *Goals* | Growth | Grandeur |
| *Culture* | Entrepreneurial | Gamesman |
| *Structure* | Divisionalized | Fractured |
| | **Inventing** | |
| | *Pioneer* ⟶ | *Escapist* |
| *Strategy* | Innovation | High-tech escapism |
| *Goals* | Science-for-society | Technical utopia |
| *Culture* | R&D | Think-tank |
| *Structure* | Organic | Chaotic |
| | **Decoupling** | |
| | *Salesman* ⟶ | *Drifter* |
| *Strategy* | Brilliant marketing | Bland proliferation |
| *Goals* | Market share | Quarterly numbers |
| *Culture* | Organization man | Insipid and political |
| *Structure* | Decentralized-bureaucratic | Oppressively bureaucratic |

● The *focusing* trajectory takes punctilious, quality-driven *Craftsmen*, organizations with masterful engineers and airtight operations, and turns them into rigidly controlled, detail-obsessed *Tinkerers*, firms whose insular, technocratic cultures alienate customers with perfect but irrelevant offerings.

- The *venturing* trajectory converts growth-driven, entrepreneurial *Builders*, companies managed by imaginative leaders and creative planning and financial staffs, into impulsive, greedy *Imperialists*, who severely overtax their resources by expanding helter-skelter into businesses they know nothing about.
- The *inventing* trajectory takes *Pioneers* with unexcelled R&D departments, flexible think-tank operations, and state-of-the-art products, and transforms them into utopian *Escapists*, run by cults of chaos-loving scientists who squander resources in the pursuit of hopelessly grandiose and futuristic inventions.
- Finally, the *decoupling* trajectory transforms *Salesmen*, organizations with unparalleled marketing skills, prominent brand names, and broad markets, into aimless, bureaucratic *Drifters*, whose sales fetish obscures design issues, and who produce a stale and disjointed line of 'me-too' offerings.

These four trajectories have trapped many firms. The names include IBM, Polaroid, Procter & Gamble, Texas Instruments, ITT, Chrysler, Dome Petroleum, Apple Computer, A&P, General Motors, Sears, Digital Equipment, Caterpillar Tractor, Montgomery Ward, Eastern Air Lines, Litton Industries, and Walt Disney Productions.

## A case history

The glorious and ultimately tragic history of ITT well demonstrates the course of the second, so-called venturing trajectory.

Harold S. Geneen was a manager's manager, a universally acclaimed financial wizard of unsurpassed energy, and the CEO and grand inquisitor of the diversified megaconglomerate ITT. It was Geneen, the entrepreneurial accountant, who took a ragtag set of stale, mostly European telecommunications operations and forged them into a cohesive corporate entity. With his accountant's scalpel, he cut out weak operations, and with his entrepreneur's wand, he revived the most promising ones. He installed state-of-the-art management information systems to monitor the burgeoning businesses. And he built a head-office corps of young turks to help him control his growing empire and identify opportunities for creative diversification.[2]

At first, this diversification paid off handsomely, as it so aptly exploited the financial, organizational, and turnaround talents of Geneen and his crack staff. Many acquisitions were purchased at bargain prices and most beautifully complemented ITT's existing operations. Also, a divisional structure in which managers were responsible for their units' profits provided a good deal of incentive for local initiative. And Geneen's legendary control and information systems – with frequent appraisal meetings and divisional accountants reporting directly to the head office – ensured that most problems could be detected early and corrected.

Unfortunately, ITT's success at diversification and controlled decentralization led to too much more of the same. Their skills at acquisition and control made Geneen and his staff ever more confident that they could master complexity. So, diversification went from a selective tactic to an engrained strategy to a fanatical religion; decentralization and head-office control were transformed from managerial tools into an all-consuming, lockstep way of life. The corporate culture worshipped growth, and it celebrated, lavishly paid, and quickly promoted only those who could attain it. The venturing trajectory had gotten under way, and the momentum behind it was awesome.

In order to achieve rapid growth, Geneen went after ever more ambitious acquisitions that were further afield from his existing operations. From 1967 to 1970, just six of ITT's larger acquisitions – Sheraton, Levitt, Rayonier, Continental Baking, Grinnell, and Canteen – brought in combined sales of $1.8 billion; and a seventh, Hartford Fire, one of the largest property and casualty insurers in the United States, was about to be added. Loads of debt had to be issued to fund these acquisitions. In less than ten years Geneen the imperialist bought a staggering one hundred companies, a proliferation so vast that it exceeded the complexity of many nation-states; 250 profit centers in all were set up. Geneen, quite simply, had created the biggest conglomerate on earth, encompassing, by 1977, 375,000 employees in eighty countries.

Even Geneen and his sophisticated staff troops, for all their mastery of detail and their status as information-system gurus, could not manage, control, or even understand so vast an empire. But they tried, meddling in the details of their divisions, and pressing home the need to meet abstract, often irrelevant, financial standards. Political games took place in which head-office controllers would try to impress Geneen by making the divisions look bad; and divisional executives would, in turn, try to fool the controllers.

This obsession with acquisitions and financial control detracted from the substance of divisional strategy. The product lines of many units were neglected and became outmoded. Return on capital fell, and by the late 1970s many of the divisions were experiencing major operating problems. A subsequent CEO, Rand Araskog, had to sell off over a hundred units in an attempt to revive the company, in the process shrinking the workforce by over 60 percent. The great ITT had become a flabby agglomeration of gangrenous parts.

The general pattern is clear. Over time, ITT's success – or, more specifically, its managers' reactions to that success – caused it to amplify its winning strategy, and to forget about everything else. It moved from sensible, measured expansion to prolific, groundless diversification; from sound accounting and financial control to oppressive dominance by head-office hit men; and from an invigorating use of divisionalization to a destructive factionalism. The substance of basic businesses – their product lines and markets – was lost in a welter of financial abstractions. By concentrating exclusively upon what it did best, ITT pushed its strategies, cultures, and structures to dangerous extremes, while failing to develop in other areas. Greatness had paved the way for excess and decline as ITT the Builder became ITT the Imperialist.

## Configuration and momentum

The example of ITT reveals two notions that surfaced again and again when we looked at outstanding companies: we call these configuration and momentum.

Outstanding organizations are a little like beautiful poems or sonatas – their parts or elements fit together harmoniously to express a theme. They are perhaps even more akin to living systems whose organs are intimately linked and tightly coordinated. Although organizations are less unified than organisms, they too constitute *configurations*: complex, evolving systems of mutually supportive elements organized around stable central themes. We found that once a theme emerges – a core mission or a central strategy, for example – a whole slew of routines, policies, tasks, and structures develops to implement and reinforce it. It is like seeding a crystal in a supersaturated solution – once a thematic particle is dropped into solution, the crystal begins to form naturally around it. Themes may derive from leaders' visions, the values and concerns of powerful departments, even from common industry practices.

ITT's configuration, like all others, had a central theme and a 'cast of players' (human, ideological, strategic, and structural) that completed the scenario. The theme was 'rapid growth through expansion'; the cast included an entrepreneurial, ambitious CEO with his strategy of diversification and acquisition, a powerful financial staff who dominated because they could best implement this strategy, elaborate information systems and sophisticated controls, even decentralized profit centers that infused expertise into the far-flung divisions amassed by diversification. All these 'players' complemented one another and were essential to the enactment of the play. And as with every configuration, the parts only make sense with reference to the entire constellation.[3]

Our research uncovered four exceptionally common but quite different configurations associated with stellar performance. We termed these Builders, Craftsmen, Pioneers, and Salesmen, and found that each was subject to its own evolutionary trajectory.

Our second finding was that organizations keep extending their themes and configurations until something earthshaking stops them, a process we call *momentum*. Firms perpetuate and amplify one particular motif above all others as they suppress its variants. They choose one set of goals, values, and champions, and focus on these more and more tightly. The powerful get more powerful; others become disenfranchised as firms move first toward consistency, then toward obsession and excess. Organizations turn into their 'evil twins' – extreme versions or caricatures of their former selves.

Once ITT began to diversify, for example, it accelerated this policy because it seemed successful, because it was very much in line with the visions of what leaders and their powerful financial staffs wanted, and because it was undergirded by a vast set of policies and programs. Similarly, having implemented its financial control systems, ITT continued to hone and develop them. After all, these systems were demanded by the expanding scope of the firm; they were favored by the growing staff of accountants; and they were the only way top managers could exert control over existing operations and still have time to scout out new acquisitions.

But momentum itself is contagious and leads to a vicious cycle of escalation. At ITT, as diversification increased, so, in order to cope, did the size of the head-office staff and the time spent on divisional meetings. The staff's role was to generate still more attractive candidates for diversification, and that's what they did. Diversification increased still further, requiring even larger legions of accountants and financial staff. And so the spiral continued. In short, momentum, by extending the Builder configuration, led to the dangerous excesses of imperialism.

Such findings led us to expect that *outstanding firms will extend their orientations until they reach dangerous extremes; their momentum will result in common trajectories of decline.* And since successful types differ so much from one another, so will their trajectories.

# The trajectories

The four trajectories emerged in a study we conducted of outstanding companies. Our earlier research suggested four very common, wonderfully coherent configurations, with powerful strategic advantages. To study the long-term evolution of these types for this project, we searched for successful companies that conformed to each type and had enough written about them to be analyzed in detail. We then tracked the companies for many years to discover what in fact happened to them. (Our research method and how we arrived at our types is summarized in the Appendix; the types themselves are described and compared in Tables 1 and 2.)

Many of the organizations will be well known to the reader. This was inevitable since we studied legendary performers that had been the subject of numerous articles and books. Also, many of our examples go back some years as we had to observe some rather protracted declines and revivals. Despite the familiarity of some of their subjects however, our narratives have a rather unusual twist. Instead of looking at how marvelous the good performers were, we will persistently be eliciting the seeds of decline from the flowers – and the fruits – of greatness.

Craftsmen, Builders, Pioneers, and Salesmen were each susceptible to their own unique trajectories. And firms of a given type followed remarkably parallel

**Table 2** The configurations compared

| | Craftsman | Builder | Pioneer | Salesman |
|---|---|---|---|---|
| *Strategies:* | Quality leadership | Expansion Diversification Acquisition | Differentiaion via innovation | Marketing differentiation |
| Product-market scope | Focused | Broad | Focused | Broad |
| Strategic change: | Stable | Dynamic | Dynamic | Stable |
| *Key goals:* | Quality | Growth | Technical progress | Market share |
| *Dominant depts.:* | Operations, production and engineering | Planning and control; finance | R&D | Marketing |
| *Structure:* | Bureaucracy Many controls | Divisional profit centers | Organic Flexible | Divisional bureaucracy |
| *Trajectory:* | *Focusing* | *Venturing* | *Inventing* | *Decoupling* |
| *Destination:* | **Tinkerer** | **Imperialist** | **Escapist** | **Drifter** |

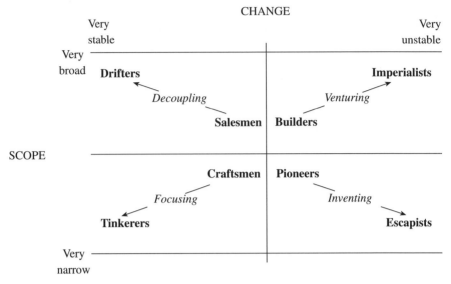

**Figure 1.** The configurations and trajectories arrayed

paths, albeit at differing speeds. For purposes of simple comparison, the four strategies are classified, in Figure 1 along two dimensions: *scope* refers to the range of products and target markets; *change* to the variability of methods and offerings. Excellent businesses are driven toward extremes along both of these dimensions (among others). Take scope. Firms that excel by focusing on one product or on a precisely targeted market come ultimately to rely on too narrow a set of customers, products, and issues. Conversely, firms that thrive by aggressively diversifying often become too complex, fragmented, and thinly spread to be effective. The same tendencies apply to strategic change as dynamic firms become hyperactive while conservative ones inch toward stagnation.

The characteristics of each of our four trajectories are summarized below.

## From craftsmen to tinkerers: the focusing trajectory

Digital Equipment Corporation made the highest quality computers in the world. Founder Ken Olsen and his brilliant team of design engineers invented the minicomputer, a cheaper, more flexible alternative to its mainframe cousins. Olsen and his staff honed their minis until they absolutely could not be beat for quality and durability. Their VAX series gave birth to an industry legend in reliability, and the profits poured in.

But Digital turned into an engineering monoculture. Its engineers became idols; its marketers and accountants were barely tolerated. Component specs and design standards were all that managers understood. In fact, technological fine-tuning became such an all-consuming obsession that customers' needs for smaller machines, more economical products, and more user-friendly systems were ignored. The Digital personal computer, for example, bombed because it was so out of sync with the budgets, preferences, and shopping habits of potential users. Performance began to slip.

Craftsmen are passionate about doing one thing incredibly well. Their leaders insist on producing the best products on the market, their engineers lose sleep over micrometers, and their quality-control staff rule with an iron, unforgiving hand. Details count. And quality is the primary source of corporate pride; it gets rewarded, and is the paramount competitive advantage. Indeed, it is what the whole corporate culture is about. Shoddiness is a capital offense.

But in becoming Tinkerers, many Craftsmen become parodies of themselves. They get so wrapped up in tiny technical details that they forget that the purpose of quality is to attract and satisfy buyers. Products become over-engineered but also overpriced; durable but stale. Yesterday's excellent designs turn into today's sacrosanct anachronisms. And an ascendant engineering culture so engrosses itself in the minutia of design and manufacture that it loses sight of the customer. Before long, marketing and R&D become the dull stepchildren, departments to be seen but not heard. And unfortunately, the bureaucratic strictures that grew up to enforce quality end up suppressing initiative and perpetuating the past.

## From builders to imperialists: the venturing trajectory

Charles 'Tex' Thornton was a young Texas entrepreneur when he expanded a tiny microwave company into Litton Industries, one of the most successful high-technology conglomerates of the 1960s. By making selective, related acquisitions, Litton achieved an explosive rate of growth. And its excellent track record helped the company to amass the resources needed to accelerate expansion still further. Sales mushroomed from $3 million to $1.8 billion in just twelve years.

But Litton began to stray too far from familiar areas, buying larger and more troubled firms in industries that it barely understood. Control systems were overtaxed, the burden of debt became unwieldy, and a wide range of problems sprang up in the proliferating divisions. The downward spiral at Litton was no less dramatic than its ascent.

Builders are growth-driven entrepreneurial companies, with a zeal for expansion, merger, and acquisition. They are dominated by aggressive managers with ambitious goals, immense energy, and an uncanny knack for spotting lucrative niches of the market. These leaders have the promotional skills to raise capital, the imagination and initiative to exploit magnificent growth opportunities, and the courage to take substantial risks. They are also master controllers who craft acute, sensitive information and incentive systems to rein in their burgeoning operations.

But many Builders develop into Imperialists, addicted to careless expansion and greedy acquisition. In the headlong rush for growth, they assume hair-raising risks, decimate their resources, and incur scads of debt. They bite off more than they can swallow, acquiring sick companies in businesses they don't understand. Structures and control systems become hopelessly overburdened. And a dominant culture of financial, legal, and accounting specialists further rivets managerial attention on expansion and diversification, while stealing time away from the production, marketing, and R&D matters that so desperately need to be addressed.

## From pioneers to escapists: the inventing trajectory

By the mid-1960s, Control Data Corporation of Minneapolis had become the paramount designer of supercomputers. Chief engineer Seymour Cray, the preeminent genius in a field of masters, had several times fulfilled his ambition to build the world's most powerful computer. He secluded himself in his lab in Chippewa Falls, working closely with a small and trusted band of brilliant designers. Cray's state-of-the-art 6600 supercomputer was so advanced that it caused wholesale firing at IBM, whose engineers had been caught completely off guard by their diminutive competitor.

CDC's early successes emboldened it to undertake new computer development projects that were increasingly futuristic, complex, and expensive. These entailed substantial lead times, major investments, and high risks. Indeed, many bugs had to be purged from the systems, long delays in delivery occurred, and costs mushroomed. Science and invention had triumphed over a proper understanding of the competition, the customers, and production and capital requirements.

Pioneers are R&D stars. Their chief goal is to be the first out with new products and new technology. Consistently at the vanguard of their industry, Pioneers are, above all, inventors. Their major strengths lie in the scientific and technological capacities of their brilliant R&D departments. Typically, Pioneers are run by missionary leaders-in-lab-coats; PhDs with a desire to change the world. These executives assemble and empower superb research and design teams, and create for them a fertile, flexible structure that promotes intensive collaboration and the free play of ideas.

Unfortunately, many Pioneers get carried away by their coups of invention and turn into Escapists – firms in hot pursuit of a technological nirvana. They introduce impractical, futuristic products that are too far ahead of their time, too expensive to develop, and too costly to buy. They also become their own toughest competitors, antiquating prematurely many of their offerings. What is worse, marketing and production come to be viewed as necessary evils; clients as unsophisticated nuisances. Escapists, it seems, become the victims of a utopian culture forged by their domineering R&D wunderkinder. Their goals, which soar to hopelessly lofty heights, are expressed in technological rather than in market or economic terms. And their loose, 'organic' structures might suffice to organize a few engineers working in a basement, but make for chaos in complex organizations.

## From salesmen to drifters: the decoupling trajectory

Lynn Townsend ascended to the presidency of Chrysler at the youthful age of forty-two. He was known to be a financial wizard and a master marketer. 'Sales just aren't made; sales are pushed,' Townsend would say. In his first five years as president, he doubled Chrysler's U.S. market share and tripled its international one. He also conceived the five-year, 50,000-mile warranty. But Townsend made very few radical changes in Chrysler's products. Mostly he just marketed aggressively with forceful selling and promotion, and sporty styling.

Chrysler's success with its image-over-substance strategy resulted in an increasing neglect of engineering and production. Also it prompted a proliferation of new models that could capitalize on the marketing program. But this made operations very complex and uneconomical. It also contributed to remote management-by-numbers, bureaucracy, and turf battles. Soon Chrysler's strategies lost focus and direction and its profits began to plummet.

Salesmen are marketers par excellence. That is their core strength. Using intensive advertising, attractive styling and packaging, and penetrating distribution channels, they create and nurture high-profile brand names that make them major players in their industries. And to place managers in especially close contact with their broad markets, Salesmen often are partitioned into manageable profit centers, each responsible for a major product line.

Unfortunately, Salesmen too are subject to a dangerous momentum that can transform them into unresponsive Drifters. They begin to substitute packaging, advertising, and aggressive distribution for good design and competent manufacture. Managers come to believe that they can sell anything as they concoct a mushrooming proliferation of bland, 'me-too' offerings. This growing diversity of product lines and divisions makes it tough for top managers to master the substance of all their businesses. So they rely increasingly on abstract financial controls and an elaborate bureaucracy to replace the hands-on management of products and manufacturing. Gradually Drifters become unwieldy, sluggish behemoths whose turf battles and factionalism impede adaptation. In scenarios that come straight from Kafka, the simplest problems take months, even years to address. Ultimately, the leader is decoupled from his company, the company from its markets, and the product lines and divisions from each other.

These four trajectories show how outstanding companies – firms with character and a terrific strategic edge – can become specialized and even monomaniacal. Strengths are amplified to the point where one goal, one strategic vision, one department, and one skill overwhelms all others. All subtlety is lost. Design-whiz Craftsmen become hyper-focused Tinkerers, entrepreneurial Builders turn into impulsive Imperialists, inventive Pioneers become utopian Escapists, and responsive Salesmen become fragmented Drifters. Nuances vanish; only the bold, exaggerated features, the core obsessions, remain.

# Forces to watch for

In reading about these four trajectories, you might want to keep in mind some of the 'subtexts' – the hidden causes at work behind the scenes that drive every one of them.

# Sources of momentum

## Leadership traps

Failure teaches leaders valuable lessons, but good results only reinforce their preconceptions and tether them more firmly to their 'tried-and-true' recipes. Success also makes managers overconfident, more prone to excess and neglect, and more given to shaping strategies to reflect their own preferences rather than those of their customers. Some leaders may even be spoiled by success – taking too much to heart their litany of conquests and the praise of their idolizing subordinates. They become conceited and obstinate, resenting challenges and, ultimately, isolating themselves from reality.

### *Monolithic cultures and skills*

The culture of the exceptional organization often becomes dominated by a few star departments and their ideologies. For example, because Craftsmen see quality as the source of success, the engineering departments that create it and are its guarantors acquire ever more influence – as do their goals and values. This erodes the status of other departments and concerns, rendering the corporate culture more monolithic, more intolerant, and more avid in its pursuit of a single goal.

To make matters worse, attractive rewards pull talented managers toward rich, dominant departments, and bleed them away from less august units. The organization's skill set soon becomes more spotty and unbalanced, compromising versatility and the capacity for reorientation.

### *Power and politics*

Dominant managers and departments resist redirecting the strategies and policies that have given them so much power. Change, they reason, would erode their status, their resources, and their influence over rival executives and departments. The powerful, then, are more likely to reinforce and amplify prevailing strategies than to change them.

### *Structural memories*

Organizations, like people, have memories – they implement successful strategies by using systems, routines, and programs. The more established and successful the strategy, the more deeply embedded it will be in such programs, and the more it will be implemented routinely, automatically, and unquestioningly. Managers will rely on ingrained habits and reflex actions rather than deliberating and reflecting on new problems. Indeed, even the premises for decision making – the cues that elicit attention and the standards used to evaluate events and actions – will be controlled by routines. Yesterday's programs will shape today's perceptions and give rise to tomorrow's actions. Again, continuity triumphs.

## Configuration and momentum

The elements of leadership, culture, power, and structural memory are by no means independent. Indeed, they interact and configure to play out a central theme. Over time, organizations become more and more consistent with that theme. So much so that an adaptable, intelligent company can turn into a specialized, monolithic machine.

Take the Pioneer. Successful innovations reward and empower their creators, who will tend to recruit and promote in their own image. The resulting horde of 'R&D types' then set up the flexible structures and design projects they find so invigorating. This further encourages innovation and the search for clients who value it. Meanwhile, other departments begin to lose influence and resources, and their skills diminish. So, cultures become monolithic, strategies more narrowly focused, skills more uneven and specialized, and blind spots more common. The firm has embarked on the inventing trajectory.

'Chain reactions' such as this make an organization more focused and cohesive. At first, the firm benefits greatly. But ultimately, concentration turns into obsession. All the prominent features become exaggerated, while everything else – auxiliary skills, supplementary values, essential substrategies, and constructive debate – vanishes.

## The paradox of Icarus

And this brings us to the Icarus paradox that traps so many outstanding firms: overconfident, complacent executives extend the very factors that contributed to success to the point where they cause decline. There are really two aspects to the paradox. The first is that *success can lead to failure*. By engendering overconfidence, carelessness, and other bad habits, success can produce excesses in strategies, leadership, culture, and structures. Icarus flew so well that he got cocky and overambitious.

The second aspect of the paradox is that many of the preceding causes of decline – galvanized cultures, efficient routines and programs, and orchestrated configurations – were initially the causes of success. Or, conversely, that *the very causes of success, when extended, may become the causes of failure*. It is simply a case of 'too much of a good thing.' For example, a focused strategy can produce wonderful competitive advantages as it mobilizes resources so efficiently; but when taken too far it becomes narrow obsession. Favoring certain departments and skills creates distinctive competences and galvanizes effort; but it can also produce intolerant corporate cultures. Similarly, routines promote efficiency and simplify coordination, but they can blind managers and mire the organization in its past. And, above all, cohesive, orchestrated configurations are indispensable for companies to operate effectively, but they can also create myopia. Icarus' wings and his courage were strengths; but when pushed to the limit, they became deadly.

*Unfortunately, it is very hard sometimes to distinguish between the focus, harmony, and passionate dedication so necessary for outstanding performance, and the excesses and extremes that lead to decline.*

# References

1   Much of the earlier research is reported in Danny Miller and Peter H. Friesen's *Organizations: A Quantum View* (Englewood Cliffs, N.J.: Prentice-Hall, 1984). See also Danny Miller, 'Configurations of Strategy and Structure', *Strategic Management Journal* (1986), 6, pp. 233–249, and 'Relating Porter's Business Strategies to Environment and Structure', *Academy of Management Journal* (June 1988), 31, pp. 280–308. The present study is described in the Appendix.
2   This vignette of ITT was compiled using the many sources on that company that are referenced in Chapter 3 of *The Icarus Paradox*. References for the other case histories in this chapter can be found in Chapters 2 through 5 of *The Icarus Paradox*.
3   Configurations are quite enduring. Try to remove or alter one piece, and the remaining parts will kick in to regenerate or restore it. For example, at ITT, any attempt to slow down diversification would have been resisted by the growth plans, the incentive system, and the staff culture. Similarly, any campaign to pay more attention to divisional product lines and operations would have faltered because of the bottom-line values of ITT, the vast amount of time divisional managers had to spend at head-office meetings, and the obsession of top management with new acquisitions.

# 7 Strategic benchmarking

## *G. H. Watson*

## Creating a benchmarking capability

### Benchmarking the benchmarking process

Most of the Malcolm Baldrige National Quality Award winners cite benchmarking as a key enabler for their quality improvement efforts. Richard W. Allen, director of quality at Solectron Corporation, the San Jose, California, company that was a 1991 winner, commented: 'Benchmarking fostered leapfrog improvements in our quality efforts by providing key learnings from leadership companies.'[1] Benchmarking is a process and, like any other process, may be studied for improvement. For instance, in 1989, when Hewlett-Packard wanted to initiate benchmarking as a business process, it first studied the Xerox approach. Because Xerox was the best early example of how to implement this methodology, many other companies benchmarked the Xerox benchmarking method and, in turn, became benchmarking models or sources of benchmarking lessons. This chapter provides advice from people who have started benchmarking in their organizations and describes, from their perspective, what to avoid and what to pursue in implementing benchmarking. The chapter closes with a description of how to implement benchmarking as a management initiative to improve business processes.

### What to avoid

Although benchmarkers often focus on learning from successes, they can also learn from implementation failures and problems observed at other companies. A variety of pitfalls await companies that are beginning a benchmarking effort. Perhaps the most important lesson to be learned is how to overcome resistance to change, in order to implement benchmarking. Executive-level excuses for not benchmarking reduce down to a single basic theme: We don't believe that we have anything to learn from other companies. An observation made of the American automotive industry by George Romney, then president of American Motors, was recalled by David Halberstam, *New York Times* journalist and author: 'Success breeds arrogance.'[2] Successful companies do not feel that they need to learn from companies that have not achieved an equivalent leadership position. Other excuses include: Our company [or industry] is different; we can't learn from others. This phrase indicates a failure to build an adequate analogy for truly understanding the process similarities between organizations. The fundamental reason for benchmarking is to learn from organizations that have experienced similar situations and dealt with them. If they have been successful, then the benchmarkers gain positive lessons from their success; if they have not succeeded, then insights are gained on the pitfalls to avoid. As Otto von Bismarck, the Prussian military strategist, observed: 'Fools you are . . . to say you learn by your own experiences . . . I prefer to profit by others' mistakes and avoid the price of my own.' Companies that do not overcome this attitude will not gain from a benchmarking effort.

Another mistake to avoid in beginning benchmarking is not factoring customer expectations into benchmark studies. The reasons for improving a company may be to provide better customer service, more adequately meet customer expectations, achieve a higher return on assets, improve the shareholders' value, and so on. It is important to remember the customer when conducting a benchmarking study; otherwise, it is possible to suboptimize the study and produce results that reflect only internal improvements that are not carried forward to the bottom line. The Ford Taurus competitive benchmarking project took this into account. Ford sought not only to achieve customer satisfaction with the design effort, but also to achieve a market success that would improve the company's financial performance. The company succeeded on both counts!

Another factor to avoid is process owners not participating in the benchmarking process. In almost every major successful company change effort, an enabling factor has been the participation of those who are charged with implementation of the change. In short, the process owner should buy into the need for the change and the proposed improvements before executing the recommendations of the study team. The best way to achieve this is through active involvement in the study effort. One reason for the success of Hewlett-Packard's best scheduling practices study, which effected change in the company's approach to new product development, was the active involvement and participation of the engineering community. Had this study been driven from a staff function, acceptance of the division level undoubtedly would have been different.

These words of advice came from Al Mierisch, manager of the quality service department of Florida Power & Light, winner of the Deming Prize in 1989: 'Don't penalize middle management or employees for the current gap in performance observed during benchmarking.'[3] Mierisch also recommended not delegating responsibility to consultants for the conduct of the study; it does not help in building internal benchmarking capability. Charles O. Lybeer, vice president of manufacturing for Stone Construction Company, a small business in Honeoye, New York, recommends that beginning benchmarkers avoid benchmarking with companies that are a poor cultural fit in any dimension: too large/small, too centralized/decentralized, too formal/informal, or too authoritarian/participative. He also underscores the need to understand one's own process and to avoid too much informality in the method of benchmarking.[4]

## What to pursue

Perhaps the best advice to encourage beginners in benchmarking was given by Samuel W. Bookhart, Jr., manager of benchmarking for DuPont Fibers and one of the authors of the Benchmarking Code of Conduct: 'Follow the Code of Conduct.'[5] Using the Code as a starting place, beginners can understand the conventions and expectations that have developed among professional benchmarkers since the early 1980s. Other experienced benchmarkers will have their own recommendations for how to begin benchmarking.

Ken Karch, manager of total quality at Weyerhauser Company, offers the following reminders for organizations beginning benchmarking efforts:[6]

- Top management commitment and participation are necessary;
- Team members often have biases that need to be dealt with;
- Team approaches are absolutely critical;
- The benchmarking process cannot be rushed;
- Education and training for the team are needed;
- Benchmarking is resource-intensive: people, travel, research, consultants, and other factors are involved;
- Process rigor is necessary for a successful study;
- Securing quantitative data is often difficult.

Florida Power & Light's Al Mierisch believes that benchmarking should be a key corporate strategy and that it should focus on corporate goals: 'Make benchmarking an ongoing process within normal business operations, e.g., business planning or strategic planning. Benchmarking should be a key to achieving your company's vision and strategies.'[7] Mierisch's advice is to get middle management to sponsor the studies and drive them from the business unit. Driving them from the staff level is ineffective because the staff does not own the process. He also believes it is important to select knowledgeable team members (people with a balance of functional, technical, analytical, and benchmarking process expertise) and empower them to implement the results. Mierisch says that benchmarkers must be sure to allow adequate time for the study and must provide sufficient resources for the team in terms of both funding and adequate training.[8]

From a small-business perspective, Charles O. Lybeer provides some sound pointers: ensure team commitment through visible management support, focus on the process being studied and on how to achieve improvement, and follow up with action. He believes that much of the benefit of benchmarking comes during the preparation process, as a team discovers the weaknesses of its own process through self-analysis.[9]

## The benefits of benchmarking

What can a management team expect to get out of benchmarking? Some significant behavioral shifts occur as a company begins to recognize that 'gaps' exist between its performance and the performance of other organizations. First, competitive benchmarking provides a better understanding of the needs of the customer and the dynamics of the particular industry. Competitive benchmarking can help to build sensitivity to changing customer needs. An example can be drawn from the Ford Taurus. Many of the comparisons that Team Taurus made for its business process improvements were against the Toyota production system; Toyota had been using a similar design methodology for years. In a recent article in *USA Today*, Chrysler's 1993 LH car series is described as the product of benchmarking studies and assessment of customer requirements. When Glenn Gardner, the chief engineer for the LH series (Dodge Intrepid, Eagle Vision, and Chrysler Concorde), came to his present job from Diamond-Star, the Chrysler joint venture with Mitsubishi, he was given free reign to build a world-class car. To ensure that it would meet this goal, Gardner's team used a combination of competitive benchmarking and customer responsiveness, making the car more amenable to the way people drive.[10]

Another advantage of benchmarking is its acknowledgment of the fact that another organization has been able to perform the same process at a higher performance level. The organization's example – especially the observation of its specific set of enabling actions – provides a vision of the potential end state for similar process improvements within one's own organization. It also helps to establish realistic, actionable objectives for the implementation of process improvements. Charles Lybeer observed a lesson learned from his experience: Benchmarking provides 'positive team member reinforcement and a feeder effect for realistic goal setting and long-range planning.'[11] The goals that represent the end state desired by an organization can be based on performance relative to observed benchmarks. This approach helps to develop realistic stretch goals as performance targets; they can be both challenging and attainable because a concrete example of this level of performance has been observed by the process owners during their benchmarking study. This experience encourages their emotional buy-in to achieving similar performance for their team. Chrysler engineers cited their observation of the 1985 Ford Taurus/Sable project as a factor in their own approach to the problem of clean-sheet automobile design.

Longer range advantages come from changing the way that an organization thinks about the need for improvement. Benchmarking provides a sense of urgency for improvement, by indicating performance levels that have been previously achieved in a study partner's process. A sense of competitiveness arises as a team recognizes improvement opportunities beyond its direct observations, and team members become motivated to strive for excellence, innovation, and the application of breakthrough thinking to achieve their own process improvement. The advice for a manager who discovers that a benchmarking team has become so motivated has a familiar ring: Lead, follow, or get out of the way!

## The role of senior management

Where does a company start, when it is interested in applying benchmarking? Many executives, like Frank Pipp, former vice president of development and manufacturing at Xerox and a champion of Xerox's first benchmarking study in 1979, want to begin with a competitive cost analysis, comparing the organization's current cost performance status against the competition. Other common starting points for management-sponsored benchmarking studies include: manufacturing cost overhead analysis, new product development cycle time, and customer service improvement. These topics are chosen according to the strategic imperatives a company is facing and its identification of the areas where the greatest need exists for performance improvement.

Once a company decides to start a benchmarking project, it should follow a time-tested, generic approach for implementation. This approach begins at the top level of the company with a presentation of an executive overview of benchmarking to the management team, to obtain its support for the pilot project. This presentation, which sets corporate expectations and establishes top-level awareness of the pilot study, will help the management team to understand the significance of the results when the completed project is reported and recommendations for change are made. One outcome of this presentation will be the identification of the pilot study's subject by the management team. Given this responsibility, the team will buy-in to the value of the methodology. In addition, the management team should review the project outline and approve the potential partners for the study. Nothing will deflate a study more quickly than a senior manager who 'doesn't respect' the benchmarking partner and is therefore unwilling to learn from the partner's example.

Experience facilitates success. It is important to select an experienced benchmarker to facilitate the first project – either an internally developed benchmarker who has practiced on some less visible projects, or an outside consultant. However, if an outside consultant is used, his or her role must allow the team to learn how to conduct the study so that a knowledge transfer takes place. Without it, the organization may become reliant on the consultant for future benchmarking studies. It is also important to get the process owner involved in the study, to ease the team's ability to implement the findings of the project.

It is especially essential that a first project follow a rigorous benchmarking process. Xerox uses a learning experience model called LUTI (Learn–Use–Train–Inspect) for its implementation of change. This PDCA-like model helps to underline the need for experiential learning to establish true understanding of process improvements. Using the LUTI approach, management would be trained, develop experience by participating in its own benchmarking project, participate in the training or mentoring of others in the benchmarking method, and, finally, inspect the use of benchmarking as part of its review of process improvements and business operations. The Xerox LUTI approach to change implementation underscores the need for continuing involvement of senior management in the process. After receiving both interim and final reports of the study progress and results, senior management should take action based on the study results and provide resources to implement the recommended change. Once the team has completed its work, management should ensure that the recommended change is facilitated and should monitor its progress to verify that the projected results are obtained. The final role of senior management, when success is observed in the pilot study, is to establish follow-on benchmarking project requirements for addressing other 'strategic issues' where improvements are needed. This will help to make benchmarking a natural part of the company's planning process.

## Benchmarking as an intervention

Specialists in the field of organizational development speak of making an *intervention* in their clients' organizations. The term intervention means a change that is imposed externally from the organization, originating either from a consultant or from management. Benchmarking is such a change to the management process of most organizations. It must be treated as a significant change and handled carefully, or, like many other systemic transformations, it may suffer rejection, much like a heart transplant that doesn't take. If benchmarking is mandated by the senior management team, it can suffer the fate of many other enforced interventions. Carla O'Dell, senior vice president at the American Productivity & Quality Center and director of the International Benchmarking Clearinghouse, proposed a tongue-in-cheek list of ways for a change agent to ensure the maximum degree of management resistance to systemic change:

● Mandate the change from the ivory tower of 'corporate' headquarters;
● Disregard the opinions of the management team;
● Make ambiguous expectations of the management team for implementing the change;
● Avoid training management in the new roles;
● Give management irrelevant training;
● Allow the management team no involvement in design;

- Provide the management team with no involvement in change;
- By-pass managers in communicating to their teams;
- Reduce or threaten to reduce the number of managers.

Resistance to change and change-blocking behavior by the management team are *not* desired behaviors. The key is to build support for the change throughout the entire management team. O'Dell also offered a prescription for obtaining support and consensus for major change:

- Invest time to prepare and plan the change;
- Involve as many of the affected parties in the change definition as possible;
- Ensure that the purpose and direction of the change are clear;
- Specify new expectations and functions for all involved;
- Clarify advantages for managers and their teams;
- Provide timely training required to perform the new activities;
- Start at the top of the organization and cascade down to the individual contributors;
- Respond to skepticism and questions with open, honest responses.

This list of change implementation behaviors should be kept in mind as a new process or methodology is being implemented in an organization.[12]

## The Weyerhauser example

The experience of Ken Karch, who led Weyerhauser's benchmarking implementation, can provide a practical lesson in what works for starting a long-term benchmarking effort. Karch recommends the following ten-point approach:[13]

1 Provide leadership from the senior management team, to communicate its support and provide resources to the pilot study; then get managers involved in a benchmarking project of their own, requiring them to actively study the strategic planning or behavioral approach of a senior manager whom they admire. The surest way to get long-term management support is to have managers involved in benchmarking. Larry Osterwise, currently director of market-driven quality for IBM and formerly general manager of IBM's Rochester, Minnesota facility (a 1990 recipient of the Malcolm Baldrige National Quality Award), tells a story about when David Kearns, former CEO of Xerox, visited his facility. Osterwise asked him if he would like to see the plant, to which Kearns replied: 'Of course, I need to keep current on my benchmarking.' Kearns's attitude, developed over years of exposure to the value of benchmarking, represents an acute awareness of each individual's responsibility to capture every learning experience as a potential stimulus for organizational change.[14]

2 'Adopt a new philosophy.' This point, modeled after Deming, means to

adopt the philosophy of continuous learning and improvement. Organizations need to eliminate any not-invented-here (NIH) syndrome that may
exist and get rid of the following attitudes (excuses):

- 'We can't learn anything from others.'
- 'We're as good as you can get.'
- 'There's no one outstanding in this area.'
- 'Our work is different – it can't be measured against others.'

One senior executive of a Fortune 500 company, discussing why his company had not entered into a benchmarking study for time-to-market of
new-products developments, summed up all of the above excuses in one
succinct phrase: 'We don't want to taint our performance by learning how
mediocre companies develop products.' The truth is: Every company has
something to learn, and few companies have provided their shareholders
with the long-term return on investment that they would like to see.

3 Create an executive steering committee that is charged with creating and
  monitoring a plan for implementing benchmarking. The role of the steering
  committee is to encourage the integration of benchmarking data into strategic planning and facilitate the establishment of common performance
  measures. Committee members should be trained in benchmarking and
  need to get excited about their involvement; they will be promoting the
  value of benchmarking to the entire organization.
4 Create a support structure. A long-term benchmarking program includes
  training for benchmarking teams; vehicles for communicating on studies
  underway and for reporting study results; access to library and information
  services; and in-house capability to facilitate benchmarking teams. These
  support services may be purchased by contract for a pilot study; however, a
  long-term benchmarking effort will require dedicated resources.
5 Find one or more pioneers who are willing to attempt a study, and support
  them from the quality office. They should be encouraged from the top of
  the organization to pursue the study, and their results should be communicated to encourage others who have a need for benchmarking. The activities of the pioneering benchmarkers should be envisioned as a paradigm
  shift toward a learning organization.
6 Educate people in the practice of benchmarking; incorporate it into the
  core quality training.
7 Communicate, through internal newsletters and company publications, the
  concept and applications of benchmarking.
8 Find and use success stories from both inside and outside the company.
9 Make benchmarking a part of the planning process. Build it into strategic
  business plans as a means for goal-setting. To do this, a company must have
  a reliable benchmarking process – one that gets both accurate measures of
  performance and good definition of performance enablers.

10 Recognize and reward successful benchmarking efforts; use an internal conference or 'benchmarking days' to spotlight individual team practices. Public acknowledgement by senior management is an important factor in reinforcing benchmarking as a desired activity. Recognition can also take the form of sending teams to conferences or entering them in a benchmarking competition such as the APQC contest for a benchmarking prize.

Karch's approach may appear to be a cookbook to some, but it provides a sound set of elements that can be tailored to an organization's culture. The goal is to have a capability to produce benchmarking studies that change the behavior of the company and increase its effectiveness and efficiency.

## What to do with a used study

Benchmarking studies are, by nature, perishable and time-sensitive. What was a standard of excellence today may be expected performance tomorrow. Thus, competitive excellence is an ever-increasing standard, and benchmarks are only observations of excellence at a particular point in time. Because the techniques and enablers that companies use to 'ratchet-up' their performance may not apply in the future, benchmarks, like any other measurement instrument, need to be recalibrated over time. Benchmarking is an evergreen process that requires revisiting studies to ensure their lasting significance. It is not an end in itself; it is a means to the end of business process excellence in a competitive environment where technology is always increasing the potential for improvement. In the electronics industry, employees once manually inserted electrical components into printed circuit boards. The next generation of improvement came when machines could perform the same function. Another level of improvement came when the machines did not have to insert the components into holes through the boards, but could place them directly on the board, thereby increasing reliability and process quality. At any point in this 'electrical component insertion process,' a different answer as to the performance benchmark for process quality, cycle time, and cost-effectiveness would have been obtained and would then have been made obsolete by the next generation of technology. Some of the earlier lessons for materials handling and component reliability would still apply and would have been carried over to the next generation. Benchmarking, therefore, must be a continuous practice for those key business processes that affect the competitiveness of the organization.

## Where to get support

As benchmarking becomes recognized as an important business practice, more and more information will become available. It will also become increasingly difficult to sort out the resources of value from those that are purely commercial in nature. Many organizations will undoubtedly attempt to imply that their capability (financial analysis or a consulting practice approach) is the true approach to benchmarking. History is the most reliable guide. The appendices of this book have been developed to provide a starting place for companies interested in benchmarking. The Benchmarking Code of Conduct is presented in Appendix A. Appendix B provides a listing of secondary research tools that can be helpful in a search for information about potential benchmarking partners. Appendix C provides the Benchmarking Recognition Award Criteria, issued by the APQC International Benchmarking Clearinghouse. These criteria can be used to assess an organization's progress in developing its benchmarking capability. Appendix D, a sample procedure for benchmarking, is intended to provide general guidance to teams on how to conduct their studies. This procedure may be appropriate for adaptation by organizations that record their processes in a formal manner, or it may be used as a guide for organizations that do not have a high degree of formality. Appendix E is a bibliography of benchmarking books, reports, and articles, compiled in cooperation with the APQC. These materials can be studied to help develop the breadth and depth of knowledge of a company's internal benchmarking experts. Appendix F provides a glossary of benchmarking terms, to aid communication with benchmarking partners by providing a common meaning of terms.

## Where is benchmarking going?

What is the future of benchmarking? Fred Bowers, corporate benchmarking program manager at Digital Equipment Corporation, predicts that benchmarking, as we know it today, will be greatly changed by the year 2000. Bowers envisions companies performing most studies by the use of information networks that connect clearinghouses and trade associations. He sees companies using benchmarking as a way to engineer competitive uniqueness. He also believes the day of the benchmarking department will pass as benchmarking becomes as natural a part of work as answering a telephone.[15]

## Benchmarking as an agent for change

This book has noted how benchmarking is a vehicle for stimulating change in an organization. Another perspective on this application of benchmarking is provided by William Lehman, managing director of the Price Waterhouse Manufacturing Management Consulting Practice. As the keynote speaker at the APQC's first benchmarking conference, Lehman commented about the root cause for some organizations' lack of success in implementing benchmarking:

> I maintain that the failure of benchmarking to generate the kind of impact that it should in most organizations is tied up with a misunderstanding of the magnitude of organizational change required to achieve that impact. The real effectiveness of a benchmarking program

lies in its ability to generate large, structural shifts in business processes, and hard benefits to the bottom line of the organization. Defining 'World Class' practices that enable the delivery of these benefits requires a benchmarking process that is specifically linked to the change planning and integration processes of the organization, its environment for change, and management's vision of the future.[16]

The challenge lies ahead. If you are in the management of a company that is not using benchmarking, you should ask yourself some hard questions:

Am I interested in driving my organization to the leadership position within our industry?

Do I believe that benchmarking can provide my company with the opportunity needed to learn about how and where to improve the organization's performance?

The recipe for successful benchmarking requires three basic ingredients: a supportive management team that has a real problem to be solved; access to prospective benchmarking partners who have previously resolved this problem; and a knowledgeable benchmarking team with the ability to use basic quality tools and research practices to investigate process problems to their root cause. To these three basic ingredients must be added a dash of research perseverance and a whole bunch of patience. If your company is beginning its benchmarking journey, I wish you the unique and abundant success that comes from both the discovery and the application of profound process knowledge!

# References

1 This quote is from Richard Allen's presentation at the APQC Conference, Benchmarking Week '92, held in Dallas, TX, May 4–8.
2 Halberstam quoted Romney in his keynote address to the GOAL/QPC Conference in 1989.
3 From Al Mierisch's presentation at the APQC Benchmarking Week '92 Conference.
4 *Ibid.*
5 *Id.*
6 *Id.*
7 *Id.*
8 *Id.*
9 *Id.*
10 As quoted in an article by James Healey, 'Firm Taps Rivals' Gains in Big Gamble', *USA Today*, October 21, 1992.
11 APQC Benchmarking week '92.
12 *Ibid.*
13 *Id.*
14 *Id.*
15 *Id.*
16 *Id.*

# 8 Business re-engineering – a strategy-driven approach

## R. Talwar

Organizations across a wide range of industries are recognizing the potential of re-engineering to deliver discontinuous leaps in performance. The competitive climate, and the pace of change within and outside the firm are also encouraging a more co-ordinated and fundamental approach to the planning and design of business activity. Two main approaches to re-engineering have emerged. The first – known as process re-engineering – offers the opportunity to rethink and streamline individual processes. The second – termed business re-engineering – provides an approach to rethinking and redesigning the entire business behind a more focused, competence based competitive strategy. The central challenge in re-engineering is to understand where and how we can create value for both customers and shareholders. This requires us to ask fundamental questions about what we do, how we do it, whether it is necessary and how it can be improved. Achieving the benefits of re-engineering demands active commitment and participation from the chief executive downwards. The re-engineering process itself needs careful planning around a clear vision of longer term goals. There are also risks inherent in undertaking these far reaching and fundamental changes. To address the risks, manage the fears, uncertainties and doubts and yet maintain motivation in the organization, demands a commitment to change management on a scale which few executives will have experienced.

The term business re-engineering has been with us since 1990 when it was first coined in an article by Michael Hammer.[1] However, many of the concepts to which it refers have been with us for 20 years or more. For some, re-engineering has become a convenient label to apply to any business project – particularly those with a substantial IT component. Others have chosen to undertake a fundamental reappraisal of where and how the company creates value for its stakeholders. Research from the USA suggests that firms which have adopted a strategy-driven approach to re-engineering generally fall into two categories:

- those who have reached crisis point – recognizing that their ability to succeed 'in spite of themselves' has run out, and
- those who are already successfully outperforming their sector.

As might be expected, the second group is far larger. They are also more likely to complete the exercise and achieve the anticipated performance improvements.

## A framework for business re-engineering

People starting their investigation of re-engineering often begin by looking for detailed methodologies and supporting tools to steer them through the process. However, as this article should demonstrate, success in re-engineering depends more on having the right management mindset than on the right tools. Given the right mindset, a framework such as that presented here can be used to guide the exercise – focusing on *what* is to be done at each stage. The organization can then choose the tools and techniques to decide *how* to do it.

This article provides an introduction to business re-engineering as a strategy-driven approach to rejuvenating and refocusing the organization by:

- explaining the concept of re-engineering,
- describing key factors which are forcing re-engineering onto the management agenda,
- outlining the basic components and principles,
- presenting a six-step framework for implementing re-engineering,
- examining the implications for the information technology (IT) function, and
- outlining approaches for continuous risk assessment and change management.

## What is business re-engineering?

Business re-engineering (Figure 1) is an approach to achieving radical improvements in customer service and business efficiency. The central challenge is to rethink and streamline the business processes and supporting architecture through which the organization creates and delivers value.

Re-engineering demands that we ignore traditional functional and organizational boundaries. Instead, it places an emphasis on designing and implementing efficient cross-functional processes. Hence, re-engineering offers the opportunity to re-examine the fundamentals of the business or key processes within it and then redesign from 'first principles'.

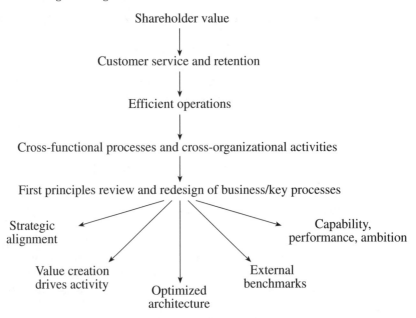

**Figure 1.** The re-engineering approach to corporate transformation

Re-engineering can bring substantial benefits – not only to the organization but to its 'partners' in the broadest sense. The key internal benefits being:

● Stronger alignment of core processes to business strategy
● The creation of customer value becomes a driver for all business activity
● The business architecture is optimized to efficient cross-functional performance
● Benchmarking is used to accelerate learning and provide a stimulus for change
● Enhanced capability and performance lead to increased ambition and conviction.

Hammer's article and his subsequent book[2] present re-engineering as a radical, IT driven approach to improving business efficiency – focusing on the redesign of key business processes. He asserts that:

> At the heart of re-engineering is the notion of discontinuous thinking – recognising and breaking away from the outdated rules and fundamental assumptions that underlie operations. Unless we change these rules, we are merely rearranging the deck chairs on the Titanic. We cannot achieve break-throughs in performance by cutting fat or automating existing processes. Rather, we must challenge old assumptions and shed the old rules that made the business underperform in the first place.[1]

In practice, 'breaking away' involves:

- examining how and why we add more or less value than our competitors:
- forcing a radical and continuous reappraisal of customer requirements and the trade-offs they make between price, functionality, quality and service;
- asking naive and challenging questions i.e. if starting again, what would we do differently?
- reappraising where and how we deliver service;
- eliminating unnecessary activities, and reducing the number of delays introduced by tasks such as reviews, authorizations, inspections and hand-offs between departments:
- minimizing the delays between processing stages by automating workflows:
- increasing flexibility by creating a multi-skilled workforce:
- reducing duplication of effort and investment by forming stronger partnerships with customers and suppliers, sharing more key information and undertaking joint development activities;
- improving internal communications by bringing different organizational functions together to speed up product and service development;
- empowering staff with greater responsibility and decision making authority;
- outsourcing activities which add no value but divert management time and energy.

## Process re-engineering or business re-engineering

From the basic concept have emerged two major categories of re-engineering initiatives. The first and most common category is *process re-engineering*. The emphasis is on identifying one or more 'core processes' (Figure 2), analysing them and then radically rethinking and redesigning their execution. While such initiatives may be supported by the chief executive, they are typically 'owned' by a senior manager or possibly a board member.

An example of this core process-driven approach is that taken by the UK health insurer Western Provident Association (WPA). The company first applied the technique to re-engineer the processing of new customer applications (Figure 3). The result was to shorten the process from one requiring 7 people, performing 45 minutes of work over 28 days to an activity involving one 'case worker' processing the entire application in four minutes.

Such approaches work best when future objectives for the process are well known. This provides a clear target for those undertaking the redesign of the selected process. However, one of the key drawbacks of such an approach lies in managing the boundaries and 'interfaces' or 'hand-offs' between the re-engineered process and the unchanged areas of the business.

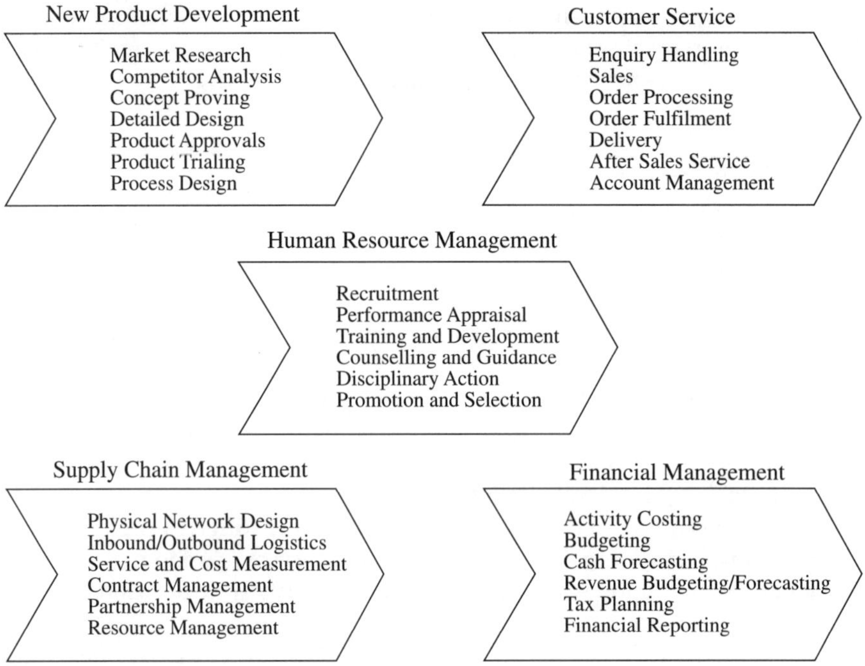

New Product Development

Market Research
Competitor Analysis
Concept Proving
Detailed Design
Product Approvals
Product Trialing
Process Design

Customer Service

Enquiry Handling
Sales
Order Processing
Order Fulfilment
Delivery
After Sales Service
Account Management

Human Resource Management

Recruitment
Performance Appraisal
Training and Development
Counselling and Guidance
Disciplinary Action
Promotion and Selection

Supply Chain Management

Physical Network Design
Inbound/Outbound Logistics
Service and Cost Measurement
Contract Management
Partnership Management
Resource Management

Financial Management

Activity Costing
Budgeting
Cash Forecasting
Revenue Budgeting/Forecasting
Tax Planning
Financial Reporting

**Figure 2.** Core business process. *Source:* BMS Bossard

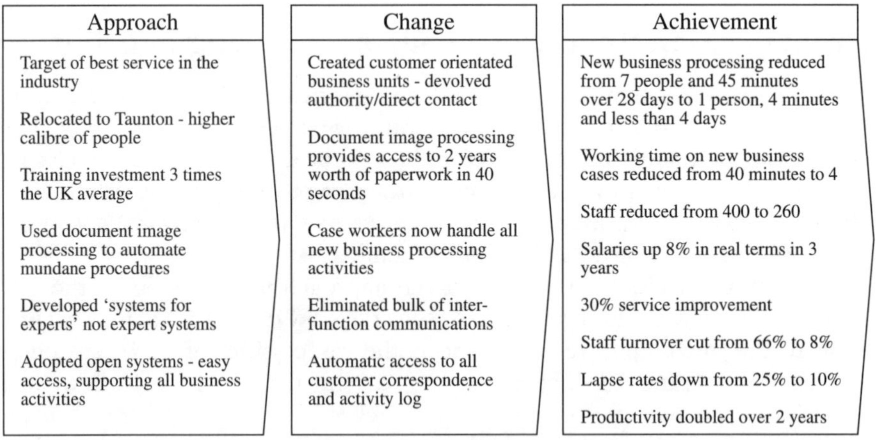

| Approach | Change | Achievement |
|---|---|---|
| Target of best service in the industry | Created customer orientated business units - devolved authority/direct contact | New business processing reduced from 7 people and 45 minutes over 28 days to 1 person, 4 minutes and less than 4 days |
| Relocated to Taunton - higher calibre of people | Document image processing provides access to 2 years worth of paperwork in 40 seconds | Working time on new business cases reduced from 40 minutes to 4 |
| Training investment 3 times the UK average | | Staff reduced from 400 to 260 |
| Used document image processing to automate mundane procedures | Case workers now handle all new business processing activities | Salaries up 8% in real terms in 3 years |
| Developed 'systems for experts' not expert systems | Eliminated bulk of inter-function communications | 30% service improvement |
| | | Staff turnover cut from 66% to 8% |
| Adopted open systems - easy access, supporting all business activities | Automatic access to all customer correspondence and activity log | Lapse rates down from 25% to 10% |
| | | Productivity doubled over 2 years |

**Figure 3.** Re-engineering core processes at Western Provident Association. *Source:* BMS Bossard

The second category – and focus of this article – is *business re-engineering*. This approach involves a strategy-driven, top-down reappraisal and redesign of the total business. Clearly, such initiatives have to be supported and driven by the Chief Executive and demand the commitment and active participation of the entire board. The more wide ranging and fundamental the rethink, the greater the impact on cross-functional activities, working practices, management systems, organization structures, motivation and reward systems, performance monitoring systems, and staff training and development. This approach (Figure 4), builds on the premise that future competitive success will be based upon a strong linkage between strategy, competence, core processes and architecture.

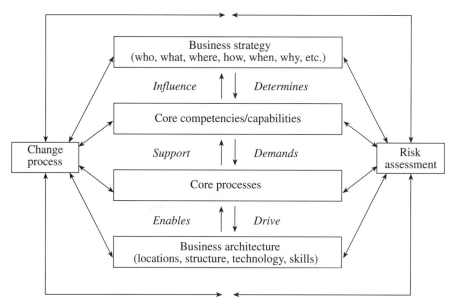

**Figure 4.** A strategy driven approach to business re-engineering. *Source:* BMS Bossard

Using this approach, the main tasks are to:

1 Clarify and communicate strategy:
   ● Who are we? What are our mission, values, etc.?
   ● On which markets, products and service should we focus?
   ● How will we respond to different market scenarios?
   ● What are the immediate priorities? etc.
2 Develop the competencies and capabilities we need to ensure effective delivery of the strategy:
   ● e.g. product management, supplier management.
3 Create the key processes to support the development and exploitation of competencies:
   ● e.g. for supplier management the key processes might be supplier identification and vetting, contracts management and supplier performance appraisal.
4 Implement the architectural changes required:

- reappraisal of physical locations,
- changes in organisational structure, rewards, and staffing,
- refinement of the technology infrastructure.

5 Assess the risks in implementing these tasks.
6 Create and implement a 'change management' plan which addresses those risks and ensures that we emerge with a motivated and committed workforce.

The more fundamental and far-reaching nature of this approach means that whilst there are examples of organizations that have undertaken such initiatives, few are willing to discuss the initiative they have undertaken. However, a number of organizations have embarked on such an initiative, including the heating equipment manufacturer Baxi Partnership and two Building Societies – National and Provincial and Birmingham Midshires.

## What is a process?

With so much emphasis in both approaches on the central concept of 'process', it is useful to propose a working definition. It is also important to distinguish between functions such as engineering, finance and marketing, and the processes which may involve one or more of those functions in their execution. Examples of such processes being new product development, order fulfilment and budgeting. Whilst individual functions may be seen as process owners – as with finance and budgeting – the success of the process lies in the involvement of multiple functions.

For the purpose of this article, a process will be taken to be *any sequence of pre-defined activities executed to achieve a pre-specified type or range of outcomes*. Ideally, that result should satisfy the diverse set of 'stake-holders' who have an interest in the process and its outcome. Those with a direct interest include customers, management and employees. The next tier of stakeholders typically includes suppliers and regulators. A third group – shareholders and analysts – are typically interested more in the overall set of processes that determine the organization's fortunes.

## Why the current interest?

The desire for streamlined business operations and greater efficiency have been with us for some time. In the past we have set about achieving them through individual actions such as cost cutting or IT investment. However, several factors have come together to encourage a more fundamental, integrated and better managed approach to planning and designing future business activity (Figure 5). In particular:

The opportunity to re-engineer has undoubtedly existed for some time. Some organizations such as Marks & Spencer and Storehouse would argue that their outstanding recent performance is the result of their having applied the concepts for many years without using the re-engineering label.

However, the rapid rise of interest over the last few years is the result of six factors combining to force firms to rethink their business operations:

## 1   Global business trends

With even the smallest of firms being affected, there is a growing recognition that global business trends are forcing us to rethink the way in which we organize and compete. The most important being:

● globalization, deregulation and liberalization of markets are enabling foreign firms – such as Nissan and Toyota – to open 'greenfield' operations;
● revolutionary rather than evolutionary developments in products, processes, technologies and management thinking (e.g. Sony with Mechatronics for camcorder production);
● a growing recognition that 'doing what we did last year but better, faster and cheaper' is no longer a viable competitive strategy – even in what were once perceived as relatively mature sectors – such as financial services;
● increasing competition between consortia, networks and alliances rather than between individual firms – which forces an emphasis on building distinctive capabilities and may lead to the formation of virtual corporations – that draw on the complementary competencies of each player to create a new commercial – but not necessary legal entity – as in the case of the relationship between Novell and Oracle;
● the growing reliance on technologies – and in particular IT – and the increasing awareness of the new business opportunities and commercial relationships that technology can make possible – if properly managed and exploited (e.g. First Direct and Telephone Banking).

## 2   Economic trends

The worldwide recession has proved deeper and longer than many would have anticipated. The result has been increases in unemployment for people at every level in society. This in turn has had a knock-on impact on both demand and price competition for firms at every stage in the value chain. However, the expectations of a diverse set of stakeholders to maintain performance against a wide range of commercial, social and strategic measures has not diminished. For example, environmental controls in the depressed petrochemicals industry are becoming increasingly stringent and costly to implement.

## 3   Operational challenges

Declining demand and increased price competition have been accompanied by growing customer sophistication. Service excellence, quality and flexibility are increasingly demanded as standard features. These in turn are forcing a growing emphasis on the reduction of operating costs and improved efficiency.

Sophisticated IT systems may have helped some organizations meet operational challenges. However, recent research suggests that there has been a negative real return on IT investment across the OECD countries over the last 20 years. There is a growing realization that IT is no longer the sole domain of the IT function. Business management must play an active part in delivering the benefits from any new investments.

## 4    Learning as a competitive weapon

The rate at which both individuals and the organization as a whole can learn has undoubtedly become a major factor in competitive survival. To build the right attitudes and behaviours and effect lasting change we have to 'unlearn' what has worked in the past and teach people how to learn. Baxi Partnership, for example, provided personal training budgets and open learning centres to help workers build the skills that would provide a 'lifetime employability' rather than jobs for life.

In many sectors the pressure is to learn how to compete given constantly changing boundaries for both firms and markets. In other sectors – such as the National Health Service – the challenge is to learn how to compete for the first time. With hospitals forced to compete for their share of a limited budget, the concepts of customer care, service, and a patient-centred approach will gain prominence over the clinical focus that has dominated to date.

Even where the firm is not re-engineering, there is a growing recognition of the need to learn about the design and management of processes. For example, in sectors such as retail there is increasing awareness of the need for tasks and processes to be executed at the most logical point of the value chain – irrespective of which firm performs them. This in turn implies learning how to monitor and influence processes, tasks and outcomes which we no longer control. Hence the growing emphasis on relationship management as a core competence for many of the leading retailers.

## 5    Continuous change

Change is not a one-off activity but a continuous process of evolutionary and revolutionary adaptation to changing business needs. Some firms – such as Western Provident Association – believe that regular programmes of re-engineering are a key way of reinforcing this message. Equally, many firms are beginning to recognize that the single most important determinant of success on any initiative is the effectiveness of the change management approach.

## 6    Past management failures

Managers as a breed – from board level downwards – are coming in for increasing criticism over failures in corporate performance. Those willing to listen to the diagnosis are beginning to recognize that 'tolerance of underperformance' has left fundamental weaknesses at the heart of the organization:

- a bias towards 'command and control' styles of management which alienate rather than motivate staff,
- a failure to manage expectations during change initiatives and address issues related to 'staff displacement' early enough,
- 'quick fix' approaches to issues which simply create problems for other business areas and future management,
- an unquestioning willingness to accept complexity that has resulted in unwieldy bureaucracies and slow decision making processes,
- a culture of 'blame avoidance' that has stifled innovation and creativity,
- a tendency to push innovative people, processes, technologies and managers into 'skunkworks' and subsidiaries – which has limited the transfer of knowledge and experience and marginalized the participants.
- a lack of understanding of the IT development process and insufficient planning have led to ill-fitting and over-priced solutions,
- empire building and the 'dead hand' of middle management have encouraged people to waste time playing politics and/or finding ways to circumvent the 'system'.

**Figure 5.** The motivations for business re-engineering

- *the globalization of business* – deregulation and liberalization are bringing increased competition from foreign entrants using greenfield operations:
- *economic pressures* – the global recession is increasing unemployment, shrinking markets and forcing greater price competition;
- *operational challenges* – shareholders are looking to management to maintain profitability whilst increasing customer service, speed, quality and flexibility despite smaller markets and lower prices;
- *competitive learning* – a recognition that the rate of learning (and unlearning) and re-skilling are powerful competitive weapons;
- *continuous change* – acceptance that change is the only constant and that the ability to manage it is a critical success factor;
- *past management failures* – a growing realization that management failure has led to creeping inefficiency and tolerance of underperformance.

## Basic components and principles

Most successful re-engineering initiatives share certain basic ingredients. These lie at the heart of the change initiative and are examined below:

*Hammer's principles*

Common to most initiatives are a set of principles which Hammer articulated in his original article (Figure 6).

The emphasis on outputs is one which requires continuous reinforcement – as evidenced by the case of the local council struggling to set nursery education budgets. On national comparisons of expenditure per nursery school place

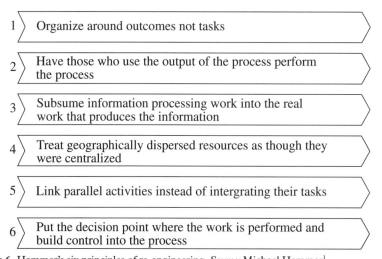

**Figure 6.** Hammer's six principles of re-engineering. *Source:* Michael Hammer[1]

*available*, the council was near the bottom of the league. In a rare example of cross-party collaboration, the council voted unanimously to undertake a radical review of all spending plans to find the funds required.

Having created a revised and controversial budget requiring massive cuts in other areas of service provision, the council set about voting the reforms through. At the crucial meeting, a lone voice in the council chamber questioned whether the review had examined the *outputs from* as well as the *inputs to* the nursery education programme.

Reluctantly a second investigation was performed. The result? The council discovered that only two thirds of places provided were occupied. On the revised *output-based* calculations the council was spending more per place than to send a child to Harrow – one of the country's leading private schools! The result has been to redesign the budgeting processes to focus on needs, outputs, and outcomes rather than inputs.

### Challenge outdated organization principles

With many organizations still basing activity design on Frederick Taylor's principles of 'Scientific Management' – the time has come to rethink the design, flow and allocation of work. Taylor advocated breaking work down into its simplest tasks, separating planning and execution. This has resulted in administrative and manufacturing organizations alike being designed on 1920s assembly line concepts with sequential workflows and strict separation of tasks.

For example, when Ford compared its operations to those of Mazda it discovered Accounts Payable employed 500 people to match 14 documents and data items before paying invoices. Mazda employed five people to perform the same task. Ford's redesign reduced the headcount by 75 per cent with payments being made based on a computerized match of three items.

### Question fundamental assumptions that underlie operations

This is one of the most interesting aspects of re-engineering as it demands that we challenge that which we have taken for granted. For example, why do management inspect every insurance policy valuation letter sent out by a clerk – unless the manager re-runs the calculation she will never know if the clerk has made a mistake.

### Set audacious objectives

The aim is to set targets that are out of reach but not out of sight. This forces discontinuous thinking – the targets should not be achievable using current improvement approaches alone.

### Simplify and annihilate

Whilst organizations might want to eliminate as many processes as possible, they typically start by attempting process simplification. Clearly, the strategy-driven framework described in this article leans towards the zero-based approach of annihilation. The emphasis is on identifying and keeping or creating only those processes which will support the execution of our core capabilities and through which we can add more value than if they were outsourced to another firm in the value chain.

*Rethink functions and processes*

In moving to greater process orientation, most organizations encounter four common challenges (Figure 7):

---

**1  Highlighting the problems of a functional orientation** – priorities may differ between functions – creating delays as work waits to be processed; functionally based accounting and control systems do not ensure a 'balanced scorecard' – little attention is given to reflecting measures of customer value and service delivery. The move towards greater use of activity and value based costing and direct product profitability analysis are helping to redress this issue; functional hierarchies also generate their own self-serving tasks and complexity as managers seek to expand their influence and power base; functional structures can also foster unhealthy competition, conflict and barriers between parts of the organization; staff are encouraged to focus on meeting the needs of their hierarchy and satisfying the targets on which they are measured – these may not coincide with doing what is best for the customer or shareholder. A classic example being the complaints department of one the recently privatized utilities. In order to meet response time targets set by the regulator, staff frequently sent out a standard letter to unanswered customers requesting 'further clarification' on their complaint. The regulator is now trying to close the 'loophole' by focusing the targets on complaint clear-up rates and not just responses.

**2  Managing the transition from a functional to a process orientated view** – there is a danger that those who grasp the problems created by a functional orientation (see Figure 8) will then try to move to a process-centred structure without the intermediate analysis and planning.

In moving to a process orientated view of the firm (see Figure 9), we have to identify the set of processes by which we manage the overall activity of taking products and services from suppliers, and add value to them in order to service customers in a profitable manner that in turn creates value for the shareholder.

In this process orientated view, we may still have functions as centres of expertise for skill groups – such as finance and sales. Their role becomes one of providing guaranteed levels of service and response to the process owner.

**3  Management must rethink its role in a process organization** – increasingly the management's role will move away from problem solving, commanding and controlling to one of empowering, enabling and motivating (see Figure 10)

**4  Understand the process architecture** – as processes tend to be split across several functions, it is often difficult to know where to start when trying to analyse or redesign them. Hence it is helpful to start with a clear checklist of the characteristics that combine to make up a process, e.g. scope, ownership, inputs, outputs and key tasks.

---

**Figure 7.** Rethinking functions and processes

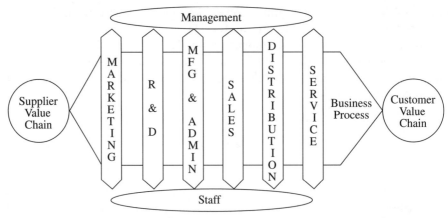

**Figure 8.** The traditional functional view of the organization. *Source:* BMS Bossard

**Figure 9.** The process view of the firm. *Source:* BMS Bossard

● highlighting the problems with a functional orientation,
● managing the transition from a functional to a process orientated view,
● rethinking management's role in a process organization,
● understanding the process architecture.

*Use IT as an enabler*

Whilst IT can clearly play a major role in the transformation process, there is a perception of failure to deliver in many organizations. The key management

| Element | Functional approach | Process approach |
|---|---|---|
| Channels of communication | Highly structured controlled information flow | Open-free flow of information |
| Operations | Uniform and restricted | Vary from business unit to business unit |
| Authority for decisions | Taken within formal line-management position | Taken by empowered individuals with relevant expertise |
| Adaptability | Slow and reluctant even when business circumstances warrant change | Changes as needed in line with continuous improvement |
| Work emphasis | Formal procedures handed down | Devise own effective processes |
| Control | Tight through strict, formal systems | Devise own measurements in line with fulfilling process role |
| Behaviour | Contained by need to follow job description | Role and responsibilities evolved to meet needs of processes |
| Participation | Little-information is handed up, decisions down | Team working with cooperation between teams |
| | Commands and controls | Empowers, enables and motivates |

**Figure 10.** Management's changing role. *Source:* Slevin and Colvin[7]

challenge is to start by looking at the opportunities which IT as a tool brings, and then defining how we want to use *IT in the business*. Armed with the knowledge of what we want, we can then look at how to manage *IT as a business* in order to achieve our objectives.

*Empowering people*

This involves both empowering to make the change and to run the business afterwards. In empowering people to re-engineer the process we must:

● Identify catalysts/change agents at all levels in the organization, involve them in the exercise and create a structure which gives them authority to:
  – make decisions,
  – implement change,
  – question the sacred cows,
  – innovate.
● Act quickly when their paths are blocked.
● Reward endeavour and achievement.
● Eliminate bureaucracy and controls that hinder progress.
● Encourage them to ignore hierarchy and then protect them if they do.
● Provide personal coaching and coaches.
● Think about how you maintain their enthusiasm after the exercise.

Empowering people to run the re-engineered business involves:

● A reappraisal of roles, responsibilities and job design,
● Training to help staff fulfil new expectations,

- Reassessment of performance measures,
- An overhaul of reward systems to reflect new expectations and performance measures,
- Training and 're-education' of management to support the newly empowered workforce,
- Wide communication of the scope and responsibility of the empowered roles,
- Reassessment of the organization/work group structures in which they will operate,
- Careful planning and management of the change,
- Regular review and refinement of the role,
- Continuous reinforcement and support throughout the transition period and beyond.

*Benchmarking*

Four key benefits can be derived from comparisons with competitors and 'best of breed' organizations in other industries;

- lessons and ideas on the design of the transformation process itself,
- insight into the design of business architecture and the execution of core processes,
- definition of targets for performance measures – and identification of new measures,
- identification of opportunities to exploit superior capabilities that exist now or that will be created through the re-engineering process.

The benchmarking findings can then be used to create the catalyst for change and provide input into key stages of the exercise.

*Creating customer focus*

Throughout the exercise we must reinforce the notion that we all have customers and if we do not meet their needs we are not adding value. If we do not create value for the customer we cannot guarantee customer retention. At the point of sale this implies lost revenue and increased cost of sales. Internally it may involve our customer looking elsewhere – within or outside the organization – for the provision of the same product or service.

Knowing the customer is not enough – particularly when dealing with the organization's end customer. We must become more astute in analysing not only their requirements but also their trade-offs between preferences. Given limited resources, we must understand where they would like to see them focused. Clearly not all customers have the same preference profile. However, by undertaking trade-off analysis we can produce a more refined segmentation and then determine if and how we should service each segment in a manner that creates value for both customer and shareholder.

# A framework for business re-engineering

Having examined the motivations for re-engineering and the component parts that form the basis of the initiative, let us examine how these can be pulled together. Most exercises typically involve six key steps (Figure 11):

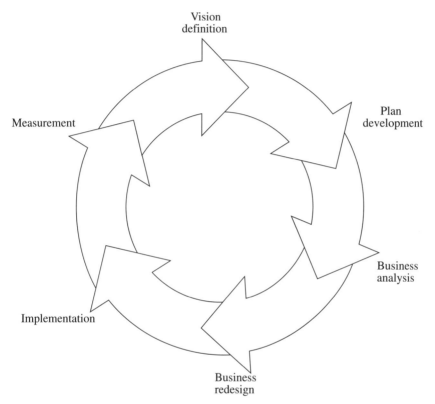

**Figure 11.** Six key steps in the re-engineering process

- building the vision of the re-engineered organization
- planning how the vision will be realized,
- analysing the current structure and processes,
- redesigning the 'business architecture',
- implementing the redesigned organization and processes,
- measuring the benefits and sharing the learning.

## Vision definition

At this stage (Figure 12), the aim is to ensure a clear focus on the products and services, competencies and processes around which the business is to be built.

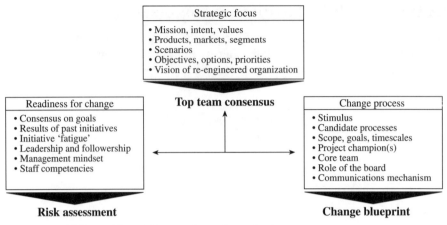

**Figure 12.** Building a vision of the re-engineered organization

Organizations generally have a range of *ad hoc* and formal techniques for undertaking this strategic analysis stage.

Of particular importance is the assessment of current and future profitability of products and services. This implies asking sensitive questions and demanding frank answers about the real value of so called 'loss leaders'. We must also decide whether there are particular segments of the market which we cannot serve profitably and assess the cost of pulling out.

The relationship between commercial offerings and competencies can become confused. We may be making money out of offerings in which we have no genuine competence-based advantage – a lesson which many in the financial services industry have learned to their cost in recent years.

The search for competence involves analysis of:

● the underlying features of our most successful products and services,
● the capabilities in which we believe we have a worthwhile and defensible edge,
● the customer requirements and hence capabilities on which we believe market dominance will hinge,
● the results of past approaches to defining and building capability.

The risk analysis and readiness for change aspects of this stage are described later on. Much has already been said about the components of the change process. A key element though is clearly the selection of candidate processes. One approach to assessing process capability is to rank its performance against the needs of both customers and shareholders (Figure 13).

A weighted ranking of performance against key criteria can be used to determine the individual value scores. So, for example, the evaluation of the customer value created by each process could be based on the contribution

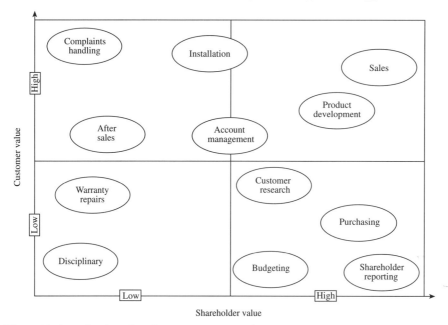

**Figure 13.** Assessing the value of a process – an example

they made against such factors as helping the customer to identify, evaluate, buy and use the product.

The resulting value index (Figure 14) can then be compared to the cost of process ownership to determine the appropriate treatment for each process in the re-engineering exercise. Experience suggests that those which fall in the central region are typically the ones which will benefit most from redesign.

## Plan development

The quality of the overall plan is a key determinant of the eventual success of the initiative. The wide ranging nature of the exercise means that those managing it must have a good understanding of the 'system' or 'business model'. This covers a range of issues such as identifying the procedure for changing salaries and bonuses and making sure the results make it through to the individual's pay cheque.

A number of the components identified have a major influence on the critical success factors for the initiative and need little elaboration.

The only aspect of planning that requires further discussion is the notion of planning incremental performance improvements (Figure 15). This again relates to the notion of the balanced scorecard. Experience suggests that those who have tried to re-engineer often fail if they focus all their attentions in one area alone such as technology – or even staff capability.

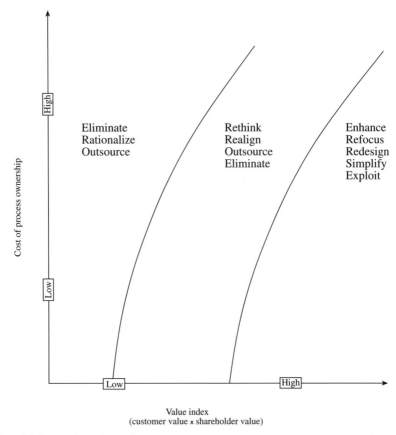

Figure 14. Comparing value and cost

Similarly, organizations which choose a balanced approach but then set targets far beyond the sights of those involved have also found the exercise failing. The problems are generally the absence of an internal reference point and a lack of belief in the organization's ability to achieve such dramatic improvements. These barriers can typically be overcome if each successive round of re-engineering has more demanding targets than the last – based on a demonstrated ability to deliver.

## Business analysis

The objective is to understand and build a high level model of the business as currently structured by:

● analysing customer requirements,
● modelling target processes,

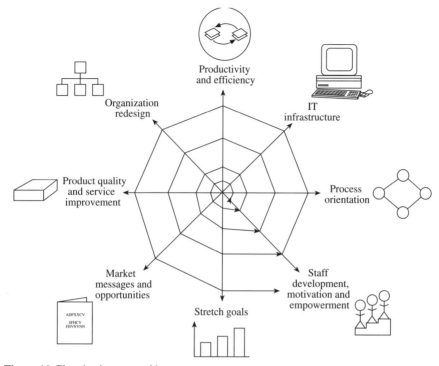

**Figure 15.** Planning incremental improvements

● assessing organizational issues,
● reviewing IT infrastructure,
● identifying candidates for improvement, elimination, outsourcing, and redesign,
● consolidating the re-engineering options.

The underlying objective is to free the firm from the shackles of past behaviour and practice. Hence the analysis phase questions why a business entity such as a process or structure exists. Next, we question how much of a process the customer sees and what value is added by each process step.

In justifying and dismantling every process, the aim is to avoid doing things just because '*we always have done*', eliminate duplication of effort and remove wasteful activities such as the rekeying of electronically generated data.

One of the questions asked most frequently is why model at all – why not go straight to redesign and re-invent everything from scratch? The answer is that there are a number of genuine benefits to be gained from understanding the current operation, including:

● defining a baseline model of existing processes with which we can plan and test future changes,

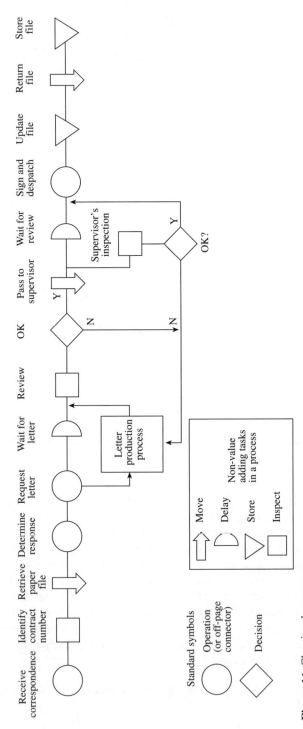

**Figure 16.** Charting the process

- identifying candidates for improvement,
- spotting current and potential problems,
- identifying improvements that can be made immediately by the process owner,
- building consensus on the steps in and problems of the current process,
- confirming interfaces to other functions, processes and organizations,
- creating the stimulus for change.

A variety of tools and techniques exist to support the modelling phase. These start with simple and easily understood pen and paper based techniques (Figure 16). They then increase in complexity and the amount of training required. At this stage the organization must decide how it will use the tools. The more sophisticated and expensive tools can be of value if key requirements are process simulation and/or the ability to support the physical enactment of the process once the business has been re-engineered.

Considerable care needs to be exercised in the selection and use of these tools. It is particularly important to avoid analysis to the lowest level of detail simply because the tool supports it. It is also dangerous to leave all system based modelling to the IT staff on the project simply because they 'understand' such tools. If the tool is required then all project staff should be able to use it. Whatever tool is chosen, the underlying process charting notation must be easily understood and applied by the users.

## Business redesign

The redesign stage can be the most fun, but also the most difficult part of the whole initiative. The objective is to create and cost the design for the re-engineered business (Figure 17). At the time of writing there is no single technique which is guaranteed to give you the optimal business design.

A number of variations on the basic concept of brainstorming are put forward. Most have the same basic elements – to allow participants the freedom to come up with a range of options of how the business process and supporting architecture should be structured. Given the basic parameters of people, procedures and technology and a physical location at which the process is executed we can vary each in turn to generate the range of options.

Examples of the results would include:

- *The insurance company* which investigated the option of eliminating all sales staff and then rewarding intermediaries on both the business generated and the accuracy of the proposal forms submitted – thereby reducing the inspection time.
- *The telecommunications company* which considered reducing the connection time for new customers down from days to seconds. The proposed approach was to install an access point and connect every premises to the

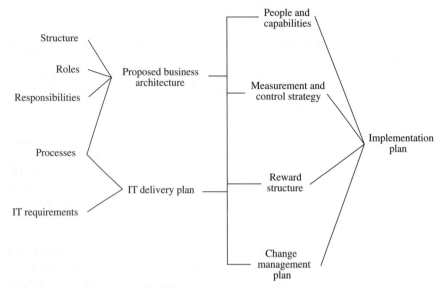

**Figure 17.** Designing the re-engineered business. *Source:* BMS Bossard

phone network using fibre optic cables and then activate the service at the time of request.

Two rules of thumb are useful when defining new processes:

● *completeness* – a well drawn process is not necessarily well defined or complete
● *conformance* – specifying a process completely does not guarantee that it will be executed that way.

## Implementation

The implementation plan typically needs to address three key areas:

● changes affecting parts of the current structure that will remain largely unchanged,
● putting in place those elements of the structure that have undergone substantial change,
● identifying changes to be made in future rounds of re-engineering.

This stage also requires a phase of bedding in and refinement:

● assessing the initial performance of the new architecture,
● making initial refinements,
● initiating a continuous review process.

## Measuring performance gains

A rigorous assessment of the results of re-engineering is vital (Figure 18). Again, measuring against a balanced scorecard of both hard and soft measures is essential. The objectives are to:

- identify and share the learning on what worked and what could be improved,
- help process owners create a continuous improvement process to support ongoing refinement,
- communicate the overall results and encourage others to spot further opportunities to be addressed in subsequent rounds of re-engineering.

# The role of IT in the re-engineering exercise

The discussion so far has promoted the view that IT can play a vital part in the exercise and highlighted some of the opportunities that IT creates. Hammer's principles also place heavy emphasis on IT's role in the re-engineering process.

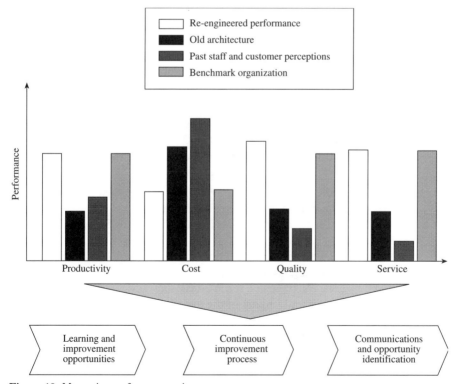

**Figure 18.** Measuring performance gains

However, it is at this point that senior managers start to become nervous – in many firms the IT function is not well respected and has a reputation for late delivery, budget overruns and poor quality systems. However, those managers have to be convinced that, just as the business can re-engineer its processes, so too can the IT function rethink its approach.

The IT function must recognize that there are a number of challenges it must meet in order to play its part effectively. IT must be seen as an enabler – not the driving force. Motivation for re-engineering has to come from the business itself.

IT's challenge is to demonstrate that it can participate fully in the experimental and iterative activity of defining new processes. Re-engineering places new demands on the IT function – for improved communication skills, greater business understanding and the use of development techniques which support experimentation/iterative development and prototyping.

## Change management and risk assessment

As we have seen, such a fundamental reappraisal of 'the way we do things' demands major changes in the organization's culture, and in the expectations, attitude, commitment and resulting behaviour of management and staff. The larger the exercise and more demanding the objectives, the higher the risk and the greater the need for effective change management. Hence, in this section a process is outlined for overcoming the risks and removing the barriers to change.

### Barriers to change

Re-engineering can cause fear, uncertainty and doubt for those most affected:

- senior and middle management may be reluctant to lose the power and authority that the current structure affords them,
- a potentially flatter structure implies less opportunities for promotion and advancement,
- those actively involved may be concerned about re-engineering both themselves and colleagues out of a job,
- those at lower levels typically receive less fact and hear more rumours about the objectives and impact of the exercise,
- re-engineering often involves headcount reduction – fear of job loss naturally diverts the attention and reduces the productivity of all who feel at risk,
- for those who survive, there is the stress induced by increased responsibility and the consequences of failure.

# A framework for managing change

Effective change management demands a clear process through which we can address concerns and build understanding, control the pace of change and maximize the value of individual contributions.

## Building vision and gaining commitment

With much of the work at the early stages being done or led by a small core team of managers and staff we must ensure that the rest of top management buy into the vision. They need an opportunity to discuss concerns, understand the change and commit to it. For those that cannot or will not buy into the vision we need to address the question of their future role in parallel to progressing the initiative.

Those who are committed need to be involved in assessing the changes which are key to achieving overall objectives.

Identification and assessment of the change barriers and priorities barriers will in turn help to determine where management time and attention should be focused.

With change priorities identified we can then define an overall structure for project management, issue resolution, project reporting and communications. These need to be supported through a set of management systems. With these in place we can then start communicating with the rest of the organization and formally launch the project.

## Project marketing

The primary role of project marketing is to build and develop organization-wide understanding and support for the initiative. This implies identifying and tackling fear, uncertainty and resistance as early as possible. Once the need for and scale of change is understood we can start trying to build the motivation and commitment to take part in implementing the proposed strategy. This in turn involves putting in place both formal and informal channels that support *two way communications*.

A key challenge here is to actually involve staff in defining a strategy and implementation plan for assisting those who will be displaced by the initiative and supporting those who will remain.

## Continuous risk assessment

The process of identifying, analysing and managing risk needs to continue throughout the project. There are two prime sources of risk in such initiatives. Firstly the risk associated with the change itself. This involves assessing factors such as the complexity of the planned change, the career risk for those involved and the speed of change. The second major source of risk is our past record on change. Prime factors here would include past attempts at implementing change, the extent to which we have learned from past failures and the level of leadership and 'followership' skills.

## Management systems

Three main systems are required in order to control progress. Firstly a system of standards helps ensure consistency across projects – guaranteeing, for example, that the risk assessment on every sub-project has the same structure. At the programme and sub-project management level, a number of tools are required to support scheduling, communication and progress reporting. Finally project owners require a reporting system which indicates progress and highlights issues requiring their attention.

## Allocating responsibility and authority

To maintain momentum on such large scale initiatives, responsibility and authority must be driven down the organization. Hence to empower people to make decisions and execute them we need a clear and widely understood structure through which they can act. The components of this structure are a steering committee and issue resolution process, clearly defined sub-projects and a mechanism through which we can integrate the output of individual projects into the business.

## People management

The human resourcing challenge is to build a high functioning team comprising resources drawn from several different functional areas. This requires an effective HR function that manages both the recruitment and release of staff from projects and monitors their performance and needs whilst there.

A second challenge lies in choosing the right balance of participants – distinguish between the differing requirements for expert, analyst and leadership roles. Where participants lack the competencies to contribute effectively the skills gap must be identified and closed rapidly through training and coaching. Finally there is an HR role to build a sense of team spirit in order to gain the loyalty and commitment of participants whose career allegiance may still lie with their functional 'parent'.

# Conclusion

The growth in interest in business re-engineering has been dramatic. The appeal lies in the simplicity of the central concept – *to rethink, restructure and streamline the business structures, processes, methods of working, management systems and external relationships through which we create and deliver value.* Such an approach can yield dramatic improvements in cycle times, efficiency, cost, quality, service, flexibility and capability. These in turn should render enhanced customer loyalty and bring increased profitability.

As with most new management tools and techniques a number of widely differing interpretations of the re-engineering concept have emerged. There is an equally large variation in the scale and scope of the business initiatives currently being labelled as re-engineering projects. These range from the far-ranging and fundamental reassessment of an entire business to small scale changes in an individual business activity such as budgeting.

Many organizations may want to consider using a strategy driven re-engineering approach. Before doing so, there are a number of simple questions that will test its appropriateness given the prevailing management style and culture. Management must decide whether it has the patience, commitment and tenacity to drive the exercise through. We must judge whether individuals within the firm can drive the exercise unaided and if not whether we understand how to manage a relationship with external consultants.

We must ask whether we are willing to change and possibly remove people, relationships, systems, products, structures and even whole departments which we may ourselves have been responsible for implementing. Finally, and crucially, only we can judge if we as top management are willing to change the culture, attitude and behaviour which got us to the elevated position we are in now.

# References

Hammer, Michael, Re-engineering Work – Don't Automate, Obliterate, *Harvard Business Review*, July–August (1990).

Hammer, Michael and Champy James, *Re-engineering the Corporation – A Manifesto for Business Revolution*, Nicholas Brearley Publishing (1993).

Talwar, Rohit, Business Re-engineering, BMS Bossard Executive Briefing, November (1992).

Talwar, Rohit, An Introduction to Business Re-engineering, BMS Bossard Presentation Guide, February (1993).

Talwar, Rohit, Issues in Process Modelling, BMS Bossard Presentation Guide, April (1993).

Talwar, Rohit, Managing Large Scale Change Initiatives, BMS Bossard Presentation Guide, May (1993).

D. P. Slevin and J. G. Colvin, Juggling Entrepreneurial Style and Organizational Structure, *Sloan Management Review*, **31** (2), Winter (1990).

# 9 Corporate diagnosis

## C. Carnall

Achieving major change is a learning process. It requires that we learn about changes in the environment and about how the organization can develop its capability to add value for customer or clients. Corporate diagnosis focuses upon the cognitive or analytical stage of the change process. Identifying what is going on, how things might be improved and creating a set of proposals for change falls within the field of corporate diagnosis. Implicit in such work are assumptions about how to measure efficiency and effectiveness and about 'models' of how organizations should function.

But is that enough? In the real world change must be defined and 'sold'. Change must be feasible and seen as such. What value is it to have the right approach if no-one will implement it? What value having plans which all agree but which do not meet the challenges presented by competition, market requirements, customer service and so on.

## Monitoring performance, measuring effectiveness

What do we mean by effective? How do we assess whether or not our organization is doing well? What do we mean by 'doing well'? Are we concerned with profit? Or sales value? Or market share? Or service levels? If so what level is satisfactory? The same as last year? Last year plus 5 per cent? Profit expressed as a percentage of turnover? Rate of growth of sales volume or of profit? Satisfactory for whom? Shareholders, managers, employees, clients, customers? What about comparing our performance with that of competing, or at least similar, organizations? A manufacturing company would compare itself to other companies in its own industry and sectors. A hospital would be compared to other hospitals of a similar size and case load and mix. We can readily see that the question of how well are we doing becomes quite complex.

We need to assess effectiveness for two reasons. First, identifying sources of ineffectiveness might lead us to restructure or reorganize in order to improve. Second, because ineffective organizations present a tougher context in which to implement technological, product or service changes. We are often involved in both. We need to introduce new technology and discover that progress will be impeded by lack of in-house expertise and by poor attitudes to change. Part of our preparation for the new technology involves bringing in the expertise (whether by forming a new department, through secondments or transfers or by hiring consultants). Also involved may be a training programme designed to introduce people to the new technology carefully, partly to allay any fears they have about the impact of change.

Dealing with sources of ineffectiveness as part of the implementation of change provides us with two advantages. First, it will allow us to implement change more effectively, and more speedily. Second, it will make future changes easier to implement because the organization will have become more adaptable. In essence, this will be because the people involved will have learned through the process of change, learned about themselves, about the new technology, and about how to prepare people to cope with change. A positive experience of change, properly exploited by all those involved, leaves people more capable of handling future change. Following Itami (1987), this means that the organization has developed its 'invisible assets'. Invisible assets are the knowledge base from which all employees operate. To quote Itami (1987):

> Invisible assets are the real source of competitive power and the key factor in corporate adaptability for three reasons: they are hard to accumulate, they are capable of simultaneous multiple uses, and they are both inputs and outputs of business activities.

Developing the knowledge base from which people operate takes time and energy. Once accumulated they have multiple uses. If a retail company develops an excellent reputation for merchandising high-quality goods, then it can use this reputation to promote products in new sectors, for example financial services. The reputation will attach to new stores, and this may help the company attract high-quality staff. Invisible assets are both inputs and outputs.

Having attracted high-quality staff to aid its development of a new market these staff bring in new ideas to the company. This enables the company to further improve its operations and therefore enhance its reputation; thus being more effective as an organization is both an input to and an output of organization change. More effective firms are more capable of handling change. Handling change effectively helps to sustain and create effectiveness in the future.

## Assessing organizational effectiveness

While considering methods of organizational effectiveness we might ask ourselves the following questions:

1 How do we assess whether or not our organization is doing well?
2 What do we mean by 'doing well'?
3 Are we concerned with profit, sales value, market share or service levels?

so, what level is satisfactory – the same as last year; last year plus 5 per cent?

5 Should profit be expressed as a percentage of turnover? (Again the latter figure compared to last year's performance.)
6 For whom is the level satisfactory – shareholders, managers, employees, clients or customers?

What about comparing our performance with that of competing or at least similar organizations? A manufacturing company would compare itself to other companies in its own industry and sectors. A hospital would be compared to other similar hospitals. We can now readily see that the question 'How well are we doing?' becomes quite complex. Indeed we increasingly utilize benchmarking as a means of ensuring that more than marginal change is being sought.

## Efficiency and effectiveness

Most people distinguish between efficiency and effectiveness. *Efficiency* comprises achieving existing goals with economical use of resources. *Effectiveness* means efficiency plus adaptability. The effective organization is both efficient and able to modify its goals as circumstances change. Consider a company manufacturing electromechanical weighing equipment in 1970. To be efficient it needed to manufacture and sell its product at economical cost in order to achieve acceptable profits (although we need to define what we mean by 'acceptable'). To be effective that company would also need to be developing electronic machines and training people in the design, manufacture, sales and maintenance of such equipment. The technology was available and could be applied to advantage. Thus the weighing machine market was likely to be moved in that direction. Effectiveness therefore implies the ability to recognize and respond to changing markets or environmental circumstances.

Argyris (1964) defines three core activities for any organization:

1 Achieving objectives
2 Maintaining the internal system
3 Adapting to the external environment.

Achieving objectives relates to the accomplishment of specific objectives such as:

1 Meeting delivery dates
2 Quality standards
3 Turnover targets

Maintaining the internal system includes activities and systems such as:

1 Appraisal
2 Training
3 Budgetary control
4 Reward systems.

Adapting to the external environment includes:

1 Marketing
2 Product/Service development
3 Public and community relations.

Effective organizations will be those achieving an appropriate balance between the various activities. The balance needed will clearly be influenced by the rate of change the organization is experiencing, both internally and externally.

Most important is to avoid narrow measures of effectiveness. For example, a famous retail store was reputed to assess store effectiveness on 'shrinkage' (loss of stock). Taken to the ultimate the best way of minimizing 'shrinkage' is to lock the stock room, and lock the store. There would be no sales but also no shrinkage! Narrow approaches can be misleading. What is needed is a wide-ranging approach and a questioning attitude. We might, for example, ask ourselves:

1 If we are making profit are we making as much as we can?
2 How are our competitors doing?
3 Where can we improve?
4 Is there any evidence of ineffectiveness?

Also we need to avoid the tendency only to 'measure' that which we can readily monitor, quantitatively. In a rapidly changing world judgement, experience and intuition are as important as quantitative analysis. The latter is needed, however. It provides the basis for systematic analysis. Trends are important, as are inter-firm or inter-organizational comparisons. But these are not enough if we wish to improve our organization. We assess performance and effectiveness in order to ensure improvement. As Will Rogers once said 'You can be on the right track but you'll get run over if you just sit there'. Thus we also need to take qualitative judgements of employee satisfaction and attitudes, corporate culture and adaptability.

# Capability

As we have seen the definition of effectiveness includes adaptability and there-fore focuses upon capability to add value and in particular to enhance or improve added value. This is vital. After all the main reason for introducing change will be to improve our capabilities whether by enhancing the added value delivered to customers or enhancing profits by reducing costs (which longer term will enhance our capability to add value by delivering higher income streams into the organization). It would be helpful therefore to look at how to assess capability more thoroughly.

## Corporate capability

One useful approach is that presented by Rowe, Mason, Dickel and Snyder (1989). In the Company Capability Profile (using their own terminology) they examine managerial factors, competitive factors, financial factors and technical factors. For example an organization which responds quickly to changing conditions, has a flexible organization structure, is aggressive in dealing with competition and has an entrepreneurial orientation is likely to possess a high level of capability. These are all managerial factors. Similarly high market share, customer loyalty are competitive aspects of capability, access to capital, cost stability and liquidity are financial aspects of capability and strength of patents and economies of scale are technical factors in capability.

Furnham and Grunter (1993) present a comprehensive treatment of corporate assessment. This presents measures of corporate culture, organizational climate, communications audits and customer audits. Elsewhere this author has presented techniques for diagnosing organizations (see Carnall 1991) with worked examples. There are a number of published 'guides' available for those wishing to take an analytical approach.

Taking account of the need to both identify and describe needed changes *and* implement them it is possible to identify not just what changes are needed but also to analyse an organization's readiness for change, as follows:

## Readiness for change

a) *Company 'track record' of changes*
   The potential problems are:

   1  Have past changes met with resistance?
   2  Were past changes poorly understood?
   3  Are employees too cautious?
   4  Did recently introduced changes have limited or little success?

   The solutions are:

   1  Keep everyone informed by making information available, explaining plans clearly and allowing access to management for questions and clarification.

2 Ensure that change is solid realistically by making a practical case for it. Explain change in terms which the employee will see as relevant and acceptable. Show how change fits business needs and plans. Spend time and effort on presentations.
3 Prepare carefully by making a full organizational diagnosis, spending time with people and groups, building trust, understanding and support.
4 Involve people by getting feedback on proposals, getting people to fill out the checklists, discussing the data from these checklists.
5 Start small and successful by piloting, with a receptive group of employees, in departments with a successful track record. Implement changes in clear phases.
6 Plan for success by starting with things that can give a quick and positive pay-off. Publicize early success. Provide positive feedback to those involved in success.

b) *Expectations of change*
   The potential problems are:

   1 Do different people hold different ideas about the change?
   2 Do people know what to expect?
   3 Are objectives clearly defined?

   The solutions are:

   1 Clarify benefits of changes by emphasizing benefits to those involved, i.e. to the company.
   2 Minimize surprises by specifying all assumptions about the change. Focus on outcomes. Identify potential problems.
   3 Communicate plans by being specific in terms that are familiar to the different groups of employees. Communicate periodically and through various media. Ask for feedback. Do not suppress negative views but listen to them carefully and deal with them openly.

c) *Who 'owns' the problem or the idea for change?*
   The potential problems are:

   1 Are the procedures, systems, departments, products, services involved seen to be a problem?
   2 Was the change planned or introduced by top management or staff departments?
   3 Is the change viewed as a matter of procedure?

   The solutions are:

   1 Specify plans in terms that people understand. Ensure that employees' problems are addressed explicitly as part of the change. Arrange for visible outcomes.

2 Clarify employees' view by exploring their concerns about the changes and examining impact on the day-to-day routines.
3 Present a clear case by specifying who wants change and why. Explain longer-term advantages. Identify common benefits. Present potential problems clearly. Listen to problems.

d) *Top management support*
The potential problems are:

1 Does top management support the change?
2 Will top management provide resources?
3 Is the management performance appraisal process an obstacle to change?

The solutions are:

1 Build a power base by becoming the expert in the problems involved. Understand top management concerns. Develop informational and formal support. Develop a strong and polished presentation in top management language.
2 Develop clear objectives and plans by establishing a clear timetable. Set up review processes to be supportive. Bring in top management and middle management to the review process. Focus meetings on specific outcomes, and specific problems.

e) *Acceptability of change*
The potential problems are:

1 Does the planned change fit other plans?
2 Is there a clear sense of direction?
3 Does the proposed change place greater demands on people?
4 Does the change involve new technology, products/services, expertise?

The solutions are:

1 Identify relevance of change to plans by reviewing plans and specifying how change fits. Incorporate changes into on-going developments. If possible, frame changes in terms of the organization's style.
2 Clarify plans for change by communicating simply and openly.
3 Implement with flexible or adaptable people, people familiar with some or all of the change, in a part of the business where there are strong supporters for change. Recognize why people support change (career, rewards, company politics).
4 Do not oversell change by being adamant about conflicts with present practices. Encourage discussion of these conflicts.

# References

Argyris, C. (1964) *Integrating the Individual and the Organization*, Wiley, New York.

Carnall, C. A. (1991) *Managing Change*, Routledge, London.

Furnham, A. and Gunter, B. (1993) *Corporate Assessment*, Routledge, London.

Itami, H. (1987) *Mobilizing Invisible Assets*, Harvard University Press, Cambridge, MA.

Rowe, A. (1989) Mason, R., Dickel, K. and Snyder, N. *Strategic Management*, 3rd edition, Addison-Wesley, Reading, MA.

# Part Four
# Transforming the Organization

---

Managing major changes successfully requires us to take an organization-wide approach. Change creates stress and strain both for those who support change (through over-work; the challenge of leading change in an uncertain world; the pressure of dealing with other, often anxious, people; the inherent uncertainties; all are subject to it in some degree, and so on) and for those who are either indifferent, opposed or fearful of change.

In the first chapter we saw how crucial organizational learning is to effective change. In this chapter we offer some views of how to implement major strategic changes. Following the work of Quinn (see in particular Quinn, 1992) organizational re-structuring and strategic change should be based upon effective diagnosis and bench-marking, information and incentive systems. A key point however in achieving strategic change amidst organizational circumstances looking less and less like traditional hier-archical structures is that 'managed incrementalism' is a strategy for change implemen-tation explicitly designed to manage risk. However, this does not need to imply that change is slow, random or gradual.

All of this assumes that change implementation requires the following:

- that we build an awareness of the need for change;
- that the case for change is made convincingly and credibly;
- that the process of change is a learning process; you don't get everything right initially;
- that dramatic changes can feel chaotic and uncertain as people seek to come to terms with new skills, etc.;
- that attention must be given to broadening and mobilizing support for change, whether through task forces and project teams, through the use of incentive systems and training, through pilot schemes and so on;
- crystallizing the vision and focus for the organization but not necessarily at the outset – indeed initially the vision may be very broad – much has yet to be learned before an *emerging* strategic vision can be articulated;
- focus on people and on the process of change.

The extracts presented approach the issue of strategic implementation in different ways. In Chapter 10 Colin Coulson-Thomas provides us with the results of three 1991 sur-veys of senior managers, the majority of whom were chief executives or on the board of their company. The surveys were entitled 'Managing the Flat Organization', 'Quality –

The Next Steps' and 'Communicating for Change'. The surveys demonstrate that developing a shared vision for a company is vital for success. However, the results also indicate '. . . that many attempts to formulate and implement visions and missions have been naïve, and in some cases destructive. A wide gulf has emerged between rhetoric and reality, and between aspirations and achievement. Instead of inspiration and motivation there is disillusionment and distrust'. Coulson-Thomas concludes that this uncertainty emerges not because people do not respond to a clear vision but rather that they find themselves unclear about how the company will achieve it.

This 'failure in implementation' appears to be derived from four principal causes:

- managers being unable to cope with the new demands being placed upon them;
- lack of real commitment to the vision throughout the organization;
- short-term measures taken by top management which appear to be inconsistent with the vision;
- in some (particularly UK and US) companies 'short-termism' demotivates managers for whom 'doing more with less' provides insufficient incentive when the only vision is about survival in the short term.

He examines the leadership role of top management (in particular the chairman or chief executive) and the need for communication.

Turning to Chapter 11 by Goodstein and Warner Burke, they look at transformation at British Airways as an example of fundamental, large-scale change in strategy and culture.

In Chapter 12 Alexander provides a review of the implementation literature. He supports the Pressman and Wildavsky idea that 'Policies are continuously transformed by implementation actions that simultaneously alter resources and objectives'. Thus strategy (or policy) and implementation interact and emerge. Alexander also notes that implementors are, or should be, concerned both with preventing failure (by avoiding the common implementation problems) and promoting success.

There are three learning modes which are of relevance to managers concerned by change, as follows:

1 *Learning by doing* – this is an internal process. We learn by experimentation, by trial and error, by pilot trials and so on.
2 *Learning by use* – this is essentially learning from the external world. We learn about how to improve our own product/services by gaining feedback from customers and by competitive benchmarking. Thus we gain from customers' experience of *using* our products/services and through comparing ourselves with competitor organizations.
3 *Learning from failure* – which speaks for itself but which, to be available to us, demands that we accept that failure will happen from time to time.

Our argument is that ideas such as transformational leadership, entrepreneurship and the learning organization each embrace these ideas.

Beyond this we recognize that major changes are typically implemented as major programmes organized around simple themes (e.g. 'right first time' for total quality programmes or 'next steps programme' for major programmes of culture change).

A good current example is that of 'time-based competition'. The key idea is that the way we manage time – whether in production, in new product development, in sales and distribution – represents a powerful source of competitive advantage. This idea has spawned another, that of 'business process re-engineering'. At the core of both is a strategy for change utilizing analytical techniques to analyse the organization seeking continuous improvements to work and information flows and to the use of time. The emphasis is upon the organization doing the work itself, utilizing its own people, empowering people at all levels to achieve change. Benchmarking is a key analytical technique utilized in such programmes, as are techniques such as 'pilots' and 'breakthrough teams'. According to Stalk and Hout (Chapter 13), breakthrough teams should be given radical goals such as reducing time by half in order that assumptions will be challenged. Bottlenecks, breakdowns, failures, unmet customer needs all become opportunities to learn. All of this implies radically new ways of thinking about the organization.

If the Stalk and Hout chapter is accepted as a source of new ways of thinking about the organization in work terms the change is simply the evolution of new attitudes and beliefs, of a new corporate culture.

Finally in Chapter 14 Argyris explains something of the constraints to achieving effective learning in organizations by pointing to the distinction between what he calls single-loop and double-loop learning. At the core of his explanation are two key points about professionals (and managers and a growing proportion of employees are professionals or quasi-professionals of one sort or another), as follows:

1 Essentially the life experience of most professionals through schooling, university and early career is characterized by success, not failure. Because they have rarely failed they have never learned how to learn from failure. Thus when things go wrong for them they become defensive, screen out criticism and put the 'blame' on others. Ironically their ability to learn shuts down just as they need it most

2 In common with our opening remarks for this book Argyris takes the view that organizations assume that learning is a problem of motivation. This creates the right structures of communication, rewards and authority and accountability – designed to create motivated and committed employees – and learning and development will follow. Sadly Argyris tells us, this is fatally flawed. People learn through how they think – through the cognitive rules or reasoning they use to design and implement their action.

For Argyris organizations can learn how to encourage learning, how to resolve these learning dilemmas. At the root of his solution is to find ways of constructively questioning the rationale or reasoning behind someone's actions.

Let me give you an example from my own experience. The day before I came to write these lines I was acting as chairman of the audit committee of the board of directors of an organization in which I am a non-executive director. The organization had, last year, subcontracted its internal audit work to an outside firm. We were discussing the report from the internal audit for the last year and considering the plan for the current financial year. We had noticed that the budget for last year had included 25 days for 'management and planning'. The out-turn had been 30 days and the budget for the current year was 32 days. In our view 25 days (which represented 10 per cent of the internal audit budget) was high. No explanation was given for the 30 days out-turn nor to justify a budget of 32 days this year. We raised a series of questions. What activities were included in 'management and planning'? What was the value of those days? We also noted that over-runs on various audit projects undertaken by the firm during last year had been due to problems of getting information – was this a sign of good planning? Or of the need for more planning? The director of the internal audit firm was defensive. He referred to industry norms of up to 20 per cent for planning audit work. We acknowledged that but pointed out that the audit needed for our organization was relatively straightforward. Eventually he said 'Well I had hoped that we could develop a co-operative approach and engage in a free and frank discussion'. To which our reply was 'That's what we are doing!' There is little doubt in my mind that the criticism had placed him on the defensive, automatically. Whilst he recognized he sought an open relationship he felt drawn to defend the number of days ascribed to 'management and planning'. More importantly he felt constrained from explaining that the reason for the high number of actual days was that there had been so many problems during the previous year (in which the organization, and, therefore the finance function, had been founded) that he and other senior colleagues had been forced to spend time on-site problem-solving in order to get things done. To say so would be to be critical of the finance director – or at least apparently so!

Argyris argues that people can be taught to reason in ways which reduce and overcome organizational defences. To quote from the extract:

> . . . *they will discover that the kind of reasoning necessary to reduce and overcome organizational defences is the same kind of 'tough reasoning' that underlies the effective use of ideas in strategy, finance, marketing, manufacturing and other management disciplines . . . it depends on collecting valid data, analysing it carefully, and constantly testing inferences drawn from the data . . . Good strategists make sure that their conclusions can withstand all kinds of critical questioning.*

At its basics then is 'productive reasoning'.

We then turn to Chapter 15 by Masuch. This chapter develops the everyday phrase 'vicious circles' into a guiding idea to explain much of what can be confusing in organizations, particularly in a period of change. Indeed let us return to the question I posed in the introduction to Part One. People are motivated by challenge, opportunity and discretion but are also seen as resistant to change. Yet change appears to create the conditions which motivate them. How can we explain this? Well if change is seen as job threatening then people may fear its consequences and thereby resist change. In turn managers concerned over much about resistance may try to keep the changes secret until the last moment thus reinforcing the fear referred to above. It is not difficult to see how vicious circles might arise out of behaviour of this type.

Overall the chapter attempts to explain something scholars often refer to as 'unintended consequences'. We establish a performance related pay scheme to motivate and reward increased performance. But unless we are very careful both in designing and managing both the scheme and the context within which it operates, people use the scheme in order to stabilize rather than increase their earnings and if we are not careful both managers and others will tacitly collude in the acceptance of a current level of performance rather than actively seek improvements.

### Reference

Quinn, J. B. (1992) *The Intelligent Enterprise*, The Free Press, New York.

# 10 Strategic vision or strategic con?: rhetoric or reality?

## *C. Coulson-Thomas*

Major companies devote considerable effort to communicating corporate visions and missions. Yet three recent surveys suggest that much of this effort has been counter-productive. A gap has emerged between rhetoric and reality. Arenas of confrontation have arisen between directors and managers, head offices and business units, holding companies and their subsidiaries, and between specialists and generalists. A widespread desire for corporate transformation is not matched by understanding of how to bring it about. The lack of top management commitment and of communication skills are major barriers to change. More competent directors and more effective boards are needed. The article suggests key roles for the chairman and the chief executive. It examines how best to share a compelling vision, and identifies a requirement for new attitudes and approaches to communication.

Most executives assume the value of a compelling corporate vision that 'grabs the attention' of customers and 'turns on' employees. Externally, the vision differentiates. Internally, it motivates people to achieve. Chief executives consider themselves negligent if their companies are without a mission statement that is generally available to all employees. Much effort has been devoted to 'communicating the vision' throughout corporate organizations.

Surely all this activity must have been worthwhile? Three recent reports,[1-3] all based on questionnaire and interview surveys completed in 1991, suggest that many attempts to formulate and implement visions and missions have been naive, and in some cases destructive. A wide gulf has emerged between rhetoric and reality, and between aspirations and achievement. Instead of inspiration and motivation there is disillusionment and distrust.

This article examines what has gone wrong, and the longer term and sometimes hidden consequences of the short term reactions of corporate boards to economic pressures. It highlights some arenas of conflict that are to be found in many companies, and emphasizes that changing attitudes and perspective generally takes longer than is first thought. Greater unity and commitment is needed in the boardroom, and new approaches to communication are required.

# The surveys

But first, the sources of the evidence, the three 1991 surveys:

1 The British Institute of Management (BIM) report *Managing the Flat Organization*,[1] is concerned with the management of the transition from a bureaucratic to a flexible organization. It is based upon a survey of 59 organizations employing 1.3 million people and with a combined turnover of £180bn.
2 The survey *Quality: The Next Steps*[2] is concerned with quality priorities and barriers. It was carried out by Adaptation Ltd, and involved over 100 organizations with a combined turnover of £85bn and employing 1.6 million people. The survey was sponsored by ODI International.
3 The survey, *Communicating for Change*[3] examines the role of communications in the management of change. It was undertaken by Adaptation Ltd, and involved 52 organizations with a combined turnover of £90bn and employing 1.2 million people. The survey was sponsored by Granada Business Services.

Table 1 gives the job titles of the individuals completing the returned questionnaires. A majority of the respondents in all three surveys[1-3] are at director level. Those completing the questionnaires were asked to categorize the main activities of their organizations. In all three surveys[1-3] the largest category of participating organization is represented by 'manufacturing/production'.

Table 2 provides a breakdown of the turnover of the participating organizations. The proportion of organizations with a turnover in excess of £1bn ranges

**Table 1**  Job titles of survey participants

|  | Managing the flat organization (%) | Quality, the next steps (%) | Communicating for change (%) |
|---|---|---|---|
| Chairman and CEOs | 61 | 26 | 33 |
| Director | 17 | 32 | 25 |
| Manager | 14 | 29 | 35 |
| Other | 8 | 13 | 7 |

**Table 2**   Turnover of respondents' organizations (£)

|  | Managing the flat organization (%) | Quality, the next steps (%) | Communicating for change (%) |
|---|---|---|---|
| 1bn+ | 65 | 24 | 33 |
| 501m–1bn | 22 | 14 | 14 |
| 101–500m | 7 | 46 | 45 |
| 51–100m | 2 | 5 | 8 |
| 11–50m | 0 | 7 | 0 |
| 0–10m | 4 | 4 | 0 |

from about a quarter in the case of 'Quality: The Next Steps',[2] to some two thirds in the 'Managing the Flat Organization'[1] survey.

There is a preponderance of 'UK headquartered' or 'UK national' organizations in all three surveys. The participation of 'non-U.K. headquartered' or 'non-UK national' companies is generally through the chief executive or a director of the UK subsidiary or operating company.

## The importance of vision

The 'Managing the Flat Organization'[1] survey is the third of a series of annual BIM surveys. The 1989 and 1990 surveys revealed that directors and managers face a turbulent and demanding business environment.[4,5] In order to survive in the face of multiple challenges and opportunities, companies are having to: (i) differentiate themselves from competitors; and (ii) become more flexible, responsive and adaptable.[4,5]

The 1991 survey[1] reveals the extent to which changes are now occurring within organizations: 'Approaching nine out of ten of the participating organizations are becoming slimmer and flatter, while in some eight out of ten more work is being undertaken in teams, and a more responsive network organization is being created' (Table 3).

In such circumstances, involving change and uncertainty, a clear vision and strategy is essential. Without it organizations can become fragmented as devolution and delegation occurs during the transition from the bureaucratic to the emerging network organization.[1,4,5] One CEO confessed: 'We almost lost control. People went off in all directions. I have had to put the old restrictions back on. They will have to stay until we can communicate or share the vision of what we are trying to do.'

The 1991 survey evidence confirms the importance of vision:

**Table 3**  What respondents' organizations are doing to better respond to challenges and opportunities within the business environment

| | |
|---|---|
| Creating a slimmer and flatter organization | 88% |
| More work is being undertaken in teams | 79% |
| Creating a more responsive network organization | 78% |
| Functions are becoming more inter-dependent | 71% |
| Procedures and permanency are giving way to flexibility and temporary arrangements | 67% |
| Organizations are becoming more inter-dependent | 55% |

- In the 'Managing the Flat Organization'[1] survey: 'Every respondent assessing it believes clear vision and mission to be important, and about threequarters of them consider it "very important"' (Table 4).

**Table 4**  Factors for creating a new philosophy of management in order of 'very important' replies

| | |
|---|---|
| Clear vision and mission | 74% |
| Customer focus | 66% |
| Harnessing human potential | 66% |
| Attitudes, values and behaviour | 52% |
| Personal integrity and ethics | 40% |
| Individual learning and development | 29% |
| Processes for ongoing adaptation and change | 29% |
| Turbulence and uncertainty | 19% |
| Organizational learning | 14% |
| Management techniques | 5% |
| Others | 3% |

- The 'Quality: The Next Steps'[2] survey concludes that: 'A clear and shared quality vision and top management commitment are essential.'
- In the 'Communicating for Change' survey,[3] 'Clear vision and strategy' and 'top management commitment' are jointly ranked as the most important requirements for the successful management of change (Table 5).
- The 'Communicating for Change' survey[3] concludes that: 'Clear vision and strategy, and top management commitment are of crucial importance in the management of change. The vision must be shared, the purpose of change communicated, and employee involvement and commitment secured.'

Sir John Harvey-Jones believes a vision should present 'an attractive and clear view of the future which can be shared. It must motivate, be ambitious, and should stretch people to achieve more than they might ever have thought possible'.[1]

**Table 5** Change requirements in order of 'very important' replies

| | |
|---|---|
| Clear vision and strategy | 86% |
| Top management commitment | 86% |
| Sharing the vision | 71% |
| Employee involvement and commitment | 65% |
| Communicating the purpose of change | 65% |
| An effective communications network | 54% |
| Communicating the expected results of change | 44% |
| Understanding the contributions required to the achievement of change | 42% |
| Communicating the timing of change | 38% |
| Linking a company's systems strategy with its management of change | 38% |
| Project management of change | 27% |
| Ongoing management education and development programmes | 23% |
| One off management education and development programmes | 8% |

# The failure of implementation

Given this agreement on the importance of vision, why is there thought to be a problem? Our family of three surveys[1-3] suggests the answer to this question lies in a failure of achievement and implementation. The 'Managing the Flat Organization'[1] survey reveals that:

- *'There is an emerging consensus concerning what is sought. The uncertainty is about how it might be achieved.'*
- Managers are not being equipped to handle the new demands that are being placed upon them. One chairman confided 'I worry that every change, every extra demand, may turn out to be the last straw'.
- In many companies both vision and mission are regarded as just 'words on paper'. As one director put it 'A document is dead'. A vision needs to live in the hearts and minds of all employees.
- The short term responses of many boards to economic recession are not always consistent with either a company's vision or the building of long term relationships with its customers. The 'gap' between rhetoric and reality suggests 'a lack of top management commitment'.
- In some (particularly UK and US) companies 'short termism' appears to have exacted a severe toll of the managerial spirit: 'Many managers appear to have "had enough" of forever "doing more with less", when the reality of the vision they are offered is corporate survival for another few months.'

These findings are not 'out of step with other results'. They are supported by the second 1991 survey 'Quality: The Next Steps'[2] which reveals that:

- Many organizations lack both a common understanding of what quality is, and a shared 'quality vision' of what it ought to be. One quality manager complained *'quality is now all things to all people'*.
- The quality message is not being effectively communicated. Over seven out of ten respondents agree that 'quality too often consists of "mother-hood" statements'.
- Quality in many organizations is largely a matter of rhetoric. One general manager described it as 'a communication device, an umbrella, an adjective, a label or a slogan'.
- Short termism, and the perceived constraints upon directors and boards to focus excessively upon financial ratios has become a significant issue. A CEO summed up the dilemma: 'I face a real conflict of interests, between the long term demands of the vision and a short term imperative to survive. I don't want the vision to become an epitaph.'
- *The main quality barrier*, by a large margin, in terms of 'very significant' replies is *'top management commitment'*. Over nine out of ten respondents consider this to be a 'very significant' barrier to the successful implementation of a quality process.

The 'Communicating for Change' survey[3] provides further support for these conclusions:

- 'There is widespread awareness of the need to change. However, commitment to significant change is rarely matched by a confident understanding of how to bring it about.'
- Simple and superficial change, such as shifting priorities, or those involving the use of words, can and sometimes do occur overnight. Fundamental changes of attitudes, values, approach and perspective usually take a longer time to achieve. The timescale to achieve such changes may extend beyond the lifetime of the change requirement.
- 'Most companies believe the communication and sharing of vision and strategy throughout their organization could be much improved.' Top management commitment emerges as a significant barrier to effective internal and external communication.
- *'In many companies there is a feeling that visions and missions are just words on paper. Directors and senior managers are not always thought to be committed to their implementation.'*
- 'The recession has increased the extent of cynicism and mistrust as boards have felt it necessary to take short term actions that conflict with longer term objectives.' A managing director confided in despair 'I know I'm doing things that will weaken us in the long term. What's worse almost everyone else knows as well. I'm surviving, but one day when the recession is over what we have done will come back to haunt us'.

# Direction and management

Respondents in all three of our 1991 surveys[1-3] emphasize the need for 'top management commitment'. It is thought essential in view of the complex nature of the change task, and the number of individuals and groups that must be involved.

Commitment begins in the boardroom. Among the key responsibilities of the board are:[6,7]

- Determining a purpose for the company, a reason for its continued existence, and articulating a vision that can be communicated.
- Establishing achievable objectives derived from the vision, and formulating a strategy for their achievement.

Both vision and strategy have to be communicated and shared.[1-3] The results of communication should be monitored to ensure that it leads to understanding. One managerial interviewee pulled a mission statement out of his wallet: 'Here it is. They put it on a piece of card. I couldn't tell you what it says. Its one of those things that doesn't stick, but we've all got one.'

A board and its directors need to be persistent. The 'Quality: The Next Steps' survey[2] concludes: 'commitment needs to be sustained if barriers to full implementation are to be identified and overcome'.

The qualities that distinguish directors from managers derive from: (i) their different legal duties and responsibilities; and (ii) the role of the board. Directors require strategic awareness, the ability to see a company as a whole and understand the context within which it operates.[8] Formulating a distinctive vision and a realistic strategy requires objectivity and the ability to look ahead.[6-8] Not surprisingly, strategic awareness, objectivity, and communication skills rank high among the qualities sought in new appointees to the board.[8]

Managers, particularly those in larger and international companies also need strategic awareness, communication and team skills etc. Increasingly, they need to understand the business environment.[9] In the 'Managing the Flat Organization'[1] survey the only 'management quality' assessed as of importance by every respondent is 'understanding the business environment'.

# Focus and horizon

A 'traditional' view has been that: 'directors . . . (focus) . . . on the external business environment . . . and are concerned with long term questions on strategy and policy', while 'in comparison the great mass of employees are thought to concentrate upon short term questions of implementation'.[6] 'In reality' both directors and managers 'concentrate upon both the outside world and the company, and also the inter-relationship between the two'.[6]

The efforts of companies to articulate and communicate a longer term and customer focused vision has shifted the focus of many managers to the extent that distinctions of perspective between many directors and managers may have become a matter of emphasis or degree. As a result 'sharing a vision' has increased the potential for conflict where vision and conduct are perceived to be incompatible.[1–3] Figure 1 illustrates the conflicting pressures at the heart of the relationship between both head office and business unit, and between holding company and subsidiary or operating company:

- Business unit managers and the directors of operating or subsidiary companies are striving: (i) to build longer term relationships with customers, and in many cases also with suppliers; and (ii) to focus externally on the customer and relationships within supply chains. Corporate visions and strategy have encouraged them to 'think long term' and to develop more of an external focus.
- At the same time, those occupying head office and main board positions feel under pressure from analysts to maintain short term performance.

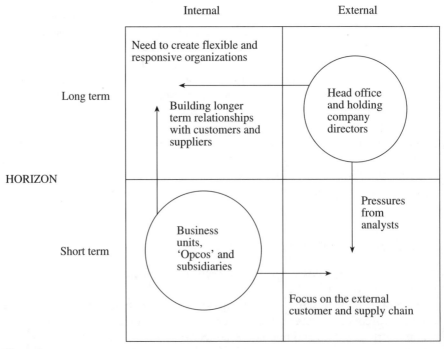

**Figure 1.**

They are also putting more emphasis upon the transformation of the internal corporate bureaucracy, as they strive to create more flexible and responsive organizations.

# Arenas of confrontation

The three 1991 surveys[1–3] suggest that four arenas of conflict have been exacerbated by the drive of CEOs to communicate and share a longer term vision:

## 1 Directors vs managers

Directors and managers do not agree on the question of where a lack of commitment is to be found within their companies:

- CEOs and directors tend to interpret the 'top management barrier' as the senior management team constituting the first couple of layers below the board.[2] While CEOs report receptive employees further down the organization, many managers, to quote one CEO, 'assess changes in terms of the impacts upon their own roles and standing in the corporate bureaucracy'.
- Interviews with CEOs suggest that 'vested interests', 'organizational politics' and 'cynicism' tend to be associated with senior rather than junior managers. Those thought by CEOs to be less committed to change are those with the greatest stake in, or having most to gain from, the 'status quo'.
- Managers have a different perspective on the source of the 'commitment barrier'. Many of those interviewed interpret 'top management' as those 'above' them, particularly the board.[2] It is felt that many boards remain sceptical and are not committed.

A CEO who 'changed companies' during the course of interviews now shares the 'managerial' view: 'Looking back I realize some of my colleagues in the boardroom were just playing with words. They would nod agreement, and then do nothing in their divisions. When people say things like "if you say so" or "you're the boss", you know you are in trouble. We should have kept at it until they were all committed.'

## 2 Head office vs business unit

Head offices and business units can have conflicting views and perspectives on the steps needed to implement a vision. The 'Quality: The Next Steps'[2] survey identified the tension which 'short-termism' can cause between a head office and operating units. One director of quality summed up the dilemma: 'Business units are confused. *We have really pushed customer satisfaction, and we have asked them to put everyone through quality training. Some of them are now quite committed. But at the moment we have frozen headcounts and new consultancy contracts so they can't do the training.*'

At the level of business units there is much dissatisfaction with the criteria used to measure performance. One divisional director complained: 'I bought into quality, and the vision, as did my team. Everyone talks about quality, but I'm measured by the same old ratios. Quality is great, and we all know its important, but numbers are real. The ratios decide my next move, not how many quality improvement projects I've got.' In many companies the relative bottom line performance of operating companies reveals little more than the basis of the allocation of 'HQ' overheads.

The need to recover the cost of head offices is also a 'bone of contention'. One business unit general manager expressed frustration: 'I'm supposed to buy and hand out corporate videos on the vision, but our prices and margins are being squeezed, and I'm being squeezed. I get memos from head office to reduce headcount and cut costs, while my re-allocated overheads have increased.'

## 3  Holding company vs subsidiary or operating company

Differences of perspective and emphasis are also endemic in the relationship between 'subsidiaries and parents'. Problems referred to in interviews during the 'Quality: The Next Steps'[2] survey include: (i) achieving 'consistency' across a group made up of diverse units; and (ii) the imposition upon a subsidiary of a group approach to quality which may not be appropriate. Some UK companies have resisted the use of a 'quality package' designed for a US parent on the grounds of incompatibility with the UK culture.

According to one international personnel director of a MNC: 'Many of my colleagues never think about how much our strategic vision is bound up with our own culture. They don't relate to it in South America. My CEO expected a problem in Europe, but not in South America. Everywhere its the same, its not their vision – its our vision. We're telling them about it, not sharing it with them.'

As corporations seek to 'slim down', many subsidiary companies believe they are bearing an unfair proportion of 'corporate savings'. One subsidiary managing director took the view: 'Who gets the misery depends upon power, and there's still a lot of it at the centre. We worry about long term vision and the investments it requires, but we make the cuts. Yet the headcount at holding company level hasn't really changed. What on earth do they all do?'

A national operating company director answered this question in the case of one global company: '1992 has a lot to answer for. We had announced a run down of central overheads, and along comes 1992. The head office politicians jumped at the opportunity to create another layer of bureaucracy at the regional level. Just when I need to cut prices to survive in a more competitive market I'm having to fund the staffing up of a European headquarters.'

## 4 Generalist vs specialist

Surveys of IT,[10] personnel,[4,11] marketing,[5] and quality[2] issues have all revealed a gap of perspective and understanding between CEOs and the heads of specialist functions. The differences of perspective appear to have been widened as a result of differing interpretations of, and commitment to, corporate vision.

Many 'functional' directors and managers are critical of their CEOs. Economic recession, particularly that in the UK, has made many specialists more aware of the gap between the rhetoric of the long term corporate vision of the CEO, as portrayed in the corporate video, and the reality of short term cuts and tactical compromise.[1-3] The 'Quality: The Next Steps'[2] survey concludes: 'recession is clearly distinguishing the companies that are committed to quality from those that pay lip service to it'.

Functional specialists are at odds with the perceived 'short termism' of CEOs. Quality is regarded by its 'champions', as a continuing process and long term commitment.[2] A director of quality claimed to be 'on a quest for the holy grail. I won't get there, but I'm obsessive. I feel, but I can't always prove, that I'm doing the right thing'. Almost all of those interviewed were experiencing some difficulty in quantifying 'benefits' and putting a satisfactory economic or 'cost-justified' case for substantial quality 'investments'.

CEOs complain that their 'specialists' lack strategic awareness and business acumen.[4,11] Their perspectives are described by CEOs as 'functional' rather than 'strategic'.[2,4,5,10,11]

## Implementing the CEO vision

*The vision of many CEOs is of a network that embraces both customers and suppliers.*[5] It is realized that in some sectors the individual company alone cannot deliver the whole of the value added sought by customers without working closely with other companies in the total supply chain.[2,5]

Customers are now regarded as a part of the organization, rather than 'outsiders'. However, many marketing directors are perceived as not sharing this vision of customers as colleagues or business partners.[5] According to one chairman: 'customers have been treated by our marketing people as cannon fodder for generalized ads and direct mail shots'.

The view of many 'generalist' CEOs, especially those trying to implement a vision, is that 'specialist' directors in the boardroom are often obstacles to, rather than facilitators of, change.[4,5,10] According to one CEO: 'Trying to transform the culture brought it home to me. They are all great as heads of a function, but they are not a team. They look at everything from their own particular perspective. I have a corporate vision. They have a marketing, or personnel, or whatever vision. It came to me one day – we don't have the same view of where we are going, or of what is important.'

Companies now compete on the flexibility and speed of their processes for responding to evolving customer requirements. Some of the CEOs interviewed consider their priority roles to be those of catalysts and facilitators of the management of continuing change. This is thought to imply responsibilities in the boardroom that are 'broader' or 'beyond' many of the 'traditional' concerns of 'functional' directors.[2]

A theme of many interviews with CEOs across a succession of surveys[1,2,4,5] has been the extent to which many issues on the boardroom agenda transcend traditional functional divisions. There is need for everyone to be involved in 'the change process',[1] and there is a requirement in many boardrooms for facilitating roles such as directors of learning or thinking.[6] A growing range of responsibilities, including 'communicating the vision' will be shared within the boardroom team, rather than be regarded as the exclusive concern of one director.

## Beginning in the boardroom

So what needs to be done? First, let us consider the articulation of, and commitment to, a common vision in the boardroom. The survey 'Quality: The Next Steps'[2] emphasizes the need for the board to: 'formulate a clear and shared quality vision, and communicate a commitment to quality'.

The board should be the source of the vision to be communicated. The Institute of Directors discussion document 'The Effective Board'[6] reveals that there is little satisfaction with the performance of many boards. Three-quarters of chairmen believe the effectiveness of the boards of their companies could be improved.

The key to sustained corporate success is an effective board, composed of competent directors who share and can communicate a common vision.[7] Yet, only one in eight companies operates a periodic, formal appraisal of personal effectiveness in the boardroom.[6] To improve the effectiveness of individual directors, and of the board as a whole, there are various checklists of questions which every company chairman should consider.[7] These include:

● Are your directors committed to a common vision and an agreed strategy?
● How effective are the members of your board at sharing the vision, and communicating with customers, employees and business partners?

Training and changing the composition of a board are the two most commonly cited means of improving the effectiveness of a board.[6,12] Poor teamwork is frequently given as a factor that is limiting the effectiveness of boards. Improved communication, open discussion, regular meetings and a shared or common purpose are all given as ways of ensuring a board works effectively as a team.[6,7]

# Who is responsible?

Within the boardroom there are two distinct and key roles and responsibilities (even if both roles are occupied by one person) which will largely determine the extent to which a compelling vision is articulated, agreed, communicated and shared:

## 1 The chairman

The chairman should be responsible for ensuring that a company has an effective board composed of directors who work well together as a team.[6,7] The chairman is generally the individual who is best equipped to form an overview of the board and its operations. At minimum:[6]

- A chairman should ensure that all directors are aware of their legal duties and responsibilities,[13] and are properly prepared to make a contribution to the board.[7,14]
- At least once a year a board ought to review its 'roles and responsibilities', size and composition, and its effectiveness.
- The personal effectiveness of all directors in the boardroom should be assessed at least once a year by the chairman.

## 2 The chief executive

The chief executive should take a lead in: (i) securing commitment; and (ii) communicating and sharing the vision. The CEO can also play a key role in preventing the occurrence of 'perspective gaps' and 'arenas of confrontation'.

Almost all those interviewed during the course of the three 1991 surveys,[1-3] and who were not CEOs, referred to the importance of CEO commitment. CEOs themselves acknowledged the importance of their 'lead', as fellow directors and many senior managers tend to base their own level of commitment upon the priority being given to 'change' or 'quality' by the CEO.

One CEO summed up the dilemma of the 'fellow traveller' director: 'I lived for too long with directors who did not really believe in what we were trying to do. They didn't raise objections in the boardroom. What's worse, they sometimes said yes, and then went away and did nothing. They didn't implement the changes in their divisions, and everyone knew it.'

# The need for more effective communication

Once agreed by a competent and committed board, a vision has to be communicated and shared.[15] Sir John Harvey-Jones believes that 'effective communication requires effort, commitment, time and courage. Full commitment is the result of integrity, openness and real two way communication'.[1]

Visible commitment is crucial. Vern Zelmer, Managing Director of Rank Xerox (UK) believes that: 'the role of the manager must change from one of managing the status quo in a command and control environment to one of managing change through active teaching, coaching, and facilitating in a participative work group'.[1]

Participants in the 'Managing the Flat Organization' survey[1] were asked to rank in importance the management qualities which will enable their organizations to respond more effectively to challenges and opportunities within the business environment. When these are ranked in order of 'very important' replies, the 'ability to communicate' comes top. Two thirds of the respondents consider it to be 'very important'.

The 'Quality: The Next Steps'[2] survey emphasizes the need for more effective communication:

● A broader view of quality needs to be communicated. Nine out of ten respondents consider 'too narrow an understanding of quality' to be either 'very significant' or 'significant' as a quality barrier.
● Managers need to be better equipped to manage change. The 'quality of management', followed closely by 'quality behaviour, attitudes and values', are the top quality priorities. Over eight out of ten respondents expect to give them a 'higher priority' over the next 5 years.

Further confirmation of the need for the more effective communication of a shared vision comes from the 'Communicating for Change'[3] survey:

● Communicating or 'sharing the vision' is considered 'very important' by over seven out of ten respondents, followed by 'communicating the purpose of change' and 'employee involvement and commitment' – both considered 'very important' by two thirds of the respondents.
● 'Communication skills' are felt by respondents to be the top barrier to both internal and external communication. A third of the respondents consider 'communication skills' to be a 'very significant' barrier to internal communication.

Whatever their boards might think or hope is the case, in reality many companies are finding it difficult to articulate and communicate a compelling vision. Words and slogans are passed on without being fully understood.

# The effective communicator

The effective communicator needs to think through what is being communicated, to whom and why. According to David O'Brien, Chief Executive of The National and Provincial Building Society, 'Often people will pick up and use the words associated with change, but without really thinking through what they mean.'[1]

Messages must be straightforward, and related to the needs and interests of the audience if they are to 'come alive'.[15,16] The communicator must be open and willing to learn. The communicator must share the vision, must feel the vision and must be visibly committed to it.

The vision itself should 'paint a picture' of a desired future that is preferable to the present, and should motivate people to strive to bring it about.[15] A vision should be succinct. It should inspire and liberate. In contrast to the compelling vision, many corporate mission statements are over long, too detailed, and bland.[7,15]

Customers and employees are attracted to those organizations whose principles they share. The vision must empathize with people's values, and it must be believed. Sir John Harvey-Jones stresses the importance of both integrity and commitment. He believes 'the manager should not be afraid to show emotion'.[1] Honesty is even more important in an era of recession and retrenchment, when there is bad news to communicate. The 'Managing the Flat Organization' report[1] concludes: 'In a few companies urgent action is needed to re-establish an atmosphere of trust.'

# Summary and conclusions

The key lessons of the three 1991 surveys[3] we have examined are that:

● Clear vision and strategy, top management commitment and communication skills are of crucial importance in the management of change.
● The vision must be compelling. It must be shared, the purpose of change communicated, and employee involvement and commitment secured. The chief executive should assume responsibility for communicating and sharing the vision.
● The distinct role of the director, and the difference between direction and management, needs to be better understood.
● The competence of directors, and the effectiveness of boards, should not be assumed. The chairman of the board should take responsibility for the effectiveness of the board as a team, and for the quality of the contributions of individual directors in the boardroom.
● The ability to communicate is an essential directorial and management quality. The focus needs to be upon changing attitudes and approaches to

communication. Significant change will not occur in many organizations unless managers are equipped with the skills to bring it about.

# References

1   Colin Coulson-Thomas and Trudy Coe, *Managing the Flat Organization*, BIM (1991).
2   Colin and Susan Coulson-Thomas, *Quality: The Next Steps*, an Adaptation Ltd survey for ODI International (1991).
3   Colin and Susan Coulson-Thomas, *Communicating for Change*, an Adaptation Ltd survey for Granada Business Services (1991).
4   Colin Coulson-Thomas and Richard Brown, *The Responsive Organization, People Management: the Challenge of the 1990s*, BIM (1989).
5   Colin Coulson-Thomas and Richard Brown, *Beyond Quality, Managing the Relationship with the Customer*, BIM (1990); Colin Coulson-Thomas, Customers, Marketing and the Network Organization, *Journal of Marketing Management*, 7, 237–255, (1991).
6   Colin Coulson-Thomas and Alan Wakelam, *Developing Directors*. A survey, funded by the Training Agency, undertaken by Adaptation Ltd with the Centre for Management Studies, University of Exeter (1990): The main findings are summarized in: Colin Coulson-Thomas and Alan Wakelam, *The Effective Board, Current Practice, Myths and Realities*, an IOD discussion document (1991).
7   Colin Coulson-Thomas, *Developing Excellence in the Boardroom*, McGraw-Hill (1992); Bernard Taylor (Ed.), *Strategic Planning: The Chief Executive and the Board*, The best of *Long Range Planning*, No. 1, Pergamon Press (1988).
8   Colin Coulson-Thomas, *Professional Development of and for the Board*, a questionnaire and interview survey undertaken by Adaptation Ltd of company chairmen: A summary has been published by the IOD, February (1990).
9   Colin Coulson-Thomas, *Human Resource Development for International Operation*, A survey sponsored by Surrey European Management School, Adaptation Ltd (1990).
10  Colin Coulson-Thomas, *Developing IT Directors*, an Adaptation Ltd report to the Department of Computing Science, Surrey University (1990); Colin Coulson-Thomas, Directors and IT, and IT Directors, *European Journal of Information Systems*, 1(1), 45–53, (1991).
11  Colin Coulson-Thomas, *The Role and Development of the Personnel Director*, An survey undertaken by Adaptation Ltd in conjunction with the Research Group of the Institute of Personnel Management (1991).
12  Alan Wakelam, *The Training & Development of Company Directors*, a report on a questionnaire survey undertaken by the Centre of Management Studies, University of Exeter for the Training Agency, December (1989); Colin Coulson-Thomas, Developing Directors, *European Management Journal*, 8(4), 488–499, December (1990).
13  Institute of Directors, *Guidelines for Directors*, Director Publications, Fourth Edition, May (1991).
14  Colin Coulson-Thomas, Career Paths to the Boardroom, *The International Journal of Career Management*, 2(3), 26–32, (1990).
15  Colin Coulson-Thomas and Didacticus Video Productions Ltd, *The Change Makers, Vision & Communication*, booklet to accompany integrated audio and video tape training programme by Sir John Harvey-Jones. Available from Video Arts (1991).
16  Peter Bartram and Colin Coulson-Thomas, *The Complete Spokesperson*, Kogan Page (1991).

# 11 Creating successful organization change

## *L. D. Goodstein and W. Warner Burke*

Buffeted at home and abroad by foreign competition that appears to produce higher-quality goods at lower prices, corporate America has now largely forsaken (at least publicly and momentarily) the traditional analogy of the organization as a machine and its organizational members as parts designed to work effectively and efficiently. Instead, many American corporations are accepting the 'New Age' view of organizations as 'a nested set of open, living systems and subsystems dependent upon the larger environment for survival.'

What is surprising about this quote is not its viewpoint, which has been normative in the organizational psychology and behavioral literature for several decades, but its source: *The Wall Street Journal.* And it is typical to find such articles in virtually every issue of most recent American business publications: articles on corporate culture, on the changing attitudes of American workers, on the need for greater employee participation in managerial decision making, and on the place of employees as an important (if not the most important) asset of the corporation.

We are not suggesting that traditionally managed organizations are now extinct in America. Corporate executives, however, have definitely begun to recognize that managing the social psychology of the workplace is a critical element in the success of any organization.

## Organizational change

Organizations tend to change primarily because of external pressure rather than an internal desire or need to change. Here are a few all-too-familiar examples of the kinds of environmental factors requiring organizations to change:

- A new competitor snares a significant portion of a firm's market share.

- An old customer is acquired by a giant conglomerate that dictates new sales arrangements.
- A new invention offers the possibility of changing the organization's existing production technology.

Other examples include (1) new government regulations on certain health-care financing programs and (2) economic and social conditions that create long-term changes in the availability of the labor force. The competent organization will be alert to early-warning signs of such external changes so that it can move promptly to make internal changes designed to keep it viable in the changing external world. Competent organizations are those that continue to change and to survive.

Thus, it is practically a cliche to state that change in organizations today is a way of life. And clearly it is not saying anything new to comment that executives and managers today are more finely attuned to change or that they more frequently view their role as that of change agent.

But even though we often state the obvious and spout cliches about change, this does not mean that we have an in-depth understanding of what we are talking about. We are only beginning to understand the nature of change and how to manage the process involved, especially with respect to organizations. The purpose of this article is to improve our understanding of organizational change by providing both some conceptual clarification and a case example that illustrates many of the concepts involved.

It is possible to conceptualize organizational change in at least three ways – levels of organizational change, strategies of organizational change and, more specifically and not mutually exclusive of strategies, models and methods of organizational change. (First we will present the concepts, second the case example, and finally some implications.)

## Levels of organizational change

A broad distinction can be made between (1) fundamental, large-scale change in the organization's strategy and culture – a transformation, refocus, reorientation, or 'bending the frame,' as David A. Nadler and Michael L. Tushman have referred to the process – and (2) fine-tuning, fixing problems, making adjustments, modifying procedures, etc.; that is, implementing modest changes that improve the organization's performance yet do not fundamentally change the organization. By far most organizational changes are designed not to transform the organization but to modify it in order to fix its problems.

In this article we address more directly the large-scale, fundamental type of organizational change. (A word of caution: 'Organizational transformation,' 'frame bending,' and other expressions indicating fundamental change do not imply wholesale, indiscriminate, and complete change. Thus when we refer to 'fundamental change,' we do not mean 'in any and all respects.')

We are concerned with transformation when an organization faces the need to survive and must do things differently to continue to exist. After polio was licked, for example, the March of Dimes had to change its mission in order to survive as an organization. Although its mission changed from one of attacking polio to one of trying to eradicate birth defects, the organization's core technology – fund raising – remained the same.

A corporate example of transformation is seen in the transition of International Harvester to Navistar. Facing bankruptcy, the company downsized drastically, completely restructured its financial situation, and overhauled its corporate culture. Although many of the company's technologies were sold off, it too retained its core technology: producing trucks and engines. Once internally focused, its culture is now significantly market-oriented – and the company is operating far more efficiently than it did in the past.

Although organizational members experience such transformations as a complete change, they rarely if ever are. Theory would suggest that if fundamental – or even significant – change is to occur with any success, some characteristic(s) of the organization must *not* change. The theory to which we refer comes from the world of individual change: psychotherapy. For organizational transformation to be achieved – for the organization to survive and eventually prosper from such change – certain fundamentals need to be retained. Some examples: the organization's ultimate purpose, the previously mentioned core technology, and key people. The principle here is that for people to be able to deal with enormous and complex change – seeming chaos – they need to have *something* to hold on to that is stable.

Conceptually, then, we can distinguish between fundamentally changing the organization and fine-tuning it. This distinction – which is a matter of degree, not necessarily a dichotomy – is useful in determining strategies and methods to be used in the change effort. When fine-tuning, for example, we do not necessarily need to clarify for organizational members what will not change – but in the case of transformation, such clarity is required for its successful achievement.

## Strategies of organizational change

Organizational change can occur in more than one way. In a 1971 book, Harvey A. Hornstein and colleagues classified six ways: individual change strategies, technostructural strategies, data-based strategies, organization development, violent and coercive strategies, and nonviolent yet direct action strategies. All of these strategies have been used to attempt, if not actually bring about, organizational change. Senior management usually chooses any one or various combinations of the first four and manages them internally. The last two – violent, coercive strategies and nonviolent yet direct-action strategies – are more often than not initiated by actions outside the organization, and the organization's executives typically manage in a reactive mode.

In this article we address some combination of the first four strategies. Yet, as previously indicated, we are assuming that the overwhelming majority of organizational changes are motivated by *external* factors – that executives are responding to the organization's external environment. But even when it is not a reaction to some social movement, organizational change is nevertheless a *response* – a response to changes or anticipated changes in the marketplace, or changes in the way technology will affect the organization's products/services, or changes in the labor market, etc.

This assumption is based on the idea that an organization is a living, open system dependent on its environment for survival. Whether it is merely to survive or eventually to prosper, an organization must monitor its external environment and align itself with changes that occur or will occur in that environment. Practically speaking, the process of alignment requires the organization to change itself.

## Models and methods of organizational change

Models of change and methods of change are quite similar in concept and often overlap – so much so that it is not always clear which one is being discussed. Kurt Lewin's three-phase model of change – unfreeze, move (or change), refreeze – also suggests method. Organization development is based on an action-research model that is, at the same time, a method.

More on the model side is the relatively simple and straightforward framework provided by Richard Beckhard and Reuben T. Harris. They have suggested that large-scale, complex organizational change can be conceptualized as movement from a present state to a future state. But the most important phase is the in-between one that they label *transition state*. Organizational change, then, is a matter of (1) assessing the current organizational situation (present state), (2) determining the desired future (future state), and (3) both planning ways to reach that desired future and implementing the plans (transition state).

Methods of implementing the change – for example, a new organizational strategy – include the following:

- Setting up a comprehensive training program (individual change strategy).
- Modifying the structure, individuals' jobs, and/or work procedures (technostructural strategy).
- Conducting a companywide survey to assess organizational culture for the purpose of using the data to pinpoint required changes (data-based strategy).

- Collecting information from organizational members about their views regarding what needs to be changed and acting accordingly (organization development strategy).
- Combining two, three, or all of these methods.

The case example we will discuss here illustrates organizational transformation in response to change initiated in the institution's external environment – excluding, however, the violent, coercive strategies and the non-violent, direct ones. The example, which is analyzed according to Lewin's three-phase model/method, highlights the use of multiple methods for change – in fact, it presents in one form or another a specific method from each of the four other change strategies mentioned earlier.

# Case example

In 1982 Margaret Thatcher's government in Great Britain decided to convert British Airways (BA) from government ownership to private ownership. BA had regularly required large subsidies from the government (almost $900 million in 1982), subsidies that the government felt it could not provide. Even more important, the Conservative government was ideologically opposed to the government's ownership of businesses – a matter they regarded as the appropriate province of private enterprise.

The growing deregulation of international air traffic was another important environmental change. Air fares were no longer fixed, and the resulting price wars placed BA at even greater risk of financial losses.

In order to be able to 'privatize' – that is, sell BA shares on the London and New York Stock Exchanges – it was necessary to make BA profitable. The pressures to change thus exerted on BA by the external environment were broad and intense. And the internal organizational changes, driven by these external pressures, have been massive and widespread. They have transformed the BA culture from what BA managers described as 'bureaucratic and militaristic' to one that is now described as 'service-oriented and market-driven.' The success of these efforts over a five-year period (1982–1987) is clearly depicted in the data presented in Table 1.

This table reflects BA's new mission in its new advertising slogan – 'The World's Favorite Airline.' Five years after the change effort began, BA had successfully moved from government ownership to private ownership, and both passenger and cargo revenues had dramatically increased, leading to a substantial increase in share price over the offering price, despite the market crash of October 1987. Indeed, in late 1987 BA acquired British Caledonian Airways, its chief domestic competitor. The steps through which this transformation was accomplished clearly fit Lewin's model of the change process.

1   The British Airways success story: creating the 'world's favorite airline'

|  | 1982 | 1987 |
|---|---|---|
| Ownership | Government | Private |
| Profit/(loss) | ($900 million) | $435 million |
| Culture | Bureaucratic and militaristic | Service-oriented and market-driven |
| Passenger load factor | Decreasing | Increasing – up 16% in 1st quarter 1988 |
| Cargo load | Stable | Increasing – up 41% in 1st quarter 1988 |
| Share price | N/A | Increased 67% (2/11/87–8/11/87) |
| Acquisitions | N/A | British Caledonian |

# Lewin's change model

According to the open-systems view, organizations – like living creatures – tend to be homeostatic, or continuously working to maintain a steady state. This helps us understand why organizations require external impetus to initiate change and, indeed, why that change will be resisted even when it is necessary.

Organizational change can occur at three levels – and, since the patterns of resistance to change are different for each, the patterns in each level require different change strategies and techniques. These levels involve:

1 Changing the *individuals* who work in the organization – that is, their skills, values, attitudes, and eventually behavior – but making sure that such individual behavioral change is always regarded as instrumental to organizational change.
2 Changing various organizational *structures and systems* – reward systems, reporting relationships, work design, and so on.
3 Directly changing the organizational *climate or interpersonal style* – how open people are with each other, how conflict is managed, how decisions are made, and so on.

According to Lewin, a pioneer in the field of social psychology of organizations, the first step of any change process is to *unfreeze* the present pattern of behavior as a way of managing resistance to change. Depending on the organizational level of change intended, such unfreezing might involve, on the individual level, selectively promoting or terminating employees; on the structural level, developing highly experiential training programs in such new organization designs as matrix management; or, on the climate level, providing data-based feedback on how employees feel about certain management practices. Whatever the level involved, each of these interventions is intended to make organizational members address that level's need for change, heighten their awareness of their own behavioral patterns, and make them more open to the change process.

The second step, *movement*, involves making the actual changes that will move the organization to another level of response. On the individual level we would expect to see people behaving differently, perhaps demonstrating new skills or new supervisory practices. On the structural level, we would expect to see changes in actual organizational structures, reporting relationships, and reward systems that affect the way people do their work. Finally, on the climate or interpersonal-style level, we would expect to see behavior patterns that indicate greater interpersonal trust and openness and fewer dysfunctional interactions.

The final stage of the change process, *refreezing*, involves stabilizing or institutionalizing these changes by establishing systems that make these behavioral patterns 'relatively secure against change,' as Lewin put it. The refreezing stage may involve, for example, redesigning the organization's recruitment process to increase the likelihood of hiring applicants who share the organization's new management style and value system. During the refreezing stage, the organization may also ensure that the new behaviors have become the operating norms at work, that the reward system actually reinforces those behaviors, or that a new, more participative management style predominates.

According to Lewin, the first step to achieving lasting organizational change is to deal with resistance to change by unblocking the present system. This unblocking usually requires some kind of confrontation and a retraining process based on planned behavioral changes in the desired direction. Finally, deliberate steps need to be taken to cement these changes in place – this 'institutionalization of change' is designed to make the changes semi-permanent until the next cycle of change occurs.

Table 2 presents an analysis of the BA change effort in terms of Lewin's model. The many and diverse steps involved in the effort are categorized both by stages (unfreezing, movement, and refreezing) and by level (individual, structures and system, and climate/interpersonal style).

## Unfreezing

In BA's change effort, the first step in unfreezing involved a massive reduction in the worldwide BA workforce (from 59,000 to 37,000). It is interesting to note that within a year after this staff reduction, virtually all BA performance indices had improved – more on-time departures and arrivals, fewer out-of-service aircraft, less time 'on hold' for telephone reservations, fewer lost bags, and so on. The consensus view at all levels within BA was that the downsizing had reduced hierarchical levels, thus giving more autonomy to operating people and allowing work to get done more easily.

The downsizing was accomplished with compassion; no one was actually laid off. Early retirement, with substantial financial settlements, was the pre-

**Table 2**   Applying Lewin's model to the British Airways (BA) change effort

| Levels | Unfreezing | Movement | Refreezing |
|---|---|---|---|
| Individual | Downsizing of workforce (59,000 to 37,000); middle management especially hard-hit.<br><br>New top management team.<br><br>'Putting People First.' | Acceptance of concept of 'emotional labor'.<br><br>Personnel staff as internal consultants.<br><br>'Managing People First.'<br><br>Peer support groups. | Continued commitment of top management.<br><br>Promotion of staff with new BA values.<br><br>'Top Flight Academies.'<br><br>'Open Learning' programs. |
| Structures and systems | Use of diagonal task forces to plan change.<br><br>Reduction in levels of hierarchy.<br><br>Modification of budgeting process. | Profit sharing (3 weeks' pay in 1987).<br><br>Opening of Terminal 4.<br><br>Purchase of Chartridge as training center.<br><br>New, 'user friendly' MIS. | New performance appraisal system based on both behavior and performance.<br><br>Performance-based compensation system.<br><br>Continued use of task forces. |
| Climate/ interpersonal style | Redefinition of the business: *service*, not *transportation*.<br><br>Top management commitment and involvement. | Greater emphasis on open communications.<br><br>Data feedback on work-unit climate.<br><br>Off-site, team-building meeting. | New uniforms.<br><br>New coat of arms.<br><br>Development and use of cabin-crew teams.<br><br>Continued use of data-based feedback on climate and management practices. |

ferred solution throughout the system. Although there is no question that the process was painful, considerable attention was paid to minimizing the pain in every possible way.

A second major change occurred in BA's top management. In 1981, Lord John King of Wartinbee, a senior British industrialist, was appointed chairman of the board, and Colin Marshall, now Sir Colin, was appointed CEO. The appointment of Marshall represented a significant departure from BA culture. An outsider to BA, Marshall had a marketing background that was quite different from that of his predecessors, many of whom were retired senior Royal Air Force officers. It was Marshall who decided, shortly after his arrival, that BA's strategy should be to become 'the World's Favorite Airline.' Without question, critical ingredients in the success of the overall change effort were Marshall's vision, the clarity of his understanding that BA's culture needed to be changed in order to carry out the vision, and his strong leadership of that change effort.

To support the unfreezing process, the first of many training programs was introduced. 'Putting People First' – the program in which all BA personnel with direct customer contact participated – was another important part of the unfreezing process. Aimed at helping line workers and managers understand the service nature of the airline industry, it was intended to challenge the prevailing wisdom about how things were to be done at BA.

## Movement

Early on, Marshall hired Nicholas Georgiades, a psychologist and former professor and consultant, as director (vice-president) of human resources. It was Georgiades who developed the specific tactics and programs required to bring Marshall's vision into reality. Thus Georgiades, along with Marshall, must be regarded as a leader of BA's successful change effort. One of the interventions that Georgiades initiated – a significant activity during the movement phase – was to establish training programs for senior and middle managers. Among these were 'Managing People First' and 'Leading the Service Business' – experiential programs that involved heavy doses of individual feedback to each participant about his or her behavior regarding management practices on the job.

These training programs all had more or less the same general purpose: to identify the organization's dysfunctional management style and begin the process of developing a new management style that would fit BA's new, competitive environment. If the organization was to be market-driven, service-based, and profit-making, it would require an open, participative management style – one that would produce employee commitment.

On the structures and systems level during the unfreezing stage, extensive use was made of diagonal task forces composed of individuals from different functions and at different levels of responsibility to deal with various aspects of the change process – the need for MIS (management information systems) support, new staffing patterns, new uniforms, and so on. A bottom-up, less centralized budgeting process – one sharply different from its predecessor – was introduced.

Redefining BA's business service rather than transportation represented a critical shift on the level of climate/interpersonal style. A service business needs an open climate and good interpersonal skills, coupled with outstanding teamwork. Off-site, team-building meetings – the process chosen to deal with these issues during the movement stage – have now been institutionalized.

None of these changes would have occurred without the commitment and involvement of top management. Marshall himself played a central role in both initiating and supporting the change process, even when problems arose. As one index of this commitment, Marshall shared information at question-and-answer sessions at most of the training programs – both 'to show the flag' and to provide his own unique perspective on what needed to be done.

An important element of the movement phase was acceptance of the concept of 'emotional labor' that Georgiades championed – that is, the high energy levels required to provide the quality of service needed in a somewhat uncertain environment, such as the airline business. Recognition that such service is emotionally draining and often can lead to burnout and permanent psychological damage is critical to developing systems of emotional support for the service workers involved.

Another important support mechanism was the retraining of traditional personnel staff to become internal change agents charged with helping and supporting line and staff managers. So too was the development of peer support groups for managers completing the 'Managing People First' training program.

To support this movement, a number of internal BA structures and systems were changed. By introducing a new bonus system, for example, Georgiades demonstrated management's commitment to sharing the financial gains of BA's success. The opening of Terminal 4 at Heathrow Airport provided a more functional work environment for staff. The purchase of Chartridge House as a permanent BA training center permitted an increase in and integration of staff training, and the new, 'user friendly' MIS enabled managers to get the information they needed to do their jobs in a timely fashion.

## Refreezing

During the refreezing phase, the continued involvement and commitment of BA's top management ensured that the changes became 'fixed' in the system. People who clearly exemplified the new BA values were much more likely to be promoted, especially at higher management levels. Georgiades introduced additional programs for educating the workforce, especially managers. 'Open Learning' programs, including orientation programs for new staff, supervisory training for new supervisors, and so on, were augmented by 'Top Flight Academies' that included training at the executive, senior management, and management levels. One of the Academies now leads to an MBA degree.

A new performance appraisal system, based on both behavior and results, was created to emphasize customer service and subordinate development. A performance-based compensation system is being installed, and task forces continue to be used to solve emerging problems, such as those resulting from the acquisition of British Caledonian Airlines.

Attention was paid to BA's symbols as well – new, upscale uniforms; refurbished aircraft; and a new corporate coat of arms with the motto 'We fly to serve.' A unique development has been the creation of teams for consistent cabin-crew staffing, rather than the ad hoc process typically used. Finally, there is continued use of data feedback on management practices throughout the system.

## Managing change

Unfortunately, the change process is not smooth even if one is attentive to Lewin's model of change. Changing behavior at both individual and organizational levels means inhibiting habitual responses and producing new responses that feel awkward and unfamiliar to those involved. It is all too easy to slip back to the familiar and comfortable.

For example, an organization may intend to manage more participatively. But when a difficult decision arises, it may not be possible to get a consensus decision – not at first, at least. Frustration to 'get on with' a decision can lead to the organization's early abandonment of the new management style.

In moving from a known present state to a desired future state, organizations must recognize that (as noted earlier) the intervening *transition* state requires careful management, especially when the planned organizational change is large and complex. An important part of this change management lies in recognizing and accepting the disorganization and temporarily lowered effectiveness that characterize the transition state.

In BA's change effort, the chaos and anger that arose during the transitional phase have abated, and clear signs of success have now emerged. But many times the outcome was not at all clear, and serious questions were raised about the wisdom of the process both inside and outside BA. At such times the commitment and courage of top management are essential.

To heighten involvement, managing such organizational changes may often require using a transition management team composed of a broad cross-section of members of the organization. Other techniques include using multiple interventions rather than just one – for example, keeping the system open to feedback about the change process and using symbols and rituals to mark significant achievements. The BA program used all of these techniques.

## Process consultation

In addition to the various change strategies discussed above, considerable use was made of all the usual organization development (OD) technologies. Structural changes, role clarification and negotiations, team building, and process consultation were all used at British Airways to facilitate change.

In process consultation – the unique OD intervention – the consultant examines the pattern of a work unit's communications. This is done most often through direct observation of staff meetings and, at opportune times, through raising questions or making observations about what has been happening. The role of the process consultant is to be counternormative – that is, to ask why others never seem to respond to Ruth's questions or why no one ever challenges Fred's remarks when he is clearly off target. Generally speaking, process consultation points out the true quality of the emperor's new clothes even when everyone is pretending that they are quite elegant. By changing the closed communication style of the work teams at British Airways to a more open, candid one, process consultation played an important role in the change process.

## The research evidence

Granted that the BA intervention appears to have been successful, what do we know generally about the impact of OD interventions on organizations and on their effectiveness? Over the past few years, the research literature has shown a sharp improvement in both research design and methodological rigor, especially in the development of such 'hard criteria' as productivity and quality indices. The findings have been surprisingly positive.

For example, Raymond Katzell and Richard Guzzo reviewed more than 200 intervention studies and reported that 87 per cent found evidence of significant increases in worker productivity as a result of the intervention. Richard Guzzo, Richard Jette, and Raymond Katzell's meta-analysis of 98 of these same studies revealed productivity increases averaging almost half a standard deviation – impressive enough 'to be visible to the naked eye,' to use their phrase. Thus it would appear that the success of BA's intervention process was not a single occurrence but one in a series of successful changes based on OD interventions.

The picture with respect to employee satisfaction, however, is not so clear. Another meta-analysis – by Barry Macy, Hiroaki Izumi, Charles Hurts, and Lawrence Norton – on how OD interventions affect performance measures and employee work satisfaction found positive effects on performance but *negative* effects on attitudes, perhaps because of the pressure exerted by new work-group norms on employee productivity. The positive effects on performance, however, are in keeping with the bulk of prior research. A recent comprehensive review of the entire field of OD by Marshall Sashkin and W. Warner Burke concluded, 'There is little doubt that, when applied properly, OD has substantial positive effects in terms of performance measures.'

## Implications and concluding remarks

We very much believe that an understanding of the social psychology of the change process gives all of us – managers, rank-and-file employees, and consultants – an important and different perspective for coping with an increasingly competitive environment. Our purpose in writing this article was to share some of this perspective – from an admittedly biased point of view.

The change effort at BA provides a recent example of how this perspective and this understanding have been applied. What should be apparent from this abbreviated overview of a massive project is that the change process at BA was based on open-systems thinking, a phased model of managing change, and multiple levels for implementing the change. Thus both the design and the implementation of this change effort relied heavily on this kind of understanding about the nature of organizations and changing them.

The change involved a multifaceted effort that used many leverage points to initiate and support the changes. The change process, which used transition teams with openness to feedback, was intentionally managed with strong support from top management. Resistance to change was actively managed by using unfreezing strategies at all three levels – individual, structural and systems, and interpersonal. Virtually all of the organizational change issues discussed in this article emerged in some measure during the course of the project.

It is quite reassuring to begin to find empirical support for these efforts in field studies and case reports of change efforts. Moreover, the recent meta-analyses of much of this work are quite supportive of what we have learned from experience. We need to use such reports to help more managers understand the worth of applying the open-systems model to their change efforts. But we also need to remember that only when proof of the intervention strategy's usefulness shows up on the firm's 'bottom line' will most line managers be persuaded that open-systems thinking is not necessarily incompatible with the real world. The BA success story is a very useful one for beginning such a dialog.

As we go to press, it seems clear that many of the changes at British Airways have stabilized the company. Perhaps the most important one is that the company's culture today can be described as having a strong customer-service focus – a focus that was decidedly lacking in 1982. The belief that marketing and service with the customer in mind will have significant payoff for the company is now endemic to the corporate culture. Another belief now fundamental to BA's culture is that the way one manages people – especially those, like ticket agents and cabin crews, with direct customer contact – directly impacts the way customers will feel about BA. For example, during 1990, Tony Clarry, then head of worldwide customer service for BA, launched a leadership program for all of his management around the globe to continue to reinforce this belief.

Yet all is not bliss at British Airways, which has its problems. Some examples:

- American Airlines is encroaching upon BA's European territory.
- The high level of customer service slips from time to time.
- Those who can afford to ride on the Concorde represent a tiny market, so it is tough to maintain a consistently strong customer base.
- Now that BA has developed a cadre of experienced managers in a

successful company, these managers are being enticed by search firms to join other companies that often pay more money.

Other problems, too, affect BA's bottom line – the cost of fuel, effectively managing internal costs, and the reactions of the financiers in London and on Wall Street, to name a few. It should be noted that since 1987 and until recently, BA's financials have remained positive with revenues and profits continuing to increase. During 1990 this bright picture began to fade, however. The combination of the continuing rise in fuel costs, the recession, and the war in the Persian Gulf have taken their toll. Constant vigilance is therefore imperative for continued success.

It may be that BA's biggest problem now is not so much to manage further change as it is to manage the change that has already occurred. In other words, the people of BA have achieved significant change and success; now they must maintain what has been achieved while concentrating on continuing to be adaptable to changes in their external environment – the further deregulation of Europe, for example. Managing momentum may be more difficult than managing change.

# Selected bibliography

The *Wall Street Journal* article referred to at the outset, 'Motivate or Alienate? Firms Have Gurus to Change Their "Cultures",' was written by Peter Waldbaum and may be found on p. 19 of the July 24, 1987 issue.

With respect to levels of organizational change, see the article by W. Warner Burke and George H. Litwin, 'A Causal Model of Organizational Performance,' in the 1989 Annual published by University Associates of San Diego. These authors describe the differences between transformational and transactional change. Along the same conceptual lines is the article by David A. Nadler and Michael L. Tushman – 'Organizational Frame Bending: Principles for Managing Reorientation' (*The Academy of Management Executive*, 1988, August, 194–204).

Regarding strategies of organizational change, see Harvey A. Hornstein, Barbara B. Bunker, W. Warner Burke, Marion Gindes, and Roy J. Lewicki's *Social Intervention: A Behavioral Science Approach* (The Free Press, 1971).

Concerning models and methods of organizational change, the classic piece is Kurt Lewin's chapter 'Group Decisions and Social Change,' in the 1958 book *Readings in Social Psychology* (Holt, Rinehart & Winston), edited by Eleanor E. Maccobby, Theodore M. Newcomb, and Eugene L. Hartley. For an explanation of organization development as action research, see W. Warner Burke's *Organization Development: Principles and Practices* (Scott, Foresman, 1982). The framework of present state-transition state-future state is explained in *Organization Transitions: Managing Complex Change*, 2nd Ed. (Addison-Wesley, 1987), by Richard Beckhard and Reuben T. Harris. A recent article by Donald C. Hambrick and Albert A. Cannella, Jr. – 'Strategy Implementation as Substance and Selling' (*The Academy of Management Executive*, 1989, November, 278–285) – is quite helpful in understanding how to implement a change in corporate strategy.

A point made in the article is that for effective organizational change, multiple leverage is required. For data to support this argument, see W. Warner Burke, Lawrence P. Clark, and Cheryl Koopman's 'Improving Your OD Project's Chances of Success' (*Training and Development Journal*, 1984, September, 62–68). More on process consultation and team building may be found in two books published by Addison-Wesley: Edgar H. Schein's *Process Consultation. Vol. 1: Its Role in Organization Development*, 1988, and W. Gibb Dyer's *Team Building: Issues and Alternatives*, 1987.

References for the research evidence are: Richard A. Guzzo, Richard D. Jette, and Raymond A. Katzell's 'The Effects of Psychologically Based Intervention Programs on Worker Productivity: A Meta-Analysis' (*Personnel Psychology*, 1985, 38, (2), Summer, 275–291); Raymond A. Katzell and Richard A. Guzzo's 'Psychological Approaches to Worker Productivity' (*American Psychologist*, 1983, 38, April. 468–472); Barry A. Macy, Hiroaki Izumi, Charles C. M. Hurts, and Lawrence W. Norton's 'Meta-Analysis of United States Empirical Change and Work Innovation Field Experiments,' a paper presented at the 1986 annual meeting of the Academy of Management, Chicago; John M. Nicholas's 'The Comparative Impact of Organization Development Interventions on Hard Criteria Issues' (*The Academy of Management Review*, 1982, 7(4) October, 531–543); John M. Nicholas and Marsha Katz's 'Research Methods and Reporting Practices in Organization Development' (*The Academy of Management Review*, 1985, October (4), 737–749); and Marshall Sashkin and W. Warner Burke's 'Organization Development in the 1980s' (*Journal of Management*, 1987, (2), 205–229).

# 12 Successfully implementing strategic decisions

*L. D. Alexander*

## Introduction

Although strategy implementation is viewed as an integral part of the strategic management process, little has been written or researched on it. The overwhelming majority of the literature so far has been on the long-range planning process itself or the actual content of the strategy being formulated. We have so far been giving lip service to the other side of the coin, namely strategy implementation. Consequently, it is not surprising that after a comprehensive strategy or single strategic decision has been formulated, significant difficulties are often encountered during the subsequent implementation process.

This study surveyed 93 private sector firms through a questionnaire to determine which implementation problems occurred most frequently as they tried to put strategic decisions into effect. Later on, in-depth telephone interviews with chief executive officers of 21 of these firms were conducted to comprehend these problems more fully. These interviews, combined later on with another 25 interviews with governmental agency heads in another study of implementation in the public sector by this researcher, help to identify factors which promote successful implementation.

## Review of the literature

The available literature on strategy implementation was reviewed in order to identify potential strategy implementation problems. Most of the 22 potential problems were identified from such helpful works as Alexander,[1] Andrews,[2] Galbraith and Nathanson,[3] Hobbs and Heany,[4] Kotter and Schlesinger,[5] Le Breton,[6] McCarthy *et al.*,[7] Quinn,[8] Steiner and Miner,[9] and Thompson and Strickland.[10] In addition, several in-depth case studies on strategy implementation by Pressman and Wildavsky[11] Murphy,[12] Quinn[13] and Alexander[14] also helped to identify more potential problems. Finally, a few of the 22 implementation problems were suggested by chief executive officers in earlier interviews conducted by this writer.

## Companies surveyed

The 93 firms participating in this survey were strategic business units of medium and large sized firms. Some 72 firms (77 per cent) were listed in the Fortune 500 list of leading industrials. If Fortune's second 500 list of industrials is included along with Fortune's top 50 listings for utilities, retailing and services, then 89 firms (96 per cent) responding were included on one Fortune list or another.

The firms' SBUs (strategic business units) sampled differed with respect to their size, industry and geographical location within the United States. For example, 26 (28 per cent) of the SBUs had less than 400 employees, 23 (25 per cent) had 400–999 employees, 29 (31 per cent) had 1000–4999 employees, 13 (14 per cent) had over 5000 employees, and 2 (2 per cent) were unidentified. While most of the corporations operated within a number of different businesses, this study was focused on implementing strategic decisions within individual SBUs.

## The strategic decisions evaluated

In the questionnaire, each responding company president (or division general manager) was asked to select one recent strategic decision that had been implemented in his SBU. He was asked to select one in which he had a great deal of personal knowledge about its subsequent implementation. Table 1 shows the types of strategic decisions that were evaluated. The main part of the questionnaire then asked the participants to evaluate the extent to which some 22 possible implementation problems actually were a problem in its

**Table 1** Types of strategic decisions implemented

| Type of strategic decision | No. | % |
|---|---|---|
| Introducing a new product or service | 29 | 31 |
| Opening and starting up a new plant or facility | 17 | 18 |
| Expanding operations to enter a new market | 15 | 16 |
| Discontinuing a product or withdrawing from a market | 11 | 12 |
| Acquiring or merging with another firm | 10 | 11 |
| Changing the strategy in functional departments | 6 | 7 |
| Other | 5 | 5 |
| | 93 | 100 |

subsequent implementation using a five-point Likert-type response scale. Finally, questions were asked to evaluate the overall success of the strategy implementation effort itself.

# Most frequently occurring problems

The 10 most commonly occurring strategy implementation problems are shown in Table 2 in descending order according to mean ratings. Two adjacent pairs of numbers on the five-point Likert response scale are combined for display purposes only as follows: minor and moderate problems (points 2 and 3), and substantial and major problems (points 4 and 5). The 10 listed items are the only ones rated as problems by over half of the sample group.

**Table 2**   Ten most frequent strategy implementation problems

| Potential strategy implementation problem | Mean | Frequency of any degree of problem | = | Frequency of minor/ moderate problems | + | Frequency of substantial/ major problems |
|---|---|---|---|---|---|---|
| Implementation took more time than originally allocated | 2·71 | 71 (76%) | | 45 (48%) | | 26 (28%) |
| Major problems surfaced during implementation that had not been identified beforehand | 2·63 | 69 (74%) | | 45 (48%) | | 24 (26%) |
| Coordination of implementation activities was not effective enough | 2·34 | 62 (66%) | | 45 (48%) | | 17 (18%) |
| Competing activities and crises distracted attention from implementing this decision | 2·29 | 60 (64%) | | 41 (44%) | | 19 (20%) |
| Capabilities of employees involved were not sufficient | 2·28 | 59 (63%) | | 40 (43%) | | 19 (20%) |
| Training and instruction given to lower level employees were not adequate | 2·14 | 58 (62%) | | 47 (50%) | | 11 (12%) |
| Uncontrollable factors in the external environment had an adverse impact on implementation | 2·28 | 56 (60%) | | 40 (43%) | | 16 (17%) |
| Leadership and direction provided by departmental managers were not adequate enough | 2·23 | 55 (59%) | | 39 (42%) | | 16 (17%) |
| Key implementation tasks and activities were not defined in enough detail | 2·09 | 52 (56%) | | 36 (39%) | | 16 (17%) |
| Information systems used to monitor implementation were not adequate | 1·94 | 52 (56%) | | 43 (46%) | | 9 (10%) |

The first seven listed implementation problems occurred to at least 60 per cent of the firms. They are:

1 implementation took more time than originally allocated by 76 per cent;
2 major problems surface during implementation that had not been identified beforehand by 74 per cent;
3 coordination of implementation activities (e.g. by task force, committees, superiors) was not effective enough by 66 per cent;
4 competing activities and crises distracted attention from implementing this strategic decision by 64 per cent;
5 capabilities (skills and abilities) of employees involved with the implementation were not sufficient by 63 per cent;
6 training and instruction given to lower level employees were not adequate by 62 per cent; and
7 uncontrollable factors in the external environment (e.g. competitive, economic, governmental) had an adverse impact on implementation by 60 per cent.

Three additional implementation problems listed in Table 2 occurred to somewhat fewer firms but still experienced by over 50 per cent of the sample firms.

Three-quarters (76 per cent) of the sampled firms found that their implementation efforts took more time than originally allocated. A number of explanations were given by CEOs in the follow-up telephone interviews. As one executive put it, 'In retrospect, we were overly optimistic in thinking now much time it would take to implement a new strategic decision. We thought that everything would work fine which it never does.' From the interviews, this problems seems to occur because top management:

1 understates how long various implementation tasks will take to complete,
2 downplays the likelihood of potential problems that may or may not occur, and
3 is blind to other problems occurring altogether.

Obviously, when all three of these occur during implementation, it can greatly lengthen the time it will take to implement the decision effectively.

Solutions to the problem of taking too much time are numerous. More time should initially be allocated from the start to handle unexpected problems and, in general, the unknown. More manpower initially can be put on important strategic decisions, and particularly later on when unexpected problems emerge. In addition, rewards and penalties can also be used to bring about the desired results.

This latter suggestion is exactly how one CEO handled a strategic decision that had been dragging on and on. As he put it,

Even though we wanted to withdraw from this particular line of fashion clothes, we kept coming up with new ideas. For every two items we'd drop from this line, we'd introduce one new one. Thus, we kept getting seduced back into this line even though I knew we had to discontinue it. After two years, I finally solved the problem by telling my staff that if you or your subordinates present me with any new sketch for this clothing line, that person will lose his job.

Major problems (and obstacles) surfaced during implementation that had not been identified beforehand were experienced by almost as many firms, specifically 74 per cent. These can be internally oriented problems brought on by the firm trying something new, insufficient advance planning, and strategy formulators not getting actively involved in implementation to name a few. Or they can be caused by externally oriented factors such as the uncertainty involved with a new product or market, uncontrollable events in the external environment, or legal/political complications introduced by new legislation or regulations among others.

Consider what happened to one domestic oil equipment firm that was implementing its strategic decision to construct oil wells in an Arab country. All sorts of problems surfaced that had not been identified beforehand as potential problems. Certain employees could not go into that country to work on the project because of their particular race or nationality. Bringing explosives into that country to blast rock in preparation for building the oil well foundation was delayed because the host government was suspicious that they could be used against the government itself. Neither of these problems had been identified beforehand by the firm or its Arab partner, who led them to believe it really knew the ropes and how to operate in the host country. In addition, another oil firm already in that country for many years tried to put up administrative road blocks by using its contacts in various governmental agencies of the Arab country.

Clearly, some of these problems could have been identified and resolved had the firm selected a better Arab partner. In addition, some of these potential problems overlooked by its Arab partner could have been identified had the firm talked with other US firms already doing business there. However, it is safe to say that some of these problems could probably never be anticipated beforehand.

The presence of competing activities and crises that distracted attention from implementing the strategic decision was yet another frequently occurring problem. Some 64 per cent of the firms experienced this implementation problem. One aerospace components firm was starting to implement one strategic decision when along came one order from an airline firm that amounted to 25 per cent of its total sales in a typical year. Obviously, considerable time and attention had to be given to this major order for about 3 months which clearly had priority over the other strategic decision. Actually, the firm decided to forget trying to implement the new strategic decision for a while and put it on hold. Given the size of the customer order, this seemed the best way to handle these competing events.

Another firm was trying to implement one strategic decision when the market for its coal-related products collapsed in 1977. Because of this unexpected crisis, pressure was put on managers at all levels to do everything possible to increase sales and profits rather than to implement this new management resource planning system. Still another firm was diverted from implementing a new overall strategy for the division and had to help a very major customer design and manufacture one of its products which was encountering major production problems. This was done to insure that this delinquent customer would get enough revenues from the sale of its products to, in turn, pay money owed to this firm. Thus, it appears that the number and type of competing activities and crises that can occur are almost limitless.

One of the three things typically occurs when competing events exist. Time and attention are taken away from implementing the new strategic decision. They are taken away from other existing programs which suffer. Or often, some time and attention are taken away from the new and existing programs.

Some 60 per cent of the firms experienced uncontrollable factors in the external environment that had an adverse impact on implementation. Some of these problems are truly surprise events. Examples of these include:

1 a hurricane tearing off a roof of a new plant which damaged equipment;
2 the Professional Airline Traffic Controllers strike and the 25 per cent reduction in flights which reduced the demand for a firm's new jet-pull-out tractor; and
3 a surprising upturn in an industry's sales when a firm was trying to move three plants into one new modern facility.

In this later example, this firm competing in the abrasives industry had planned to make this move during a time of slackened demand. All economic forecasts for 1978/1979 suggested a softness in the economy; consequently, the firm thought this would be an excellent time to consolidate operations. Unfortunately, after the move got started, that year turned out to be the best year ever for the industry which caused added problems trying to satisfy high customer demand while moving operations.

While most uncontrollable problems in the external environment cannot be anticipated, contingency plans can be developed for some of them. Then, if that problem does occur, at least the firm will be in a better position to take corrective action to minimize its impact on the firm.

Two somewhat lower rated items, which are:

1 advocates and supporters of the strategic decision left (the division or company) during implementation (experienced by only 27 per cent of the firms) and
2 the key people who developed and made the strategic decision, did not play an active enough role in its subsequent implementation (40 per cent),

illustrate how two problems can combine to make things even worse. One company president put it this way,

> Our company was acquired by another parent firm with no background in this business. A new group vice president was installed to straighten out the mess here. He and I developed a strategy to break even in about 15 months with proper equipment, but then 6 months later, this group vice president was replaced for reasons beyond my knowledge. His replacement was not familiar with our operations, wants us now to go in about a 180 degree different direction, and only looks at bottom line results.

In another firm, a company president appointed a key subordinate to be the project manager, directly overseeing the implementation of the strategic decision. Half way through its implementation, that subordinate got so frustrated with the whole thing that he took a job elsewhere which really ground things to a halt. While the loss of a key person implementing a strategic decision can cause problems and lengthen the implementation time, the loss of the key architect of the decision can potentially stop the implementation forever.

## High versus low implementation success

The sample of 93 firms was then divided into high ($n = 33$), medium ($n = 29$), and low ($n = 31$) success depending on the strategic degree of success in implementing the strategic decision. This was based on an implementation success index made up of an average of three questions rated on a five-point scale ranging from 'low extent' to 'high extent'. These questions sought to determine the extent to which the actual implementation effort:

1 achieved the initial goals and objectives of the strategic decision;
2 achieved the financial results (sales, income, and/or profits) that were expected; and
3 was carried out within the various resources (money, manpower, time, etc.) initially budgeted for it.

Analysis of variance and student $t$-tests were calculated for each of the 22 potential implementation problems to determine whether there were first significant overall differences and then specific significant differences between the high-success and low-success groups. In 21 instances, the high-success group in implementing their respective strategic decisions had lower mean scores than the low-success group for the respective problem.

Seven of the same 10 problems shown in Table 2 along with five new problems were found to be significantly different with the analysis of variance comparing high-, medium- and low-success groups. Then, in 11 instances (marked by asterisks) as shown in Figure 1, the Student $t$-test showed that the mean

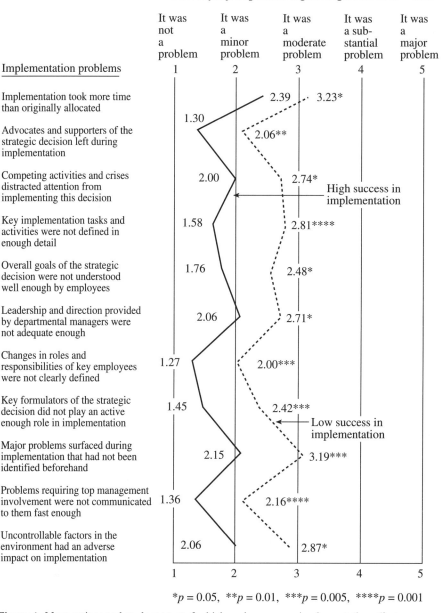

**Figure 1.** Mean ratings and student *t*-tests for high- vs low-success implementation efforts

score for high-success implementing firms (as shown by the solid line) was significantly less than that for the low-success group of firms (as shown by the dashed line). The five implementation problems that had *t*-test significance at the 0·005 level or above are:

1 key implementation tasks and activities were not defined in enough detail;
2 problems requiring top management involvement were not communicated to them fast enough;
3 changes in roles and responsibilities of key employees were not clearly defined;
4 key formulators of the strategic decision did not play an active enough role in implementation; and
5 major problems surfaced during implementation that had not been identified beforehand.

Thus, Figure 1 clearly suggests that the presence of more higher rated implementation problems has a negative effect on implementation success. Low-success firms experienced an average of 12·8 problems rated at any intensity level. In addition, 5·0 of these same 12·8 implementation items were rated as substantial or major problems by low-success firms. Conversely, high-success implementation firms experienced an average of only 9·2 problems, of which only 1·5 of them were rated at the substantial or major level.

## Promoting successful strategy implementation

In the follow-up telephone interviews with CEOs, one major purpose was to understand better various implementation problems that did hinder the implementation effort. However, another reason for these interviews was to get these executives to draw on their extensive experience and speculate on the things that help to promote successful strategy implementation. Although these generalizations are not statistically valid, they were mentioned most frequently by 21 CEOs plus 25 additional interviews with agency heads from federal and state governments in a comparison study.

### Communication, communication, communication

This seemingly simple suggestion was mentioned more frequently by CEOs than any other single item. The reason it is repeated three times is to reflect exactly what was said by a number of these company presidents. They felt that top management must first of all clearly communicate with all employees what the new strategic decision is all about. Hopefully, it involves two-way communication that permits and solicits questions from affected employees about the formulated strategy, issues to be considered, or potential problems that might occur. In addition, communication includes clearly explaining what new responsibilities, tasks, and duties need to be performed by the affected employees. It also includes the why behind changed job activities, and more fundamentally the reasons why the new strategic decision was made in the first place. Finally, CEOs mentioned that two-way communication is needed throughout the implementation process to monitor what is actually happening, analyze how to deal with emerging problems, and in deciding what modifications might be needed in the program to make it work.

## Start with a good concept or idea

The need to start with a formulated strategy that involves a good idea or concept was mentioned next most often in helping promote successful implementation. In a nut shell, what this idea suggests is that no amount of time and effort spent on implementation can rescue a strategic decision that is not well formulated to begin with. More than being thoroughly planned out, the idea must be fundamentally sound. Thus, this suggests that strategy implementation can fail for one of two reasons. One is caused by a failure to do things required during implementation to insure that a well-formulated strategy is successful. The other cause of failure is due to a poorly conceived formulated plan that no amount of implementation effort can help rescue.

## Obtain employee commitment and involvement

This third suggestion builds on the first two and interrelates with them. CEOs suggested that one way to accomplish this is to involve affected employees and managers right from the start in the strategy formulation process. On the contrary, when a strategic decision has been developed in a vacuum by a few people, top management should not be surprised that it is resisted during implementation by the affected employees. Top management should not be surprised if the formulated plan has major flaws in it because key employees and affected groups did not participate in its formulation. In fact, just the opposite may be true. Top management ought to be surprised if a formulated strategy, developed pretty much without key employee involvement, is implemented successfully.

Involvement and commitment should also be developed and maintained throughout the implementation process. If middle and lower level managers and key subordinates are permitted to be involved with the detailed implementation planning, their commitment typically will tend to increase. The workability of the specific action plan should also be improved simply by getting the affected employees involved – and committed – early on as well as throughout the implementation process.

## Provide sufficent resources

CEOs mentioned at least four different kinds of resources. The obvious one is money, which, considering the sizeable scope of many strategic decisions, is a bottom line requirement. Conversely, failure to provide adequate funding may contribute to limited success or outright failure. Manpower is another key resource which can have either a positive or a negative effect on implementation. Technical expertise (or knowledge), as related to the new strategic decision, is still another resource mentioned by some CEOs. The idea suggested here is that firms need to have in-house expertise or hire a few new employees who possess it in order to implement strategic decisions involving new endeavours. A final resource mentioned is time. Sufficient time to accomplish the implementation, adequate time and attention given by top management to the new effort, and hopefully not too many other competing programs demanding the time of affected employees who will implement this one.

## Develop an implementation plan

This final suggestion is a plea to develop many of the specifics to be done during implementation. In essence, this details who is to do what and when it is to be accomplished. A few CEOs mentioned that this plan must strike the right balance. If the implementation plan is too vague, it is of little practical use. Conversely, if the plan is too detailed, it may tend to force various functional departments to follow it precisely, even when it clearly needs to be modified.

Several CEOs also mentioned that a part of that plan should be to identify likely implementation problems. Instead of being blindly optimistic that nothing will go wrong while implementing a strategic decision, do just the opposite. Try to identify the most likely problems that might occur and then develop contingency responses for those eventualities.

## Summary and conclusions

A number of strategy implementation problems do seem to occur on a regular basis. In fact, 10 of the 22 potential problems rated occurred to at least 50 per cent of the sampled firms. While problems do occur frequently, the vast majority of firms experience them as minor or moderate problems. However, when a firm encounters several implementation problems, rated at the substantial or major level, it can have a very adverse impact on the implementation process.

Surprisingly, some of the traditional strategy implementation factors mentioned in the literature were not judged as frequently to be problems. Rated among the least frequent of the 22 implementation problems were:

- rewards and incentives utilized to get employee conformance to program were not sufficient (cited as a problem by only 18 per cent of the respondents);
- support and backing by top management in this SBU and at the corporate level were not adequate (21 per cent);
- financial resources made available were not sufficient (27 per cent);

- organizational structural changes made were not effective (33 per cent); and
- changes in roles and responsibilities of key employees were not clearly defined (38 per cent).

It may be that firms do such a good job in these areas than problems are prevented. Or it may suggest that other implementation problems identified in this study are more important than what the literature has somewhat led us to believe.

High-success firms experience implementation problems to a significantly less extent than do low-success implementation firms. In fact, some 11 problems were experienced to a significantly less extent by high-success firms when compared with low-success firms. In addition, high-success firms experienced problems rated at the substantial or major problem intensity level three times less frequently than did low-success firms. In addition, high-success firms also encountered fewer total problems during implementation.

Successful implementation in part involves preventing various implementation problems from occurring in the first place. It also involves taking quick action of resolve and address problems that do occur. Obviously, the faster corrective action is initiated during implementation, the more likely it can be resolved before it impacts adversely on the firm.

Successful implementation also involves doing the things that help promote success rather than just preventing problems from occurring. Although the five suggestions presented here are not statistically significant, they do help reinforce the importance of satisfying basic managerial tasks to help bring about success.

# References

1   L. Alexander, *Strategy Implementation Annotated Bibliography*, Harvard's HBS Case Services, Case No. 9–380–797 (1980), plus 1983 Supplement.
2   K. Andrews, *The Concept of Corporate Strategy*, Dow Jones-Irwin, Homewood, IL (1971).
3   J. Galbraith and D. Nathanson, *Strategy Implementation: The Role of Structure and Process*, West Publishing Co., St Paul, MN (1978).
4   J. Hobbs and D. Heany, Coupling strategy to operating plans, *Harvard Business Review*, pp. 119–126, May–June (1977).
5   J. Kotter and L. Schlesinger, Choosing strategies for change, *Harvard Business Review*, pp. 106–114, March–April (1979).
6   P. Le Breton, *General Administration: Planning and Implementation*, Holt, Rinehart and Winston, New York (1965).
7   D. McCarthy, R. Minichiello and J. Curran, *Business Policy and Strategy: Concepts and Readings*, Richard D. Irwin, Homewood, IL (1979).
8   J. Quinn, *Strategies for Change: Logical Incrementalism*, Richard D. Irwin, Homewood, IL (1980).
9   G. Steiner and J. Miner, *Management Policy and Strategy: Text, Readings, and Cases*, Macmillan, New York (1977).

10   A. Thompson and A. Strickland, *Strategy Formulation and Implementation: Tasks of the General Manager*, Business Publications, Dallas (1981).

11   J. Pressman and A. Wildavsky, *Implementation*, University of California Press, Berkeley, CA (1973).

12   J. Murphy, Title I of ESEA: The politics of implementing federal education reform, *Harvard Educational Review*, pp. 35–63, February (1971).

13   J. Quinn, General Motors' downsizing decision. In D. Harvey's *Business Policy and Strategic Management*, pp. 669–695. Charles E. Merrill, Columbus. OH (1982).

14   L. Alexander, Pacific power and light: Implementation of an innovative home weatherization program. In A. Thompson and A. Strickland's *Strategic Management: Concepts and Cases*, pp. 880–905, Business Publications, Dallas (1984).

# 13  Competing against time

## *G. Stalk and T. M. Hout*

## Making the change

Once top executives and key managers develop a vision and decide their company is going to become a time-based competitor, two questions face them: (1) How do we overcome the organization's natural barriers to change? (2) How do we engage the organization to develop the solutions – the new ways of doing things – that we want? Fundamental change is exhilarating but also difficult. For some people it's a great release of energy, for others it's a threat. It is manageable if senior people are candid about what the problems are and persistent in communicating the market opportunities. Let's first address barriers to change, by differentiating between the two kinds and talking about how they are ultimately overcome.

One group of barriers to becoming a time-based company stems from the actions and policies of senior management. There may be a lack of imagination that starts right at the top. The organization's structure may undermine time compression – too many departments that break up the main sequence or functional lines of authority that are too strong. Measurements and rewards may be counterproductive. Old mythologies of the company – such as, our products are better so customers will wait for ours to come out – will confuse employees unless laid to rest. Inadequate leadership and, in particular, weak people in managers' roles, who are seen as not being able to solve the problems and make the changes they're talking about, will set any time-based effort back. All of these barriers are senior management's job to eliminate. The company can't ignore them and then talk about teamwork and fast cycles and expect much to happen.

The change from cost-based to time-based competition is fundamental and places new, sometimes conflicting demands on the company's managers, a factor that top management may under-estimate at first. Profit-center managers can find the time-based message appealing but still take comfort in rising backlogs and greater use of fixed assets. Functional heads who got promoted on the strength of protecting the company from costly mistakes may find multifunctional approaches hard to accept. Data processing managers may be excellent at keeping the old systems running but see PC-centered networks and electronic data interchange with suppliers as threats to the firm's data integrity. Top executives have to be clear on what the new expectations are and help their managers through the transition.

The absolutely first step in senior management's design of the change process should be to assess the capability of managers at least three levels down. The most capable should be given strong roles in managing the task groups that remove the company-imposed barriers and design the new solution. The currently less able managers should be encouraged but left off the critical path, at least early on. The least able should be removed. Senior management has to tackle the barriers under its control right away.

The second group of barriers to change comprises the beliefs, habits, and concerns of employees that are ultimately under the control of employees themselves. There is a wide range of legitimate problems here. Many employees fear operations will collapse if serious changes are made. Some will see the concept but not the payoff. A large number will simply not know how to make the change and work under a new set of rules; the new paradigms will frighten them. Others will see the new rules as a loss of turf or status or as a downgrading of their skills. And some will simply be immobilized by grief over the end of a way of working with colleagues that they loved.

Although some of these problems must take time to heal or require individual counseling, most employees will respond to positive involvement in the change process and to clear, consistent communication from those they recognize as leaders. Fears and skepticism or disbelief for most employees simply indicate that they haven't *seen* a different approach in practice or that they haven't heard their immediate leaders endorse it. It's easy for management to underestimate how many exposures to the new message and to early pilot successes employees need. The reason is that there are a lot of countermessages – years of doing it the old way, short-timers who say it isn't worth it, concerns that certain job classifications and specialists will be gone, and so on. We have found that management has to communicate to all levels between three and five times more often than it may have thought necessary at the start.

It's a good idea for management to address doubts about the time-based concept directly. Employees, especially long-term people, have strong beliefs about how the business works, and unless these are specifically challenged they can undermine everything you're trying to do. Many employees will find the time-based vision runs counter to the facts. For example, they will believe that better service will mean more inventory. It always has in the past. It is not intuitive to most people the first time they hear it that synchronized, continuous flow operations can shorten cycle times, which in turn reduces the lead time needed to give customers what they want. Others will believe that yours is a commodity business where no one makes good returns. To counter this perspective, the idea of time-sensitive segments where higher prices and profits are available will have to be laid out in detail and examples shown.

Another firmly rooted belief may be that while the company 'wastes a little time,' it is impossible to reduce by one half or more the time it takes to service orders or to develop new products. Such prospects are unbelievable. In response to this opinion, management needs to shift employees from thinking about wasting time in an efficiency expert's sense to compressing time in a strategic sense. This takes a lot of explaining. Pictures and flow charts with boxes and arrows help.

The second question posed at the beginning of this section was how do we engage the organization to develop solutions that we want? This question brings us to the heart of the change process. There are lots of ways, and in every successful case that we know of, management used several. In some parts of the company, experiments and pilots that can generate solutions spontaneously down in the organization should get started right away. In others, especially where complex cross-functional issues are involved, a more deliberate process of bringing people from various parts of the organization together to design solutions is the right approach. And, nothing concentrates the mind of the company more effectively than focusing a cross-functional group on customers: What do they want, and how can we better serve them?

Focusing a group on how to create more value for customers should produce new insights. The aim is to locate the best customers, those who will reward you for taking time and uncertainty out of their businesses. One approach here is to ask the question: What difference would it make to customer X if we could customize our product for him in a particular way or deliver to him in one-half the time it now takes? For example, if we are a magazine publisher, what is it worth to our largest advertiser if we develop a new variant of an existing magazine whose content and format are targeted directly to a particularly important customer group? This line of thought gets you into your customer's imagination and what he or she could do with the right product or channel. It allows you to hypothetically manipulate revenue streams and capture rates, and figure out what would radically change the customer's business. Then you can more readily help him or her do that. It's likely that if you become a big link in the revolutionizing of that business, the first move was yours, not theirs. It's hard to find a more win/win situation than showing your customers a way to higher profits via your help.

A case in point is a building materials producer who sells to distributors, who in turn sell to several customer groups. The distributors' two largest customer groups are large contractors and small prefab manufacturers. Since these two customer groups provide the distributors' volume base load, distributors pay most attention to them. The building materials producer assigned two people – one from marketing, the other from production – to do a time-based segmentation of distributors' customers. By going to distributors and watching various customer groups' lead time and product mix demands, they found a group – small contractors on upscale jobs – who demanded exactly what the building materials producer's new flexible plant could produce and who were willing to pay 20–30 percent more to get small quantities of what they needed the same day. The two people brought this to the attention of selected distributors, and together they set up an ordering and delivery channel to service this segment. It's now the most profitable customer group for both the manufacturer and distributor.

Learning to think in terms of small segments is part of becoming a time-based competitor. Think about how more speed might change your best customers' fortunes and then figure out how to do it. It helps to have the stretch goal in a concrete form with a well-considered dollar value attached. Organizations respond to this better than to abstract targets.

## Pilots and breakthrough teams

Pilots are a good way to energize those parts of the organization where good people are ready to go and where local trial-and-error experimentation is the right way to get solutions. It's important to keep the rest of the company out of the pilot undertaking. This means buffering it physically and politically. If necessary, build up a temporary stock of materials or data between the pilot unit and those with which it interacts. Keep senior people with turf issues out of the pilot itself and put them on a group at the end that interprets the pilots' results. Let specialists into the pilots only at the request of the operators.

*Examples.* Six salespeople in a field office decide that they need to spend more time with customers and less in administration. They come up with a plan, which includes new data links and better software for field reporting, and review it with the regional head. One company information system specialist of their choosing is included in the pilot, and together they rig up prototype data links and buy the closest off-the-shelf software. Only after they demonstrate that it works and get other sales offices excited do they bring in the information systems department and the controller to start to budget and build something, based on the pilot concept, suitable for the whole company. Experiment before specifying, and involve small groups before large groups.

A construction equipment company decides it needs to take half the time out of its new product development process. There are at least seven key functions – product marketing, product engineering, research center, manufacturing engineering, tooling, purchasing, and test engineering – involved. This product line manager had earlier tried to reduce development time but had failed. His process had involved all seven heads at once and had gotten bogged down in complexity; in addition, two heads – test and tooling – had opposed any change in procedure. This time the line manager took three heads committed to change – marketing, product engineering, and manufacturing engineering – and told them to simply begin developing a new product around some basic time-based principles and to shape the process as they went. They were given permission to go outside the organization to buy any services they wanted if internal functions weren't flexible. The three did just that when tooling and test people said what they wanted couldn't or shouldn't be done. The pilot was a success, vindicating the product-line manager's hard ball approach. Tooling and testing have managed to change. A set of old chestnuts has been broken.

Pilots work best when demonstration is the right first step and when a local manager already has a pretty good broad idea of the change he or she wants and knows it can get done if not exactly how. Having the critical pilot drivers in place, in this case the three function heads, is a prerequisite.

There are, however, other cross-functional situations where issues are harder to define, where no one has a general solution in mind, and where there is no natural champion to whom everyone involved reports. Here breakthrough teams can be useful. They are select groups of usually four to six leading middle managers chartered for a few months to think through new, radical solutions. A typical large company might have several breakthrough teams operating in the early stages of a time-based transition. Following are some typical charters:

- How to cut the customer order-to-shipment cycle in half
- How to accelerate cost estimating for new products and engineering changes
- How to establish an around-the-clock global short-term money management function in the company
- How to ensure that all suppliers get the same order and schedule information at the same time the company does
- How to accelerate the transfer of a successful product from one country's organization to another inside a multinational company

These teams are one-time solution-finding teams, not permanent working teams. Their members are the most capable middle managers from the parts of the organization involved in the cycle, so they know the problems and the difference between paper and real solutions. Part of the breakthrough team experience is to get them talking without day-to-day problems grinding at them, to get them to see the whole system. Their charter is to drop assumptions about how the company works and to come up with a better way. The aim is not a highly polished, no-loose-ends presentation, but rather the core workings of a way to do things that is dramatically better and faster.

Experience suggests that these teams must be given radical goals, like collapsing time in half. Otherwise, assumptions aren't challenged. The whole premise is using bottlenecks, breakdowns, and unmet customer needs as opportunities to learn. The teams use a variety of techniques – root-cause analysis, scenario building, pursuing conflict between two people until the real problem crystalizes, and old-fashioned imagination. Between regular meetings, research into technical or other problems is done. There are no formal reports to the team members' superiors. The teams report to a senior steering group that is responsible for all the breakthrough teams operating. This steering group is responsible for managing change under the time-based vision that the management team has decided to pursue.

One example is a breakthrough team that was chartered to compress the cost-estimating cycle for new parts inside an automobile company. Formerly, the cycle took two to three weeks as each function added its step serially and passed the work package on. Figure 1 shows this. Product engineering prepared the blueprints, manufacturing engineering developed routings, industrial engineering added labor standards, purchasing quoted purchased parts, finance added burden rates, and sales priced the part. This cost-estimating cycle had the classic earmarks of a loosely managed serial process. No one was accountable for the cycle; it was buried among many others. There were numerous handoffs, with each function playing a limited role. Because decision rules were formal and timely interaction was difficult, it was hard to catch inappropriate numbers until late in the process. And it slowed down the whole process of quoting prices for new parts.

A breakthrough team representing these functions developed a solution over a set of five meetings. Looking at several case histories, the team determined that new parts fell into a few classes, and that parts within a class had similar costing characteristics. The team developed a set of procedures and rules, including notes on how to identify problems. It had interviewed all users of the cost estimates and their functional department heads, so it knew the real issues.

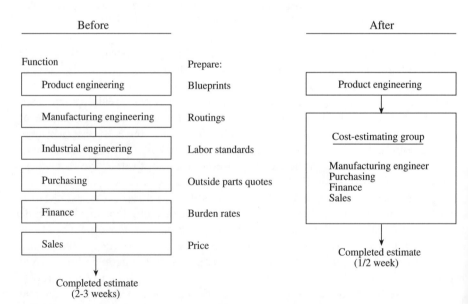

**Figure 1.** Cost estimating procedure – before and after breakthrough team

The team's recommendation was a standing closed-loop cost-estimating cell of four members that met twice a week to process all of product engineering's new blueprints. All the work was done in one room, with no formal handoffs. Difficult cases were researched off-line and settled at the next meeting. The group had a chairman. Once the cell was up and running, the members rotated off every six months in staggered fashion. The average cycle time dropped to one-half week, and the quality of work improved.

Each problem breakthrough teams address is different, but here are some common principles of solutions applied in time-based companies:

- Align organizations, authority, data collection, scheduling, etc., with the main sequence.
- Pass the best information upstream fast.
- Continuously measure performance and performance improvements.
- Make debottlenecking investments in people and in equipment.
- Do not allow a support activity to gate the main sequence. Either eliminate it, carry deliberate excess capacity, or take it off-line.
- Work out a triage among required processes and tasks, and realign work flow.
- Use parallel processing as much as possible.
- Reduce batch sizes, and execute each batch more frequently.
- Synchronize operations; especially, balance the cycle time across different mix loads so that downstream activities are not held up by mix variations.
- Do not allow incomplete work to be passed on.
- Eliminate causes of rework at the source.
- Understand the process and where its performance leverage points are before you prescribe changes.
- Do not compromise the above principles for the sake of keeping peace among team members.

Breakthrough teams, taken together, redesign the work of the company. Each charter has to be sufficiently large and cross-functional to make a real difference in time compression that customers can see and that strategists can exploit. Cost estimating in the example above was a modest-sized charter and took only five weeks to design and be up and running. Designing new simultaneous information systems for suppliers, in contrast, can take several months to crack and involve twice as many people. The steering group that charters and integrates the breakthroughs becomes the principal orchestrator of the change. The number of teams is important. Setting up too many teams will fragment the problem and fail to confront the real issues of organizational complexity and distance. Too few teams will overwhelm each team with an impossible charter. Breakthrough teams should be set up to succeed.

Breakthrough teams, or something comparable, are especially useful for making organizationally complex changes, where analysis should precede action. Analysis is needed because the solution isn't obvious and different parts of the company have to be involved. These teams are the backbone of a company's move toward time compression and can be mobilized quickly. Teams can shape recommendations early and draw reaction. Once a solution takes shape, it can be refined during implementation. Breakthrough teams lose effectiveness if they stand too long.

In this way, the change process is neither top down nor bottom up, but really driven from the middle and coordinated at the top by those who settled on the vision. The able middle managers are in the best position to do the cutting-edge learning that will reshape the company's practices. They are junior enough to know the particulars of what will work and what won't, and senior enough to grasp the larger picture. Equally important, they will be among those implementing the new systems that they design, positioning them to continue learning. Companies don't become time-based in one shot, and it's the capacity to compound learning – the learning to learn – that distinguishes successful time-based companies. Keeping the best middle managers in the learning loop from design through implementation gives them the feedback they need to come up with the next round of improvements.

## Reorganization emerges

The best approach to becoming time-based is to structure the company around the flow of work that customers value and to depend more on the middle of the organization to discover this flow and reshape the company's operations accordingly. This method rests on the belief that senior management can only create visions and motivate change; it cannot prescribe the solutions and reorganize operations from the top. Scholars and practitioners often observe that American companies are stronger on control than on coordination, and that Japanese companies look more to management process and sources of leverage than to tidy structure. Time-based companies build coordination and process strength. Companies whose first instinct when trying to improve performance is to reorganize or restructure operations will usually compromise their opportunities.

Reorganizing or restructuring operations should generally follow, not precede, pilots and breakthrough teams. These exploratory mechanisms help management decide such questions as – What should departments have in them? Where should authority and responsibility rest? How many layers are necessary? Operations are organisms, not mechanisms; no one can correctly design them at much of a distance. The right organizational structure should emerge after operating managers have wrestled with meeting radical time-based goals. Becoming time based is more of a creative and less of a formal process than is a one-time management event like overhead value analysis. It happens in an irregular series of big and little steps. Improving a big step at the wrong time – like installing an expensive new information system or organizing too many product-based profit centers that share a main sequence – can be expensive.

At the same time, the process of becoming a time-based company requires strong senior management leadership and steering. It involves several senior actions – developing a vision, assessing managers several levels down, chartering pilots and breakthrough teams, reading their results, and modifying the whole process as it proceeds. Senior management must also resolve major tensions that surface along the way. For example, radical prescriptions will usually challenge the prerogatives of some decentralized line managers or senior function heads. At this point, these people have to be reminded that decentralization of operations doesn't preclude rethinking, or mean that some operations cannot occasionally be centralized.

And senior managers who begin to move their organizations toward time compression face an inescapable dilemma: How do we achieve faster cycles in the long run without being badly damaged by work interruptions in the short term? Most organizations cover their delays and errors with slack resources and loosely fitting interfaces. But when a company begins to compress its cycles, the delays and errors can rarely be fixed as quickly as the slack is taken away. Temporary breakdowns occur, and fast response to customers – the whole objective – is undermined. Every management must find its own pace and mechanisms to walk this tightrope. More pilots can be done. Dynamic computer simulations can help predict problems. More temporary buffers can be added. But what's critical is that managers keep pushing the change process and not suspend their efforts when the inevitable problems arise.

## Sustaining improvement

The foregoing prescription for becoming a time-based competitor – radical vision, breakthrough teams, with top management involved and leading the way – is the jump-start. A large organization at any given time is invested in a way of doing business that carries with it a set of expectations and implied standards for what is good. The slower the industry rate of change, the more is invested. Even successful organizations experience inertia. The companies that over a period of years dramatically compress time start by overcoming inertia: They set new goals, discard old routines, and celebrate new approaches that work better. Leaders get this done by mobilizing the best people in their organization. This is the jump-start, and it is always a radical, stressful period. It is also eventually highly satisfying.

This high energy start-up does change measurable performance in the short term, but its main function is to overcome inertia by establishing the new paradigm and by building momentum in new directions. It puts more energy into the organization than will show up early in improved numbers. But the short-term improvement can still be significant. Table 1 shows what several

**Table 1** Examples of successful jump-starts

| Industry | Early time-based focus | Early benefits | Time frame (months) |
|---|---|---|---|
| Auto components | Order processing; plant operations | Cycle time reduced 50%; market share slide arrested | 8 |
| Telephone equipment | New product development | Cycle time cut 40%; new product introductions up 55% | 9 |
| Insurance | New policy applications; claims processing | Cycle time reduced 45%; productivity up 15% | 10 |
| Specialty paper | Total system, from order to distribution to customer | Cycle time reduced 30%; price realization up 10%; reversed market share slide | 8 |
| Commercial bank | Consumer loan approvals | Cycle time reduced 70%; new applications up 25% | 7 |
| Packaged food product | Transplanting successful products to global markets | Cycle time reduced 65%; preempt growth segment in Europe, profits up 25% | 5 |

companies accomplished during their jump-start periods, which ranged from five to ten months. Most were able to halve the cycle time of the activities they targeted, and they got measurable benefits in the market, ranging from better price realization to share gains.

The early momentum is by no means self-sustaining, however. Early successes are often achieved in those parts of the company where thoughtful people knew big improvements could be made (although not exactly how), and they are the work of the company's more able, motivated employees. But momentum can be blunted if tough problems go unsolved or if hastily convened teams compromise their solutions for easy, incremental gains that leave the company basically unchanged. If key managers stop driving the process, if the old measures are still the ones that really matter, and if problem people aren't taken off the critical path, progress will grind to a halt. The same thing may happen if time-compression efforts grow mainly out of an earnings short-fall. Once the market comes back, the effort will probably die.

Sustaining the effort requires institutionalizing the basics of the process:

● Monitoring progress against the vision, and emphasizing the gap that still exists

● Continuing to benchmark the best time-based performers (They won't stand still; they'll get better.)
● Involving key managers in driving the next set of pilots and breakthrough teams and making sure that goals are not compromised
● Taking people from early teams that completed their work successfully and seeding new teams that are attacking difficult problems with them, demonstrating that the company values the process, not just the first results
● Following up by formally instituting a new set of measures and rewards, and phasing out the old ones
● Granting capital spending authorizations for proposals that promote time compression, like distributed information networking; and denying proposals for new plant and equipment that won't be necessary if cycle times are reduced
● Communicating the principles and objectives to all constituencies again and again, including employees, suppliers, customers, union leaders, and others.

The real benefits come from sustained effort over years, not months. This applies not just to the numbers, but to the learning as well. Companies learn how to learn by having a group make a difficult change, by thinking and talking about what the group did that made the difference, then by continuing to use elsewhere the practices that made the difference. The dramatic time-based improvements made by major divisions of big companies – the consumer products division of AT&T, the copier business at Xerox, and the construction equipment division of Deere – worked just this way. These businesses are different now because their people *expect* each other to continue to entertain changes and therefore to make continuous improvements. Once this expectation is lost, continuous improvement will stop.

Good companies have always made continuous improvement. It's implicit in the experience curve institutionalized in many companies' thinking in the 1970s. The experience curve traced the rate of decline in real costs per unit for aggressive competitors in an industry and found costs continued to decline as experience in the business accumulated. The best operations, like Hillenbrand Industries, which dominates in hospital beds and coffins, or ICI in chemical fertilizers, maintain their rate of improvement over years and years. It happens in low-tech as well as in high-tech industries, and in low-growth as well as in high-growth markets. Continuous improvement is a function of management – not of technologies or growth rates.

The experience curve applies to time as well as to cost. For example, the automobile company shown in Table 1 cut its cost-estimating cycle from two or three weeks to one-half week by moving from loosely managed functional specialists working independently to a closed-loop cell. The next move was to automate some of the information flow and to reduce the team by one member. Some team members had become multifunctional enough to allow this. This reduced cycle time even more. Future time compressions will probably involve simplifying and standardizing the information that comes from the engineers upstream. Eventually, the whole cost-estimating function may be folded into the organization and disappear as a discrete cycle.

Where continuous improvement will come from in the future is not always clear. In fact, if companies knew what the next changes had to be, they would make them. But there is a tool that can help, especially with processes that can be studied, such as production or distribution. Root-cause diagrams can help lay out a continuous improvement agenda for the future. Figure 2 shows such a diagram for a typical machine setup in a high-variety plant. Each step going from left to right takes the problem back further into root causes. The exhibit shows causes four levels down, and each level compounds the number of things to get done. Such a chart can organize the relevant challenges for coordinating the efforts of a machine cell crew.

Institutionalizing the management process that gets time compression started is the first condition for sustaining time improvement. But to keep time-based learning going, a company needs rapid feedback loops in all its activities.

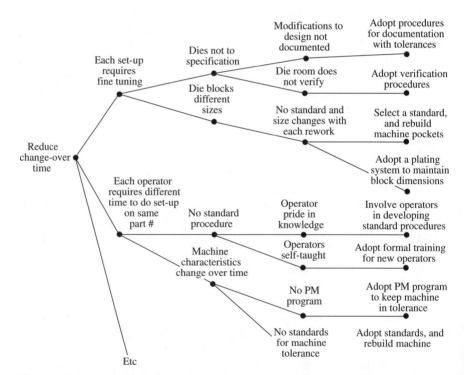

**Figure 2.** Root cause analysis showing path of continuing improvement for a factory set-up

Learning slows and dissipates when the results of decisions or actions are late reaching the people directly involved.

Here are some examples of rapid feedback loops:

● Implement early prototyping in everything from new-product develop-ment to competitive intelligence research projects. Force participants to put together preliminary product early, even when major issues are still unresolved. This gives everyone involved the big picture and shows where the holes are.

● Apply continuous market research at low levels of intensity using people from various functions, as opposed to conducting episodic big studies. With the latter, too much is missed and attitudes harden in between. At Du Pont, even production workers, not just salespeople and product engineers, visit key customers to learn their needs firsthand.

● Organize colocation of as many parts of a business as possible.

● Require a continuous flow of proposed engineering changes to super-visors, with no dollar value minimum on submitted changes. One engin-eering supervisor told his engineers to concentrate on major changes, so no small ones were forthcoming. Competitors were hurting the company badly in the market with a stream of small but useful changes.

● Monitor new-product launches early, tracking not just sales and customer satisfaction, but engineering, packaging, and other aspects of perform-ance. The sooner the company can learn which product versions and sales approaches are working best, the more it can emphasize them and the faster it can build volume. This is true regardless of how long the market conversion is projected to take.

● Shorten the economic lives of equipment. Many companies bias their purchases toward longer-lived equipment, citing lower depreciation costs. But shorter-lived equipment may force more frequent process reviews among key departments, opening opportunities for improvement.

● Conduct frequent performance evaluations, both between supervisor and subordinate and among peer team members.

● Develop in-house proprietary techniques, such as engineering design algorithms, performance evaluation forms, and market research segmen-tation descripters. Using mainly off-the-shelf techniques simply perpetu-ates someone else's view of the problem and prevents the company's employees' light bulbs from switching on.

There is one other condition for continuous improvement, and that is growth of the business. Market share is nice and in many businesses it's a major advan-tage, but growth is essential. Vital organizations grow regardless of the indus-try's growth rate. Growth forces you to get new customers and new problems. Growth makes your people change the way they spend their day. Growth makes your company create new segments or cross existing boundaries to encounter new competitors. The longer you grow, the longer you can put off the day when your business is 'mature' and your organization is 'settled'. If that day comes, you have a real management problem on your hands.

Reprinted with the permission of The Free Press, an imprint of Simon & Schuster from *Competing Against Time: How Time-Based Competition is Reshaping Global Markets* by George Stalk Jr. and Thomas M. Hout. Copyright © 1990 by The Free Press.

# 14 Teaching smart people how to learn

*C. Argyris*

Any company that aspires to succeed in the tougher business environment of the 1990s must first resolve a basic dilemma: success in the marketplace increasingly depends on learning, yet most people don't know how to learn. What's more, those members of the organization that many assume to be the best at learning are, in fact, not very good at it. I am talking about the well-educated, high-powered, high-commitment professionals who occupy key leadership positions in the modern corporation.

Most companies not only have tremendous difficulty addressing this learning dilemma; they aren't even aware that it exists. The reason: they misunderstand what learning is and how to bring it about. As a result, they tend to make two mistakes in their efforts to become a learning organization.

First, most people define learning too narrowly as mere 'problem solving', so they focus on identifying and correcting errors in the external environment. Solving problems is important. But if learning is to persist, managers and employees must also look inward. They need to reflect critically on their own behavior, identify the ways they often inadvertently contribute to the organization's problems, and then change how they act. In particular, they must learn how the very way they go about defining and solving problems can be a source of problems in its own right.

I have coined the terms 'single loop' and 'double loop' learning to capture this crucial distinction. To give a simple analogy: a thermostat that automatically turns on the heat whenever the temperature in a room drops below 68 degrees is a good example of single-loop learning. A thermostat that could ask, 'Why am I set at 68 degrees?' and then explore whether or not some other temperature might more economically achieve the goal of heating the room would be engaging in double-loop learning.

Highly skilled professionals are frequently very good at single-loop learning. After all, they have spent much of their lives acquiring academic credentials, mastering one or a number of intellectual disciplines, and applying those disciplines to solve real-world problems. But ironically, this very fact helps explain why professionals are often so bad at double-loop learning.

Put simply, because many professionals are almost always successful at what they do, they rarely experience failure. And because they have rarely failed, they have never learned how to learn from failure. So whenever their single-loop learning strategies go wrong, they become defensive, screen out criticism, and put the 'blame' on anyone and everyone but themselves. In short, their ability to learn shuts down precisely at the moment they need it the most.

The propensity among professionals to behave defensively helps shed light on the second mistake that companies make about learning. The common assumption is that getting people to learn is largely a matter of motivation. When people have the right attitudes and commitment, learning automatically follows. So companies focus on creating new organizational structures – compensation programs, performance reviews, corporate cultures, and the like – that are designed to create motivated and committed employees.

But effective double-loop learning is not simply a function of how people feel. It is a reflection of how they think – that is, the cognitive rules or reasoning they use to design and implement their actions. Think of these rules as a kind of 'master program' stored in the brain, governing all behavior. Defensive reasoning can block learning even when the individual commitment to it is high, just as a computer program with hidden bugs can produce results exactly the opposite of what its designers had planned.

Companies can learn how to resolve the learning dilemma. What it takes is to make the ways managers and employees reason about their behavior a focus of organizational learning and continuous improvement programs. Teaching people how to reason about their behavior in new and more effective ways breaks down the defenses that block learning.

All of the examples that follow involve a particular kind of professional: fast-track consultants at major management consulting companies. But the implications of my argument go far beyond this specific occupational group. The fact is, more and more jobs – no matter what the title – are taking on the contours of 'knowledge work'. People at all levels of the organization must combine the mastery of some highly specialized technical expertise with the ability to work effectively in teams, form productive relationships with clients and customers, and critically reflect on and then change their own organizational practices. And the nuts and bolts of management – whether of high-powered consultants or service representatives, senior managers or factory technicians – increasingly consists of guiding and integrating the autonomous but interconnected work of highly skilled people.

## How professionals avoid learning

For 15 years I have been conducting in-depth studies of management consultants. I decided to study consultants for a few simple reasons. First, they are the epitome of the highly educated professionals who play an increasingly central role in all organizations. Almost all of the consultants I've studied have MBAs from the top three or four US business schools. They are also highly committed to their work. For instance, at one company, more than 90 per cent of the consultants responded in a survey that they were 'highly satisfied' with their jobs and with the company.

I also assumed that such professional consultants would be good at learning. After all, the essence of their job is to teach others how to do things differently. I found, however, that these consultants embodied the learning dilemma. The most enthusiastic about continuous improvement in their own organizations, they were also often the biggest obstacle to its complete success.

As long as efforts at learning and change focused on external organizational factors – job redesign, compensation programs, performance reviews, and leadership training – the professionals were enthusiastic participants. Indeed, creating new systems and structures was precisely the kind of challenge that well-educated, highly motivated professionals thrived on.

And yet the moment the quest for continuous improvement turned to the professionals' *own* performance, something went wrong. It wasn't a matter of bad attitude. The professionals' commitment to excellence was genuine, and the vision of the company was clear. Nevertheless, continuous improvement did not persist. And the longer the continuous improvement efforts continued, the greater the likelihood that they would produce ever-diminishing returns.

What happened? The professionals began to feel embarrassed. They were threatened by the prospect of critically examining their own role in the organization. Indeed, because they were so well paid (and generally believed that their employers were supportive and fair), the idea that their performance might not be at its best made them feel guilty.

Far from being a catalyst for real change, such feelings caused most to react defensively. They projected the blame for any problems away from themselves and onto what they said were unclear goals, insensitive and unfair leaders, and stupid clients.

Consider this example. At a premier management consulting company, the manager of a case team called a meeting to examine the team's performance on a recent consulting project. The client was largely satisfied and had given the team relatively high marks, but the manager believed the team had not created the value added that it was capable of and that the consulting company had promised. In the spirit of continuous improvement, he felt that the team could do better. Indeed, so did some of the team members.

The manager knew how difficult it was for people to reflect critically on their own work performance, especially in the presence of their manager, so he took a number of steps to make possible a frank and open discussion. He invited to the meeting an outside consultant whom team members knew and trusted – 'just to keep me honest,' he said. He also agreed to have the entire meeting tape-recorded. That way, any subsequent confusions or disagreements about what went on at the meeting could be checked against the transcript. Finally, the manager opened the meeting by emphasizing that no subject was off limits – including his own behavior.

'I realize that you may believe you cannot confront me,' the manager said. 'But I encourage you to challenge me. You have a responsibility to tell me where you think the leadership made mistakes, just as I have the responsibility to identify any I believe you made. And all of us must acknowledge our own mistakes. If we do not have an open dialogue, we will not learn.'

The professionals took the manager up on the first half of his invitation but quietly ignored the second. When asked to pinpoint the key problems in the experience with the client, they looked entirely outside themselves. The clients were uncooperative and arrogant. 'They didn't think we could help them.' The team's own managers were unavailable and poorly prepared. 'At times, our managers were not up to speed before they walked into the client meetings.' In effect, the professionals asserted that they were helpless to act differently – not because of any limitations of their own but because of the limitations of others.

The manager listened carefully to the team members and tried to respond to their criticisms. He talked about the mistakes that he had made during the consulting process. For example, one professional objected to the way the manager had run the project meetings. 'I see that the way I asked questions closed down discussions,' responded the manager. 'I didn't mean to do that, but I can see how you might have believed that I had already made up my mind.' Another team member complained that the manager had caved in to pressure from his superior to produce the project report far too quickly, considering the team's heavy work load. 'I think that it was my responsibility to have said no,' admitted the manager. 'It was clear that we all had an immense amount of work.'

Finally, after some three hours of discussion about his own behavior, the manager began to ask the team members if there were any errors *they* might have made. 'After all,' he said, 'this client was not different from many others. How can we be more effective in the future?'

The professionals repeated that it was really the clients' and their own managers' fault. As one put it, 'They have to be open to change and want to learn.' The more the manager tried to get the team to examine its own responsibility for the outcome, the more the professionals bypassed his concerns. The best one team member could suggest was for the case team to 'promise less' – implying that there was really no way for the group to improve its performance.

The case team members were reacting defensively to protect themselves, even though their manager was not acting in ways that an outsider would consider threatening. Even if there were some truth to their charges – the clients may well have been arrogant and closed, their own managers distant – the *way* they presented these claims was guaranteed to stop learning. With few exceptions, the professionals made attributions about the behavior of the clients and the managers but never publicly tested their claims. For instance, they said that the clients weren't motivated to learn but never really presented any evidence supporting that assertion. When their lack of concrete evidence was pointed out to them, they simply repeated their criticisms more vehemently.

If the professionals had felt so strongly about these issues, why had they never mentioned them during the project? According to the professionals, even this was the fault of others. 'We didn't want to alienate the client,' argued one. 'We didn't want to be seen as whining,' said another.

The professionals were using their criticisms of others to protect themselves from the potential embarrassment of having to admit that perhaps they too had contributed to the team's less-than-perfect performance. What's more, the fact that they kept repeating their defensive actions in the face of the manager's efforts to turn the group's attention to its own role shows that this defensiveness had become a reflexive routine. From the professionals' perspective, they weren't resisting; they were focusing on the 'real' causes. Indeed, they were to be respected, if not congratulated, for working as well as they did under such difficult conditions.

The end result was an unproductive parallel conversation. Both the manager and the professionals were candid; they expressed their views forcefully. But they talked past each other, never finding a common language to describe what had happened with the client. The professionals kept insisting that the fault lay with others. The manager kept trying, unsuccessfully, to get the professionals to see how they contributed to the state of affairs they were criticizing. The dialogue of this parallel conversation looks like this:

*Professionals*: 'The clients have to be open. They must want to change.'

*Manager*: 'It's our task to help them see that change is in their interest.'

*Professionals*: 'But the clients didn't agree with our analyses.'

*Manager*: 'If they didn't think our ideas were right, how might we have convinced them?'

*Professionals*: 'Maybe we need to have more meetings with the client.'

*Manager*: 'If we aren't adequately prepared and if the clients don't think we're credible, how will more meetings help?'

*Professionals*: 'There should be better communication between case team members and management.'

*Manager*: 'I agree. But professionals should take the initiative to educate the manager about the problems they are experiencing.'

*Professionals*: 'Our leaders are unavailable and distant.'

*Manager*: 'How do you expect us to know that if you don't tell us?'

Conversations such as this one dramatically illustrate the learning dilemma. The problem with the professionals' claims is not that they are wrong but that they aren't useful. By constantly turning the focus away from their own behavior to that of others, the professionals bring learning to a grinding halt. The manager understands the trap but does not know how to get out of it. To learn how to do that requires going deeper into the dynamics of defensive reasoning – and into the special causes that make professionals so prone to it.

# Defensive reasoning and the doom loop

What explains the professionals' defensiveness? Not their attitudes about change or commitment to continuous improvement; they really wanted to work more effectively. Rather, the key factor is the way they reasoned about their behavior and that of others.

It is impossible to reason anew in every situation. If we had to think through all the possible responses every time someone asked, 'How are you?' the world would pass us by. Therefore, everyone develops a theory of action – a set of rules that individuals use to design and implement their own behavior as well as to understand the behavior of others. Usually, these theories of actions become so taken for granted that people don't even realize they are using them.

One of the paradoxes of human behavior, however, is that the master program people actually use is rarely the one they think they use. Ask people in an interview or questionnaire to articulate the rules they use to govern their actions, and they will give you what I call their 'espoused' theory of action. But observe these same people's behavior, and you will quickly see that this espoused theory has very little to do with how they actually behave. For example, the professionals on the case team said they believed in continuous improvement, and yet they consistently acted in ways that made improvement impossible.

When you observe people's behavior and try to come up with rules that would make sense of it, you discover a very different theory of action – what I call the individual's 'theory-in-use.' Put simply, people consistently act inconsistently, unaware of the contradiction between their espoused theory and their theory-in-use, between the way they think they are acting and the way they really act.

What's more, most theories-in-use rest on the same set of governing values. There seems to be a universal human tendency to design one's actions consistently according to four basic values:

1 To remain in unilateral control;
2 To maximize 'winning' and minimize 'losing';
3 To suppress negative feelings; and
4 To be as 'rational' as possible – by which people mean defining clear objectives and evaluating their behavior in terms of whether or not they have achieved them.

The purpose of all these values is to avoid embarrassment or threat, feeling vulnerable or incompetent. In this respect, the master program that most people use is profoundly defensive. Defensive reasoning encourages individuals to keep private the premises, inferences, and conclusions that shape their behavior and to avoid testing them in a truly independent, objective fashion.

Because the attributions that go into defensive reasoning are never really tested, it is a closed loop, remarkably impervious to conflicting points of view. The inevitable response to the observation that somebody is reasoning defensively is yet more defensive reasoning. With the case team, for example, whenever anyone pointed out the professionals' defensive behavior to them, their initial reaction was to look for the cause in somebody else – clients who were so sensitive that they would have been alienated if the consultants had criticized them or a manager so weak that he couldn't have taken it had the consultants raised their concerns with him. In other words, the case team members once again denied their own responsibility by externalizing the problem and putting it on someone else.

In such situations, the simple act of encouraging more open inquiry is often attacked by others as 'intimidating'. Those who do the attacking deal with their feelings about possibly being wrong by blaming the more open individual for arousing these feelings and upsetting them.

Needless to say, such a master program inevitably short-circuits learning. And for a number of reasons unique to their psychology, well-educated professionals are especially susceptible to this.

Nearly all the consultants I have studied have stellar academic records. Ironically, their very success at education helps explain the problems they have with learning. Before they enter the world of work, their lives are primarily full of successes, so they have rarely experienced the embarrassment and sense of threat that comes with failure. As a result, their defensive reasoning has rarely been activated. People who rarely experience failure, however, end up not knowing how to deal with it effectively. And this serves to reinforce the normal human tendency to reason defensively.

In a survey of several hundred young consultants at the organizations I have been studying, these professionals describe themselves as driven internally by an unrealistically high ideal of performance: 'Pressure on the job is self-imposed.' 'I must not only do a good job; I must also be the best.' 'People around here are very bright and hardworking; they are highly motivated to do an outstanding job.' 'Most of us want not only to succeed but also to do so at maximum speed.'

These consultants are always comparing themselves with the best around them and constantly trying to better their own performance. And yet they do not appreciate being required to compete openly with each other. They feel it is somehow inhumane. They prefer to be the individual contributor – what might be termed a 'productive loner.'

Behind this high aspiration for success is an equally high fear of failure and a propensity to feel shame and guilt when they do fail to meet their high standards. 'You must avoid mistakes,' said one. 'I hate making them. Many of us fear failure, whether we admit it or not.'

To the extent that these consultants have experienced success in their lives, they have not had to be concerned about failure and the attendant feelings of shame and guilt. But to exactly the same extent, they also have never developed the tolerance for feelings of failure or the skills to deal with these feelings. This in turn has led them not only to fear failure but also to fear the fear of failure itself. For they know that they will not cope with it superlatively – their usual level of aspiration.

The consultants use two intriguing metaphors to describe this phenomenon. They talk about the 'doom loop' and 'doom zoom.' Often, consultants will perform well on the case team, but because they don't do the jobs perfectly or receive accolades from their managers, they go into a doom loop of despair. And they don't ease into the doom loop, they zoom into it.

As a result, many professionals have extremely 'brittle' personalities. When suddenly faced with a situation they cannot immediately handle, they tend to fall apart. They cover up their distress in front of the client. They talk about it constantly with their fellow case team members. Interestingly, these conversations commonly take the form of bad-mouthing clients.

Such brittleness leads to an inappropriately high sense of despondency or even despair when people don't achieve the high levels of performance they aspire to. Such despondency is rarely psychologically devastating, but when combined with defensive reasoning, it can result in a formidable predisposition against learning.

There is no better example of how this brittleness can disrupt an organization than performance evaluations. Because it represents the one moment when a professional must measure his or her own behavior against some formal standard, a performance evaluation is almost tailor-made to push a professional into the doom loop. Indeed, a poor evaluation can reverberate far beyond the particular individual involved to spark defensive reasoning throughout an entire organization.

At one consulting company, management established a new performance-evaluation process that was designed to make evaluations both more objective and more useful to those being evaluated. The consultants participated in the design of the new system and in general were enthusiastic because it corresponded to their espoused values of objectivity and fairness. A brief two years into the new process, however, it had become the object of dissatisfaction. The catalyst for this about-face was the first unsatisfactory rating.

Senior managers had identified six consultants whose performance they considered below standard. In keeping with the new evaluation process, they did all they could to communicate their concerns to the six and to help them improve. Managers met with each individual separately for as long and as often as the professional requested to explain the reasons behind the rating and to discuss what needed to be done to improve – but to no avail. Performance continued at the same low level and, eventually, the six were let go.

When word of the dismissal spread through the company, people responded with confusion and anxiety. After about a dozen consultants angrily complained to management, the CEO held two lengthy meetings where employees could air their concerns.

At the meetings, the professionals made a variety of claims. Some said the performance-evaluation process was unfair because judgments were subjective and biased and the criteria for minimum performance unclear. Others suspected that the real cause for the dismissals was economic and that the performance-evaluation procedure was just a fig leaf to hide the fact that the company was in trouble. Still others argued that the evaluation process was antilearning. If the company were truly a learning organization, as it claimed, then people performing below the minimum standard should be taught how to reach it. As one professional put it: 'We were told that the company did not have an up-or-out policy. Up-or-out is inconsistent with learning. You misled us.'

The CEO tried to explain the logic behind management's decision by grounding it in the facts of the case and by asking the professionals for any evidence that might contradict these facts.

Is there subjectivity and bias in the evaluation process? Yes, responded the CEO, but 'we strive hard to reduce them. We are constantly trying to improve the process. If you have any ideas, please tell us. If you know of someone treated unfairly, please bring it up. If any of you feel that you have been treated unfairly, let's discuss it now or, if you wish, privately.'

Is the level of minimum competence too vague? 'We are working to define minimum competence more clearly,' he answered. 'In the case of the six, however, their performance was so poor that it wasn't difficult to reach a decision.' Most of the six had received timely feedback about their problems. And in the two cases where people had not, the reason was that they had never taken the responsibility to seek out evaluations – and, indeed, had actively avoided them. 'If you have any data to the contrary,' the CEO added, 'let's talk about it.'

Were the six asked to leave for economic reasons? No, said the CEO. 'We have more work than we can do, and letting professionals go is extremely costly for us. Do any of you have any information to the contrary?'

As to the company being antilearning, in fact, the entire evaluation process was designed to encourage learning. When a professional is performing below the minimum level, the CEO explained, 'we jointly design remedial experiences with the individual. Then we look for signs of improvement. In these cases, either the professionals were reluctant to take on such assignments or they repeatedly failed when they did. Again, if you have information or evidence to the contrary, I'd like to hear about it.'

The CEO concluded: 'It's regrettable, but sometimes we make mistakes and hire the wrong people. If individuals don't produce and repeatedly prove themselves unable to improve, we don't know what else to do except dismiss them. It's just not fair to keep poorly performing individuals in the company. They earn an unfair share of the financial rewards.'

Instead of responding with data of their own, the professionals simply repeated their accusations but in ways that consistently contradicted their claims. They said that a genuinely fair evaluation process would contain clear and documentable data about performance – but they were unable to provide first-hand examples of the unfairness that they implied colored the evaluation of the six dismissed employees. They argued that people shouldn't be judged by inferences unconnected to their actual performance – but they judged management in precisely this way. They insisted that management define clear, objective, and unambiguous performance standards – but they argued that any humane system would take into account that the performance of a professional cannot be precisely measured. Finally, they presented themselves as champions of learning – but they never proposed any criteria for assessing whether an individual might be unable to learn.

In short, the professionals seemed to hold management to a different level of performance than they held themselves. In their conversation at the meetings, they used many of the features of ineffective evaluation that they condemned – the absence of concrete data, for example, and the dependence on a circular logic of 'heads we win, tails you lose.' It is as if they were saying, 'Here are the features of a fair performance-evaluation system. You should abide by them. But we don't have to when we are evaluating you.'

Indeed, if we were to explain the professionals' behavior by articulating rules that would have to be in their heads in order for them to act the way they did, the rules would look something like this:

1  When criticizing the company, state your criticism in ways that you believe are valid – but also in ways that prevent others from deciding for themselves whether your claim to validity is correct.
2  When asked to illustrate your criticisms, don't include any data that others could use to decide for themselves whether the illustrations are valid.
3  State your conclusions in ways that disguise their logical implications. If others point out those implications to you, deny them.

Of course, when such rules were described to the professionals, they found them abhorrent. It was inconceivable that these rules might explain their actions. And yet in defending themselves against this observation, they almost always inadvertently confirmed the rules.

## Learning how to reason productively

If defensive reasoning is as widespread as I believe, then focusing on an individual's attitudes or commitment is never enough to produce real change. And as the previous example illustrates, neither is creating new organizational structures or systems. The problem is that even when people are genuinely committed to improving their performance and management has changed its structures in order to encourage the 'right' kind of behavior, people still remain locked in defensive reasoning. Either they remain unaware of this fact, or if they do become aware of it, they blame others.

There is, however, reason to believe that organizations can break out of this vicious circle. Despite the strength of defensive reasoning, people genuinely strive to produce what they intend. They value acting competently. Their self-esteem is intimately tied up with behaving consistently and performing effect-ively. Companies can use these universal human tendencies to teach people how to reason in a new way – in effect, to change the master programs in their heads and thus reshape their behavior.

People can be taught how to recognize the reasoning they use when they design and implement their actions. They can begin to identify the inconsistencies between their espoused and actual theories of action. They can face up to the fact that they unconsciously design and implement actions that they do not intend. Finally, people can learn how to identify what individuals and groups do to create organizational defenses and how these defenses contribute to an organization's problems.

Once companies embark on this learning process, they will discover that the kind of reasoning necessary to reduce and overcome organizational defenses is the same kind of 'tough reasoning' that underlies the effective use of ideas in strategy, finance, marketing, manufacturing, and other management discip-lines. Any sophisticated strategic analysis, for example, depends on collecting valid data, analyzing it carefully, and constantly testing the inferences drawn from the data. The toughest tests are reserved for the conclusions. Good strat-egists make sure that their conclusions can withstand all kinds of critical questioning.

So too with productive reasoning about human behavior. The standard of analysis is just as high. Human resource programs no longer need to be based on "soft" reasoning but should be as analytical and as data-driven as any other management discipline.

Of course, that is not the kind of reasoning the consultants used when they encountered problems that were embarrassing or threatening. The data they collected was hardly objective. The inferences they made rarely became explicit. The conclusions they reached were largely self-serving, impossible for others to test, and as a result, 'self-sealing,' impervious to change.

How can an organization begin to turn this situation around, to teach its members how to reason productively? The first step is for managers at the top to examine critically and change their own theories-in-use. Until senior man-agers become aware of how they reason defensively and the counterproductive consequences that result, there will be little real progress. Any change activity is likely to be just a fad.

Change has to start at the top because otherwise defensive senior managers are likely to disown any transformation in reasoning patterns coming from below. If professionals or middle managers begin to change the way they reason and act, such changes are likely to appear strange – if not actually dangerous –

to those at the top. The result is an unstable situation where senior managers still believe that it is a sign of caring and sensitivity to bypass and cover up difficult issues, while their subordinates see the very same actions as defensive.

The key to any educational experience designed to teach senior managers how to reason productively is to connect the program to real business problems. The best demonstration of the usefulness of productive reasoning is for busy managers to see how it can make a direct difference in their own performance and in that of the organization. This will not happen overnight. Managers need plenty of opportunity to practise the new skills. But once they grasp the powerful impact that productive reasoning can have on actual performance, they will have a strong incentive to reason productively not just in a training session but in all their work relationships.

One simple approach I have used to get this process started is to have participants produce a kind of rudimentary case study. The subject is a real business problem that the manager either wants to deal with or has tried unsuccessfully to address in the past. Writing the actual case usually takes less than an hour. But then the case becomes the focal point of an extended analysis.

For example, a CEO at a large organizational-development consulting company was preoccupied with the problems caused by the intense competition among the various business functions represented by his four direct reports. Not only was he tired of having the problems dumped in his lap, but he was also worried about the impact the interfunctional conflicts were having on the organization's flexibility. He had even calculated that the money being spent to iron out disagreements amounted to hundreds of thousands of dollars every year. And the more fights there were, the more defensive people became, which only increased the costs to the organization.

In a paragraph or so, the CEO described a meeting he intended to have with his direct reports to address the problem. Next, he divided the paper in half, and on the right-hand side of the page, he wrote a scenario for the meeting – much like the script for a movie or play – describing what he would say and how his subordinates would likely respond. On the left-hand side of the page, he wrote down any thoughts and feelings that he would be likely to have during the meeting but that he wouldn't express for fear they would derail the discussion.

But instead of holding the meeting, the CEO analyzed this scenario *with* his direct reports. The case became the catalyst for a discussion in which the CEO learned several things about the way he acted with his management team.

He discovered that his four direct reports often perceived his conversations as counterproductive. In the guise of being 'diplomatic,' he would pretend that a consensus about the problem existed, when in fact none existed. The unintended result: instead of feeling reassured, his subordinates felt wary and tried to figure out 'what is he *really* getting at.'

The CEO also realized that the way he dealt with the competitiveness among department heads was completely contradictory. On the one hand, he kept urging them to 'think of the organization as a whole.' On the other, he kept calling for actions – department budget cuts, for example – that placed them directly in competition with each other.

Finally, the CEO discovered that many of the tacit evaluations and attributions he had listed turned out to be wrong. Since he had never expressed these assumptions, he had never found out just how wrong they were. What's more, he learned that much of what he thought he was hiding came through to his subordinates anyway – but with the added message that the boss was covering up.

The CEO's colleagues also learned about their own ineffective behavior. They learned by examining their own behavior as they tried to help the CEO analyze his case. They also learned by writing and analyzing cases of their own. They began to see that they too tended to bypass and cover up the real issues and that the CEO was often aware of it but did not say so. They too made inaccurate attributions and evaluations that they did not express. Moreover, the belief that they had to hide important ideas and feelings from the CEO and from each other in order not to upset anyone turned out to be mistaken. In the context of the case discussions, the entire senior management team was quite willing to discuss what had always been undiscussable.

In effect, the case study exercise legitimizes talking about issues that people have never been able to address before. Such a discussion can be emotional – even painful. But for managers with the courage to persist, the payoff is great: management teams and entire organizations work more openly and more effectively and have greater options for behaving flexibly and adapting to particular situations.

When senior managers are trained in new reasoning skills, they can have a big impact on the performance of the entire organization – even when other employees are still reasoning defensively. The CEO who led the meetings on the performance-evaluation procedure was able to defuse dissatisfaction because he didn't respond to professionals' criticisms in kind but instead gave a clear presentation of relevant data. Indeed, most participants took the CEO's behavior to be a sign that the company really acted on the values of participation and employee involvement that it espoused.

Of course, the ideal is for all the members of an organization to learn how to reason productively. This has happened at the company where the case team meeting took place. Consultants and their managers are now able to confront some of the most difficult issues of the consultant-client relationship. To get a sense of the difference productive reasoning can make, imagine how the original conversation between the manager and case team might have gone had everyone engaged in effective reasoning. (The following dialogue is based on actual sessions I have attended with other case teams at the same company since the training has been completed.)

First, the consultants would have demonstrated their commitment to continuous improvement by being willing to examine their own role in the difficulties that arose during the consulting project. No doubt they would have identified their managers and the clients as part of the problem, but they would have gone on to admit that they had contributed to it as well. More important, they would have agreed with the manager that as they explored the various roles of clients, managers, and professionals, they would make sure to test any evaluations or attributions they might make against the data. Each individual would have encouraged the others to question his or her reasoning. Indeed, they would have insisted on it. And in turn, everyone would have understood that act of questioning not as a sign of mistrust or an invasion of privacy but as a valuable opportunity for learning.

The conversation about the manager's unwillingness to say no might look something like this:

*Professional #1*: 'One of the biggest problems I had with the way you managed this case was that you seemed to be unable to say no when either the client or your superior made unfair demands.' [Gives an example.]

*Professional #2*: 'I have another example to add. [Describes a second example.] But I'd also like to say that we never really told you how we felt about this. Behind your back we were bad-mouthing you – you know, "he's being such a wimp" – but we never came right out and said it.'

*Manager*: 'It certainly would have been helpful if you had said something. Was there anything I said or did that gave you the idea that you had better not raise this with me?'

*Professional #3*: 'Not really. I think we didn't want to sound like we were whining.'

*Manager*: 'Well, I certainly don't think you sound like you're whining. But two thoughts come to mind. If I understand you correctly, you *were* complaining, but the complaining about me and my inability to say no was covered up. Second, if we had discussed this, I might have gotten the data I needed to be able to say no.'

Notice that when the second professional describes how the consultants had covered up their complaints, the manager doesn't criticize her. Rather, he rewards her for being open by responding in kind. He focuses on the ways that he too may have contributed to the cover-up. Reflecting undefensively about his own role in the problem then makes it possible for the professionals to talk about their fears of appearing to be whining. The manager then agrees with the professionals that they shouldn't become complainers. At the same time, he points out the counterproductive consequences of covering up their complaints.

Another unresolved issue in the case team meeting concerned the supposed arrogance of the clients. A more productive conversation about that problem might go like this:

*Manager*: 'You said that the clients were arrogant and uncooperative. What did they say and do?'

*Professional #1*: 'One asked me if I had ever met a payroll. Another asked how long I've been out of school.'

*Professional #2*: 'One even asked me how old I was!'

*Professional #3*: 'That's nothing. The worst is when they say that all we do is interview people, write a report based on what they tell us, and then collect our fees.'

*Manager*: 'The fact that we tend to be so young is a real problem for many of our clients. They get very defensive about it. But I'd like to explore whether there is a way for them to freely express their views without our getting defensive.

'What troubled me about your original responses was that you assumed you were right in calling the clients stupid. One thing I've noticed about consultants – in this company and others – is that we tend to defend ourselves by bad-mouthing the client.'

*Professional #1*: 'Right. After all, if they are genuinely stupid, then it's obviously not our fault that they aren't getting it!'

*Professional #2*: 'Of course, that stance is anti-learning and overprotective. By assuming that they can't learn, we absolve ourselves from having to.'

*Professional #3*: 'And the more we all go along with the bad-mouthing, the more we reinforce each other's defensiveness.'

*Manager*: 'So what's the alternative? How can we encourage our clients to express their defensiveness and at the same time constructively build on it?'

*Professional #1*: 'We all know that the real issue isn't our age; it's whether or not we are able to add value to the client's organization. They should judge us by what we produce. And if we aren't adding value, they should get rid of us – no matter how young or old we happen to be.'

*Manager*: 'Perhaps that is exactly what we should tell them.'

In both these examples, the consultants and their manager are doing real work. They are learning about their own group dynamics and addressing some generic problems in client-consultant relationships. The insights they gain will allow them to act more effectively in the future – both as individuals and as a team. They are not just solving problems but developing a far deeper and more textured understanding of their role as members of the organization. They are laying the groundwork for continuous improvement that is truly continuous. They are learning how to learn.

# 15   Vicious circles[1]

## *M. Masuch*

## Introduction

Today, most social scientists agree on the nature of social systems. They contend that neither Divine Will, nor legal statutes, nor the assemblage of architectural artifacts is sufficient to keep such systems alive. They hold that human activity determines the character and behavior of these systems. The first to express this view clearly was Max Weber (1947), who insisted that any specifically social phenomenon should be understood as a network of individual yet reciprocal human actions. Parsons (1937), dubbing this approach 'action theory,' showed that the same view was implicitly present in the writings of Weber's major contemporaries such as Durkheim, Pareto, and Marshall. He suggested that this convergence may reflect some fundamental truth that manifests itself in any serious thinking about societies. And even today, while many social scientists agree to disagree, most of them, regardless of their paradigm, still stick to the action perspective.[2]

Unfortunately, it has proven difficult to apply this view consistently to organizations or other social systems. It often appears impossible to trace the behavior of such systems back to the actions of individuals. The problem, sometimes referred to as 'the transformation problem,' is rooted in the intentionality of individual actions. Supposedly, individuals act with some degree of purpose, yet the sum total of their interactions is often at variance with their intentions. In short, their activities have side effects. Such side effects may create nothing but random outcomes. Frequently, however, social systems display regularities that make little sense in terms of individual intentions. Side effects sometimes follow a logic of their own (Platt, 1973; Boudon, 1977, 1981;

[1] This is a revision of a paper presented at the 78th Annual Meeting of the American Sociological Association, Detroit, September 1983. The author gratefully acknowledges comments on earlier drafts by J. Bonomo, M. Ellman, D. Garling, P. de Greef, J. Goudsblom, R. D. Hall, T. Korver, A. Mowitz, N. Luhmann, D. Pels. C. Perrow, D. L. Phillips, A. de Swaan, A. Teulings, and S. Udy.
[2] Action theory is evident in the systems theory of Luhmann (1982), in Schutz's (1967) phenomenology, in Habermas' (1984) critical theory, in the symbolic interactionism of Blumer (1969), and in Giddens' (1979) post-Marxism.

Schelling, 1978; Elster, 1980). They are in concert, although neither a conductor nor a score appears to be present.

Side effects are not necessarily undesirable – the marketplace, for example, has proven a superb orchestra in transforming private vices into public virtues – but frequently they are. Business cycles upset economies and economists alike. Arms races accelerate. Many organizations decline or underperform consistently. Some hidden score is present, but it is not the request program that is played. Yet, whose program is it? How is it possible that human beings can act purposefully in ways that frustrate their purposes?

Metaphysical approaches aside, two answers are possible. People ask for too much, or they don't know what they are doing. In the first case, they cling to standards of desired outcomes that are unattainable. Their 'normative expectations' (Luhmann, 1972) are unrealistic. In the second case, however, they do have more promising alternatives. They *should* do better because the outcomes are (partially) undesired; they *could* do better because better alternatives are available; and they are *trying* to do better because their actions are held to be purposeful, thus rational. But they don't do better. They are somehow trapped in the web of their own actions. The hidden score is their own, but they don't like the music. Unable to stop, they play the unpleasant tune over and over again.

The emerging picture begins to resemble a vicious circle. By trying to avoid undesired outcomes, human actors actually create these outcomes. And by continuing their activities, they continue to reproduce those undesired outcomes. Understanding the logic of vicious circles should therefore increase the understanding of undesired organizational behavior (as well as the behavior of other social systems) and possibly help to improve it.

## Action loops and vicious circles

The singular human act, or 'unit act,' is usually regarded as the basic element of a social system (Parsons, 1937). It comprises an individual actor, a situation to act upon, the actor's purpose, and the activity itself. In pursuing his or her purpose, the actor may behave more or less consciously, although not every singular act coincides with the ideal of rational action, i.e., action that follows the logic of optimal choice. Irrational action, on the other hand, is absurd from the point of view of the individual actor, since it implies the paradox of someone purposefully frustrating his or her own purpose.

A singular act brings change. By changing a given situation, however, a unit act does not yield the structure necessary to build a social system. To create a structure, actions have to be repeated (Weick, 1969). A change, generated by a single act, has to be neutralized by a counterchange that reproduces the original situation. In short, the basic element of any action structure is the action loop, not the singular act. An action loop occurs when an activity entails a chain of other activities which, in turn, ultimately re-create the original situation. With the re-creation of the original situation, the loop can repeat itself, and a network of activities can emerge that can develop and maintain its own identity in a given environment. Such networks are here understood as systems. The foremost example of social systems are formal organizations (Parsons, 1956; Katz and Kahn, 1966; Thompson, 1967; Pfeffer and Salancik, 1978).

The theoretical analysis of action loops has primarily been undertaken in cybernetics (for an overview, see Richardson, 1983), where they are referred to as feedback loops. Feedback loops are action loops that are either approaching some arbitrary reference point or moving away from that point. Usually, they are called negative or positive feedback loops, depending on whether they are moving away from or approaching the reference point. The reference point itself can be determined in two different ways: by making value judgments (i.e., by defining some desired standard) or by assessing facts (i.e., by referring to some factual state of affairs). Some additional terminology may help to make the point more explicit. Negative feedback loops are called 'deviation-counteracting' when related to normative standards and 'self-correcting' when related to a factual point of reference. Positive feedback loops, on the other hand, are called 'deviation-amplifying' when related to norms and 'self-reinforcing' when related to facts (Figure 1). Predator-prey interaction is self-correcting, for example, whereas a nuclear chain reaction is self-reinforcing. A runaway nuclear arms race is deviation-amplifying (if peace is the normative point of reference), whereas successful arms talks are deviation-counteracting, given the same point of reference (see Figure 2). In this paper, vicious circles are defined as deviation-amplifying loops, i.e., action loops with counterproductive results.

Factual and normative behavior of action loops often coincide, but not always. A desired state of affairs can also reflect change, as economic growth does, for instance (Kuhn and Beam, 1982). On the other hand, some deviation-amplifying loops are self-correcting. For example, zero growth in an

|  | **Point of reference** | |
|  | Normative | Factual |
| --- | --- | --- |
| Positive movement | Deviation-amplifying loop | Self-reinforcing loop |
| Negative movement | Deviation-counteracting loop | Self-correcting loop |

**Figure 1.** Positive and negative feedback loops

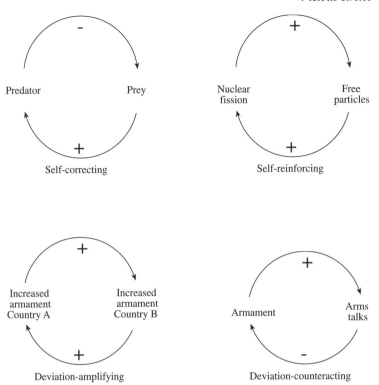

**Figure 2.** Examples of positive and negative feedback loops

**Feedback**

|  | Deviation-amplifying | Deviation-counteracting |
|---|---|---|
| Self-reinforcing feedback | Undesired change (crisis) | Desired change (development) |
| Self-correcting feedback | Undesired performance (stagnation) | Desired performance (stability) |

**Figure 3.** Typology of factual and normative aspects of action loops.

economy is usually assessed as stagnation, as a self-correcting process that deviates more and more from the desired path of expansion. The cross-tabulation of the factual and the normative aspects of action loops yields the simple typology illustrated in Figure 3. Note that although two kinds of deviation-amplifying loops are distinguished here, only one of them ('crisis') exhibits the typical features of such a loop. The other one ('stagnation') may be hidden under the surface of factual inertia.

Whether an action loop has the properties of a vicious circle depends on the normative point of reference. A clear-cut identification of an action loop as a vicious circle presupposes the opportunity to state clearly what the purpose of an action is and who is justified to make such statements. Many actions, however, are not accompanied by goal statements; many goals are not clearly stated; many statements are not clearly justified; and too many people make too many different statements. Economic growth, for example, may be welcomed by those who fear unemployment, while environmentalists may disapprove of it. In addition, the evaluation of any activity in normative terms is a matter of judging the judgment of those who participate in that particular activity. One may even ask whether a vicious circle could continue to exist were it known to its participants.

Unfortunately, little can be done about these ambiguities. Any classification of an action loop remains somewhat arbitrary, depending on which and how many actors are involved, how conflicting their goals are, and other factors. There are, nevertheless, many instances in which the counterproductivity of a feedback loop is hardly disputable.

## Dynamics of vicious circles

Vicious circles are usually conceived as spiraling processes, like Merton's (1957) famous 'tragic circle of self-fulfilling prophecy.' In times of crisis, rumors cause nervous clients to rush to the counters of a bank. Its liquidity is endangered as more and more clients become more and more nervous. Finally, bankruptcy is imminent. The vicious circle involved describes the interaction between two variables that are crucial for the organization's survival: trust and cash flow. The bank needs the trust of its depositors, since its operation is based on the principle of lending out the deposits. But it also needs a certain amount of cash in order to meet the actual demand for liquidity that the depositors may have.

Initially, trust and cash flow may be sufficient to keep the system in equilibrium and to prevent a significant number of clients from panicking. As the general economic condition deteriorates, however, the likelihood increases that rumors may be taken seriously. A critical threshold may be crossed sooner or later. Then, a contracting circle sets off. Declining trust leads to a smaller cash flow, which, in turn, reduces the level of trust further, and so on. Ultimately, trust as well as cash flow are reduced to zero and the bank is forced out of business. Unless brought to a halt by exogenous forces, all contracting circles will display the same self-terminating dynamic. Once set in motion, a decrease in one variable will cause similar decreases in other variables. Once the critical threshold is crossed, nothing can stop contracting circles. They are bound to a self-terminating dynamic.

Expanding circles have a different dynamic. Their growth depends on itera-tively increasing variables. This process has to be fed by outside resources, yet resources are scarce in a finite world. Eventually, every expanding circle will reach a ceiling when no additional resources are available to feed further expansion (Mazur, 1978). Borrowing from the jargon of economics, one might say that the marginal causality of an expansive loop will decline past a certain point to become zero in the end.

An example of the dynamics of expanding vicious circles can be seen in the 'vicious circle of bureaucracy,' the only deviation-amplifying feedback that has been extensively examined in the literature. Originally discovered by Merton (1957), it has been subsequently discussed and refined by such authors as Gouldner (1954), Argyris (1957, 1964), March and Simon (1958), Thompson (1961), Crozier (1964), Downs (1967), Lawler (1976), and Dunbar (1981), among others. The circle has the following general shape. The management of an organization attempts to bring about some change, such as raising product-ivity. It does so by rule making, close supervision, or other bureaucratic meas-ures – in short, by increasing formalization. Instead of helping the organization reach its goal, these measures trigger apathy, alienation, or other dysfunctional reactions in the work force. Management, unsatisfied with the results but unaware of the real causality, further increases the pressure on the system, and around comes the circle.

At some point, however, management will have exhausted its repertoire of control techniques, and the circle slows down. The prevailing apathy is 'walled in' (Gouldner, 1954), and the system gets 'blocked' (Crozier, 1964). Finally, the circle stagnates. The circle is nevertheless still active. Control measures are constantly enacted, as is apathy. The circle has become a normal, yet sub-optimal state of affairs. Acquiescing, the organization goes Sisyphus.

The vicious circle of bureaucracy is not the only stagnating circle that upsets organizations. Four other well-known organizational pathologies also illustrate this point.

*Pathological status systems* (Barnard, 1946; Türk, 1975; Neuberger and Duffy, 1976). Organizations make use of status systems in order to induce high performance. Once granted, a given status is not easily revoked, how-ever. Additional status stimuli are created and status inflation results. The meaning of status decreases, until the status system has lost its stimulating function.

*Pathological communication systems* (Downs, 1967; Altheide and Johnson, 1980; Fischhoff, 1982; Wildavsky, 1983). Information becomes biased while floating up the organization's hierarchy. Counterbiasing techniques are applied to compensate for that tendency. This evokes additional biasing as well as counterbiasing. Officially reported information loses its significance, and the organization falls back on rumors and other intelligence techniques to gather information.

*Pathological growth* (Parkinson, 1958; Downs, 1967; Breton and Wintrobe, 1982). Administrative units in organizations expand due to Parkinson's Law (bureaucrats tend to multiply subordinates, not rivals, and make work for each other). As the organization grows top-heavy, further expansion is increasingly difficult to support. Ultimately, a ceiling on size is attained. Buchanan and Tullock (1977) have pointed out that the same logic may also apply on a macroscale. While growing, public bureaucracies may absorb more and more resources until taxpayers finally run out of money.

*Pathological conflict* (Vickers, 1968; Reich, 1981; Masuch, 1984). Bureaucratic activities (e.g., regulation) trigger the installation of counterbureaucracies. The conflict seesaws, until all bureaucratic energy is absorbed and further escalation becomes impossible.

These pathologies suggest that stagnating vicious circles are not infrequent in social systems. Such a statement is hard to verify empirically, but it follows analytically from the implications of the action perspective. Action structures are reproductive, by definition. Consequently, any nuisance that is not simply a passing problem, but is a structural suboptimality (e.g., overbureaucratization, overcentralization, underdevlopment), is also reproduced. Since suboptimality cannot, by definition, be intended, any structural suboptimality must somehow be based on stable vicious circles.

# Vicious circles in combination

Within social systems, action loops are embedded in a network of other action loops; stagnating circles even depend, in a paradoxical sense, on their environment for survival. There is an infinite variety of possible combinations of action loops, but two elementary clusters can be singled out.

## Explosive clusters

Explosive clusters combine two or more positive feedbacks, at least one of which is deviation-amplifying. Parkinson's law illustrates the most simple case in which two circles (bureaucrats multiply bureaucrats, and bureaucrats make work for each other) reinforce each other. Yet, explosive clusters are not restricted to such simple combinations.

In the case of a declining university, as discussed by Cyert (1978), the organization faces decreasing growth rates. This reduces promotion opportunities within the organization and weakens its attractiveness to outstanding new participants (the first vicious circle). Quality inside the organization declines, so that the organization is forced to look elsewhere in order to fulfill the few top positions, thus decreasing promotion opportunities further (a second circle). The organization cannot maintain the former standards of excellence and loses students (a third circle). More financial problems creep up and are dealt with by raising tuition and reducing salaries. Two additional circles (four and five) are thus triggered: more students stay away, while more good faculty members depart for better positions elsewhere. The explosion – or, more precisely, the implosion of vicious circles – may eventually lead to the actual collapse of the organization.

Organizations of somewhat longer standing usually possess considerable reserve buffers, slack, emergency procedures, and the like to weather the storms of organizational life. They do not walk a tightrope. However, their deviation-counteracting capacity is not unlimited. If a number of deviation-counteracting loops break down at the same time or if the pressure becomes too great, this capacity may be exhausted (Turner, 1976). Once a critical threshold is passed, one vicious circle gets its chance and triggers other circles, thereby exhausting whatever remains of the organization's resiliency. A 'vicious' chain reaction runs through the already scattered action structure and destroys it. In the disaster literature, this is termed 'nonlinearity' (Perrow, 1984).

All declining organizations must pass that threshold before they collapse, because the threshold is the point of no return. It is the dividing line between a situation in which rescue might still be possible and one in which it is too late. The existence of the threshold allows one to formulate a general survival condition for organizations. To avoid collapse, an organization must merely avoid reaching the threshold. In order to do so, the organization must perform three tasks: (1) identify the threshold condition, (2) identify possible dangers in the environment and their potential impact (i.e., the distance over which they may push the organization closer to that threshold), and (3) muster sufficient reserves to be able to buffer adverse effects.

The literature on organization failure shows that every collapsing organization has, in fact, violated at least one of these three conditions (Whetten, 1980; Greenhalgh, 1983). Either organizations have lost their capacity to identify hazards in a changing environment or they are no longer able to calculate the risks (i.e., the threshold condition) correctly (Aguilar, 1967; Hall, 1976; Starbuck, 1983). Or, they have not been able to muster sufficient buffers, which is the major cause for the 'liability of newness' of young organizations (Stinchcombe, 1965; Kaufman, 1975; Perrow, 1979). Or, they have inadvertently used up their buffer resources, for example, by engaging in a large high-risk development project (Argenti, 1976).

## Monitored clusters

Monitored clusters combine one or more deviation-amplifying circles with one or more negative feedbacks. Monitored clusters account for the existence of stagnating vicious circles. Such circles are, in fact, expanding loops that encounter one or more negative feedbacks during their career. The vicious circle of bureaucracy (Crozier, 1964; Vroom, 1980) illustrates this point. During its expanding phase, apathy increases along with the level of control. Past a certain point, however, additional control devices become scarce and a negative feedback is created. It puts a check on the circle's further expansion, as shown in Figure 4.

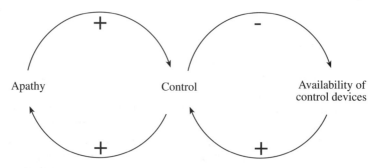

**Figure 4.** The vicious circle of bureaucracy

Scarce resources guarantee that any expanding loop will be brought to a halt, even without the purposeful interference of human actors. Such interference may nonetheless occur. The consequences of a circle may be perceived, while the cause, the circle itself, remains obscure. Measures are taken to keep the problem under control, but they do not really solve it. This is a classic case of treating the symptoms. A better cure could be administered were the true causality known to the participants.

A variant of the formalization loop is that analyzed by Argyris and Schön (1978) and Argyris (1982). Apathy is a problem, but its true cause remains undiscovered. Human relations devices are applied to counteract it and do yield some effect, so that the loop comes to a halt before management has exhausted the available instruments of control. Yet, the situation is suboptimal. A lower level of apathy could have been obtained more effectively by lowering the level of formalization than by the human relations treatment, as shown in Figure 5.

Because it represents in a nutshell the logic of irrational (i.e., unnecessary) conflict, one more specific form of monitored clusters should also be noted here. Such a cluster is created when a simple two-loop cluster triggers an additional negative loop (of ambiguous normative standing). Crozier's own interpretation of the 'vicious circle of bureaucracy,' as he labeled it, illustrates this possibility. He observed that in some organizations increased formalization reduces the elbow room of all participants, not solely that of the work force (Crozier, 1964, 1970). A third loop is created, once the workers or their unions discover the appeasing effect of high formalization. Then, the unions may push for even more formalization in order to restrict management's power, as illustrated in Figure 6.

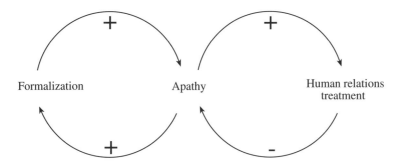

**Figure 5.** Variant of the formalization loop of bureaucracy

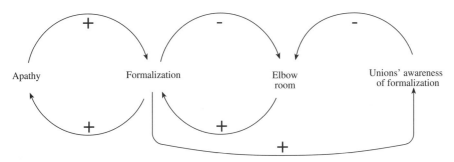

**Figure 6.** Irrational conflict: Crozier's 'blockage.'

Crozier used the term 'blockage' to describe this structure. The label is well chosen, since it conveys what the cluster does – or, more precisely, what it cannot do. The return to a more rational state of the system is blocked because the second, self-correcting circle obscures the effect of the first (vicious) one. The second circle misleads the participants to accept the present level of apathy as the bottom line. Aware of worse alternatives, but unaware of better ones, they start to defend the present suboptimal state of affairs and create the third circle. What is blocked is, in fact, the escape route to a better solution.

All elements of an irrational conflict are present (Dunbar, Dutton, and Torbert, 1982). In the first loop, inadequate understanding of the situation leads to irrational action and creates a potential for conflict. The second and the third loops then produce the stalemate: the second creates the illusion that things can only get worse, and a third circle is then created to prevent them from getting worse. But it also prevents things from getting better. The structure has provoked a cleavage of interest, so that one side (in this case, management or organized labor) is 'right,' under the assumption that the other side is 'wrong.' Both are wrong, though, because a better solution (in this case, higher productivity with less control) is attainable.

# Emergence and persistence of vicious circles

Vicious circles lead an absurd existence, since everyone should avoid deviation-amplifying feedbacks. Yet, once caught in a vicious circle, human actors continue on a path of action that leads further and further away from the desired state of affairs. Why this happens has already been suggested implicitly. Human actors create a vicious circle because they lack an adequate understanding of their situation. For example, were the managers in the vicious circle of bureaucracy aware of the counterproductive effects of overcontrol, they would pursue a different policy. But, instead, they cling to a machine model (March and Simon, 1958) of human behavior. Subordinates are treated like machines, but they don't react like machines. Not understanding the underlying causality, management continues on the once-chosen path, and the circle comes around again.

Whenever a single actor or a group, behaving virtually as one actor, is causing the circle and the counteraction necessary to complete it can be seen as reactive behavior, the deviation-amplifying feedback can be attributed to an inaccurate definition of the situation. If the actor were aware of the circle, he or she would prefer to avoid it and could do so either by doing nothing or by choosing a better available alternative.

The same holds for strategic interaction, that is, when the outcome is jointly created by two or more independent actors. The best-known strategic interaction is perhaps the arms race (Schelling, 1960; Kahn, 1965). The elementary action structure in this case is a conflict between two parties. Each side dedicates a certain part of its resources to that conflict. At any given moment, both sides have to ponder whether they should escalate. Escalation may bring superiority if the other side does not escalate. If both sides act in the same way, the status quo is maintained, either at a higher and more costly level or at a lower level of conflict intensity. Given that inferiority is worse than spending additional resources on the conflict, the payoff matrix shown in Figure 7 results.

In this interaction, which has the structure of the 'prisoner's dilemma' game, both sides could stop the escalation by acting jointly. But because the conflict prevents them from doing so, it may appear that both will have to opt for escalation; otherwise, they risk being duped by the other side. Yet, the future of the conflict should make both actors think twice. Each round of the game starts at the level of the previous round, so that payoffs decrease; less and less resources can be dedicated to the organization's original mission. This, in fact, is the vicious circle. Figure 8a shows the sequence of payoffs in five consecutive rounds of the conflict. As long as both players follow the minimax rationality recommended by game theorists for this case, both must try to avoid the worst possible outcome and choose escalation (the southeastern quadrant). This is also the nonescalation payoff for the second round of the game. In the next round played, the conflict moves to the next southeastern

**Organization B**

| | Nonescalation | Escalation |
|---|---|---|
| | | |

|  | Nonescalation | Escalation |
|---|---|---|
| Nonescalation | 95,  95 | 85,  100 |
| Escalation | 100,  85 | 90,  90 |

**Organization A**

**Figure 7.** Payoff matrix of a two-organization conflict. The payoffs are given in absolute numbers. Here, only the ordinal order is important. 100 is the best, 95 the second best, 90 the third best, and 85 the worst outcome. The first number in a quadrant gives the payoff for A and the second one that for B.

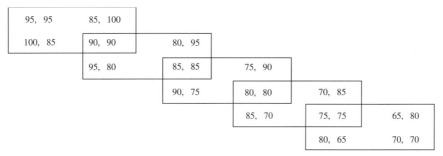

**Figure 8a.** Sequence of payoffs in five consecutive rounds of the conflict shown in Figure 7

| 95,  95 | 65,  80 |
|---|---|
| 80,  65 | 70,  70 |

**Figure 8b.** Payoff matrix in which nonescalation in first round is confronted with payoffs from repeating the escalation four times

quadrant and so forth. Figure 8b gives the payoff matrix in which nonescalation in the first round is confronted with the payoffs that result when the escalation has been repeated four times.

Both sides should discover that the best payoff obtainable after a certain number of repetitions is worse than the worst was at the beginning (Figure 8b). Consequently, both will avoid escalation, even at the risk of the other side gaining superiority. What makes them escape is the fact that payoffs actually decline, as opposed to what would happen in a tit-for-tat metagame situation in which the payoffs are the same in every round played.

This result can be generalized to other strategic interactions in which payoffs deteriorate.[1] Past some point in the evolution of the game, payoffs will become poor enough so that both sides accept the risk of the fourth-best outcome at the start. The knowledge of the vicious circle should be sufficient for each side to avoid it (Axelrod, 1981). If vicious circles persist in strategic situations, some misperception must be present. For example opponents may overestimate each other's aggressiveness and underestimate each other's rationality (Jervis, 1976).

The ramifications of vicious circles put pressure on the participating actors to consider their original understanding of the situation and to search actively for the hidden cause of the problem. Why do they fail to find it? There are three factors that explain why a feedback loop, the very model of inductive or enactive learning, might derail in such a way as to keep a vicious circle alive: (1) participants' cognitive disposition, (2) the complexity of the situation, and (3) the self-sealing structure of vicious circles.

## Cognitive dispositions

Many cognitive dispositions bias actors against perceiving vicious circles. First, people find it less difficult to think in chains than in networks or loops (Dörner, 1975, 1980; Axelrod, 1976; Simon, 1979). Second, they are perceptually biased against inconsistencies, i.e., causal relations between events that they like and others they dislike (Abelson et al., 1968; Salancik, 1982). Yet, since vicious circles frustrate the good intentions of their originators, they always imply psychologically unacceptable causalities. Third, individuals are prone to attribution errors (Kelley, 1971; Staw, 1975; Kelley and Michela, 1980). Failure is more likely to be attributed to others than is success; this increases the likelihood that the counterproductive consequences of one's own actions will be seen as the faults of others. Fourth, human actors tend to avoid cognitive dissonance (Festinger, 1957; Staw, 1976; Aronson, 1978; Staw and Ross, 1978). They may reiterate an unsuccessful definition of the situation for the very reason that it failed earlier. Fifth, their cognitive capacities are reduced under threat (Smart and Vertinsky, 1977; Staw, Sandelands, and Dutton, 1981). The more threatening the ramifications of a vicious circle, the less likely that it will be detected in time. Sixth, they tend to adjust their aspiration level to the facts (Helson, 1964; Janis and Mann, 1977). They may come to accept a problem as normal, before discovering its source.

## Complexity

Complexity, here understood as the number of possible causal links within an action structure, enhances the birth rate as well as the life expectancy of vicious circles. First, complexity increases the likelihood of side effects, and because

---

[1] Among the 78 different 2×2 games are approximately 30 that can be played with circular results (Rapoport and Guyer, 1966), not to mention those that are possible in more complex games.

vicious circles always result from side effects, complexity will increase the birth rate of vicious circles. Second, as complexity increases the probability that intricate causal structures will occur, it increases the likelihood of long, multi-linked circles. These are especially difficult to discover, since they may complete themselves beyond the horizon of each of the participants (Baumgartner and Burns, 1980, 1981). Third, except in highly munificent environments (understood here as those in which there is a higher than 50 percent chance that any random action generates positive, desired outcomes), complexity decreases the chance that enactive, trial-and-error learning will be successful. Once caught by complexity in a vicious circle, the participants will find it difficult to escape by mere chance (Perrow, 1984).

## Self-sealing structures

Certain vicious circles affect the perception just as some diseases affect the immune system of the body. First, vicious circles can generate a complexity that both creates them and hides them. Overregulation, for example, creates overcomplexity in the legal system and triggers demand for additional regulation, while the same complexity complicates adequately understanding the situation (Wahl, 1980; Mitnick, 1980; Reich, 1981). Overcentralization creates decision overload or 'switchboard' problems, so that inundated decision makers at the center make poor decisions. Additional problems and more decision overload are the result (Deutsch, 1966; Mintzberg, 1973). Second, vicious circles can create a variety of threat-rigidity or threat-anxiety loops in which the actual danger is aggravated by anxiety-affected decision making (Janis and Mann, 1977; Argyris and Schön, 1978; Staw, Sandelands, and Dutton, 1981; Perrow, 1984). Third, vicious circles may induce pathological perceptions with self-aggravating consequences (Kets de Vries, 1980). For example, the cohesion of an organization may depend on mythical fantasies about the leader's supernatural abilities in such a way that each of the leader's failures necessitates a reinforcement of those fantasies (Smith and Simmons, 1983). Or cohesion may depend on an exotic interpretation of the outside world that triggers exotic behavior with consequences that are self-fulfilling prophecies (Neidhardt, 1983).

These factors do not rule out the possibility that vicious circles may be anticipated, and avoided, by proactive learning or be discovered in time by alert participants. The literature on learning shows, furthermore, that failure increases the readiness of individuals to redefine their situation (Hedberg, 1981), and this should increase the chances of detecting vicious circles. Yet perceptual biases, complexity, and self-sealing loops can explain why vicious circles survive. Whether vicious circles persist depends on their surrounding network. Action loops depend on an action structure for survival, which is only provided by systems. But, in systems, vicious circles can build up like malignant tumors in the body.

The accumulation of vicious circles may explain organizational stagnation. Within action structures that are not highly munificent, side effects have more negative than positive ramifications. Consequently, within a slowly, incrementally changing action structure – as is typical in normal, stable organizations – more and more action loops are accidentally created that have negative effects on the balance (Miller, 1982; Forrester, 1975). Figure 9, a diagram from Peters and Waterman (1982) illustrates this point. This diagram, drawn by a manager of a would-be new venture in a moderately high-tech business, outlines the clearance procedure for a new product. The circles in the diagram represent organizational units and the straight lines depict formal linkages. There are 223 such formal linkages. As Peters and Waterman pointed out:

> Needless to say, the company is hardly first to the marketplace with any new product. The irony, and the tragedy, is that each of the 223 linkages taken by itself makes perfectly good sense. Well-meaning, rational people designed each link for a reason that made sense at the time – for example, a committee was formed to ensure that a glitch between sales and marketing, arising in the last product rollout, is not repeated . . . The other sad fact is that when we use this diagram in presentations, we don't draw shouts of 'Absurd.' Instead, we draw sighs, nervous laughter, and the occasional volunteer who says, 'If you really want a humdinger, you should map our process.' (1982: 17–19)

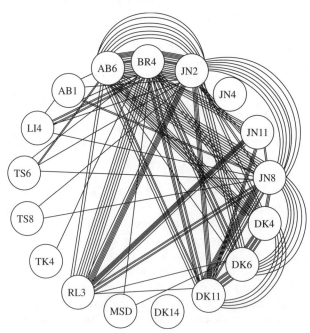

**Figure 9.** New product sign-off procedure. (Reproduction from Peters and Waterman, *In Search of Excellence*, p. 18. © 1982 by Thomas J. Peters and Robert H. Waterman, Jr. Used with permission of the authors and Harper & Row, Publishers, Inc.)

What Peters and Waterman describe is nothing less than the accumulation of counterproductive side effects, in short, stagnating vicious circles. The normal, incrementally developing organization will always exhibit a tendency toward stagnation, unless this is offset by high munificence or by repeated reorganizations that break the ties and the circles of stagnation (Olson, 1982).

## Vicious circles in complex organizations

In order to summarize, a simple model of the transitory stages in the history of an organization (Figure 10) is constructed, based on Miller and Friesen's (1980) 'Archetypes of Organizational Transition.'

*Growth → Bold Leadership → Collapse.* It is assumed that the organization, like many other successful ones, has been erected by a talented entrepreneur. It has survived the hazards of young age and seen a considerable period of rapid, eventually too rapid, expansion. Relying on the dynamics of self-sustained growth, the leader pushes for further expansion. Two dangers are present. First, normal errors, some disadvantageous acquisitions, for example, exhaust

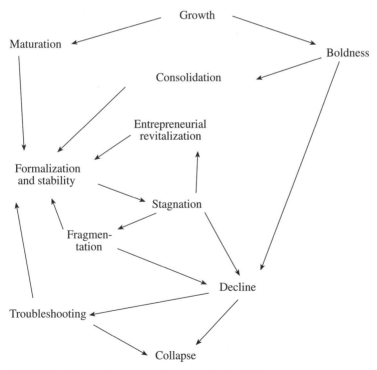

**Figure 10.** Model of the transitory stages in an organization's history

the organization's buffers. Second, the environment, which must have been munificent in the past to sustain high growth rates, may change and become less benevolent. The pace of expansion is too fast under the new conditions; again, buffers may be exhausted, so that collapse is imminent.

*Growth* → *Bold Leadership* → *Decline* → *Collapse*. A similar development may occur as the result of a leader's age. Having had his best times, he may become less flexible, his intellectual capacities may shrink, and his behavior may change. For example, he may be more hesitant to delegate authority, and his attitudes toward bad news may encourage information biasing. Various circles of suboptimality such as overcentralization, formalization, or information biasing develop. High performers leave, while outside talent stays away, so that a vicious circle of mediocrity forms. Under more extreme circumstances, psychotic organizational cultures develop. For example, to survive in the leader's entourage, managers may have to reaffirm the leader's crotchety viewpoints. Contact with reality is gradually lost. Only the leader's death or his forced retirement may forestall decline and collapse.

*Formalization* → *Stagnation* → *Decline*. Not all aging leaders act irresponsibly. They may manage their retreat successfully so that the organization can reach the phase of formalization and stability through consolidation and maturation. The primary threat now is stagnation. All incrementally developing organizations will experience a tendency toward stagnation under normal conditions. Successful organizations can maintain high performance by revolving through the triangle of formalization and stability, stagnation, and entrepreneurial revitalization. As some uncertainty is involved in the process, however, success in maintaining high performance depends to a certain extent on chance factors. Organizations that maintain high performance indefinitely are indefinitely lucky. All others will fail to shift toward revitalization occasionally and decline begins. Cultures of mediocrity develop that justify lower performance and regulate the declining aspiration levels. The quality of management and the work force declines, until low performance becomes the standard.

*Decline* → *Collapse*. Decline and collapse are intimately connected, although the borderline of collapse may be hidden to the participants. Decline verges on collapse when the organization has been pushed to the lower limit of acceptable performance. Then, contracting circles are triggered by the competitive disadvantages that the organization suffers. Deviation-counteracting capacity is exhausted to fill the gaps. New vicious circles are created, and chain reactions evolve, until collapse takes place, as illustrated in Figure 11.

*Stagnation* → *Fragmentation* → *Decline* → *Collapse*. Another possible reaction to stagnation is fragmentation. The organization's subunits may fight the growing entanglement of stagnation by striving for independence. Fiefdoms evolve. Independence is gained, but synergy from interdependence is lost. Bureaucratic conflicts, thus far mitigated, surface and absorb more energies. Buffers

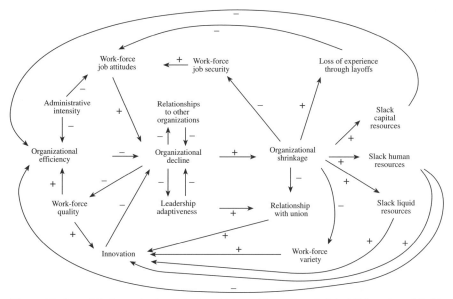

**Figure 11.** A model of organizational decline. (Adapted from Greenhalgh, 1983, and modified in accordance with him by the author.)

dissolve, and collapse may be triggered incidentally. But this is not the only possible outcome. The gains from independence may exceed the benefits from interdependence. Disintegration may continue, until the old subunits have gained formal independence and the old organization is dissolved.

*Decline → Troubleshooting → Collapse.* As decline verges on collapse, attempts may be made to turn the organization around. Troubleshooters are hired. If successful, the process resembles the stability-fragmentation-revitalization triangle starting at a low-performance level. But troubleshooting can also hasten the pace of decline if the new management overacts or commits too many new errors. Then, complexity circles, decision-overload situations, and, eventually, threat-rigidity problems multiply. Collapse becomes imminent.

## Discussion and implications

Vicious circles are dangerous. They destroy organizations, careers, and people. Yet they do serve some purpose. First, as the locus of many structural problems in organizations, vicious circles provide a target for organizational improvement. Although it's hard to detect them, it is not impossible. Individuals are intuitively biased against vicious circles, but by being aware of their potential presence, individuals may help to create counterbiases. By approaching organizations counterintuitively, and by routinely checking their circular structures, practitioners can improve upon organizations. Also, efforts can be made to refine knowledge about vicious circles. Up to the present day, the empirical inference of circular structures has been hampered by mathematical problems. The tools to represent formally a network of action loops are simultaneous differential equations. These rarely have general solutions when nonlinearities occur. The common way to avoid the mathematical intricacies is numerical simulation (Forrester, 1961, 1968). So far, however, this technique depends on face validity for model validation. Efforts should be made to develop tools for less intuitive validation methods. Also, more fundamental research is needed to develop models that allow for an inductive inference of the loop structure of a given system. Points of departure are to be found in network theory (Schwartz and Sprinzen, 1984) and especially in topological algebra (Casti, 1979).

Second, vicious circles help to solve the transformation problem – the problem of bridging the gap between individual action and the behavior of organizations or other social systems. There is a twist to the transformation problem which, so far, has hampered its solution: it's not always there. At times, individuals manage to bridge the gap between their own actions and the system's behavior; oftentimes, they don't. Social scientists have largely ignored this fact. Either they claim that social systems are merely a 'construction of reality' that can be reduced to (inter)actions on the individual level (Weber, 1947; Berger and Luckmann, 1966), or they insist that social systems reside on their own 'emanation level' and have nothing to do with individual action (Lévi-Strauss, 1977; Durkheim, 1982). Both kinds of explanations thus ignore the volatility of the transformation problem. They explain too little or too much. Vicious circles explain just the right amount: Individual actions are transformed into systems by two kinds of loops: deviation-counteracting loops and vicious circles. Only the latter destroy the actor's intention in the transformation process. If the transformation problem arises, vicious circles must be present.

Third, vicious circles are not always present. Not all problems can be solved by detecting and avoiding vicious circles. People may simply expect too much. For a circle to qualify as 'vicious,' its participants must share frustrated goals. If goals are not shared, that is, if conflict is rational, the behavior of an organization itself is subject to conflicting expectations. What is a vicious circle for one party, then, is a virtuous circle for another. In a world of scarce resources, many conflicts are rational. Knowing the difference between vicious circles and rational conflicts may help individuals avoid at least one deviation-amplifying loop – the vicious circle of futile efforts.

# References

Abelson, Robert P., and Associates 1968 Theories of Cognitive Consistency: A Sourcebook. Chicago: Rand McNally.

Aguilar, Francis Joseph 1967 Scanning the Business Environment. New York: Macmillan.

Altheide, David L., and J. M. Johnson 1980 Bureaucratic Propaganda. Boston: Allyn & Bacon.

Argenti, John 1976 Corporate Collapse: The Causes and Symptoms. New York: Halstead Press.

Argyris, Chris 1957 Personality and Organization. New York: Harper & Row. 1964 Integrating the Individual and the Organization. New York: Wiley. 1982 Reasoning, Learning and Action. San Francisco: Jossey-Bass.

Argyris, Chris, and Donald Schön 1978 Organizational Learning: A Theory of Action Perspective. Reading, MA: Addison-Wesley.

Aronson, Elliot 1978 'The theory of cognitive dissonance: A current perspective.' In L. Berkowitz (ed.), Theories in Social Psychology: 181–220. New York: Academic Press.

Axelrod, Robert 1976 Structure of Decisions: The Cognitive Maps of Political Elites. Princeton, NJ: Princeton University Press. 1981 'The emergence of cooperation among egoists.' American Political Science Review, 75: 306–318.

Barnard, Charles 1946 'Functions and pathology of status systems.' In W. F. Wythe (ed.), Industry and Society: 46–83. New York: McGraw-Hill.

Baumgartner, Thomas, and Tom R. Burns 1980 'Inflation as the institutional struggle over income distribution.' Acta Sociologica, 23: 177–186. 1981 'Inflationary pressure and societal responses.' Mimeographed paper, SIAR Inflation Project, University of Oslo.

Berger, Peter L., and Thomas Luckmann 1966 The Social Construction of Reality. New York: Doubleday.

Blumer, Herbert 1969 Symbolic Interactionism: Perspective and Methods. Englewood Cliffs, NJ: Prentice-Hall.

Boudon, René 1977 *Effets pervers et ordre social*. Paris: PUF. 1981 'Undesired consequences and types of structures of systems of interdependence.' In P. M. Blau and R. K. Merton (eds.), Continuity in Structural Inquiry: 255–284. London: Sage.

Breton, Albert, and Ronald Wintrobe 1982 The Logic of Bureaucratic Conduct. Cambridge: Cambridge University Press.

Buchanan, James M., and Gordon Tullock 1977 'The expanding public sector: Wagner squared.' Public Choice, 31: 147–150.

Casti, John 1979 Connectivity, Complexity, and Catastrophe in Large Scale Systems. London: International Institute for Applied Systems Analysis.

Crozier, Michel 1964 The Bureaucratic Phenomenon. Chicago: University of Chicago Press. 1970 *La société bloquée*. Paris: Seuil.

Cyert, Richard M. 1978 'The management of universities of constant or decreasing size.' Public Administration Review, 38: 344–349.

Deutsch, Karl W. 1966 The Nerves of Government. New York: Wiley.

Dörner, Dietrich 1975 '*Wie Menschen eine Welt verbessern wollten.*' Bild der Wissenschaft, 12(2): 48–53. 1980 'On the difficulties people have in dealing with complexity.' Simulation and Games, 11: 87–106.

Downs, Anthony 1967 Inside Bureaucracy. Boston: Little, Brown.

Dunbar, Roger L. M. 1981 'Design for organizational control.' In P. C. Nystrom and W. H. Starbuck (eds.), Handbook of Organizational Design, 2: 85–115. New York: Oxford University Press.

Dunbar, Roger L. M., John M. Dutton, and William R. Torbert 1982 'Crossing mother: Ideological constraints on organizational improvements.' Journal of Management Studies, 19: 91–108.

Durkheim, Emile 1982 The Rules of Sociological Method. London: Macmillan.

Elster, Jon 1980 Logic and Society: Contradictions and Possible Worlds. New York: Wiley.

Festinger, Leon 1957 A Theory of Cognitive Dissonance. Stanford, CA: Stanford University Press.

Fischhoff, Baruch 1982 'Debiasing.' In D. Kahnemann, P. Slovic, and A. Tversky (eds.), Judgment under Uncertainty: Heuristics and Biases: 422–444. Cambridge: Cambridge University Press.

Forrester, Jay W. 1961 Industrial Dynamics. Cambridge, MA: MIT Press. 1968 Principles of Systems. Cambridge, MA: MIT Press. 1975 'Counterintuitive behavior of social systems.' In J.W. Forrester: Collected Papers. Cambridge, MA: Wright-Allen Press.

Giddens, Anthony 1979 Central Problems in Social Theory: Action, Structures, and Contradiction in Social Analysis. Berkeley, CA: University of California Press.

Gouldner, Alvin W. 1954 Patterns of Industrial Bureaucracy. Glencoe, IL: Free Press.

Greenhalgh, Leonard 1983 'Organization decline.' In Samuel B. Bacharach (ed.), Research in the Sociology of Organizations, 2: 231–276.

Habermas, Jürgen 1984 The Theory of Communicative Action. Boston: Beacon Press.

Hall, Roger I. 1976 'A system pathology of an organization: The rise and fall of the old *Saturday Evening Post.*' Administrative Science Quarterly, 21: 185–211.

Hedberg, Bo L. T. 1981 'How organizations learn and unlearn.' In P. C. Nystrom and W. H. Starbuck (eds.), Handbook of Organizational Design, 1: 3–27. New York: Oxford University Press.

Helson, Harry 1964 Adaptation-Level Theory: An Experimental and Systematic Approach to Behavior. New York: Harper & Row.

Janis, Irving L., and Leon Mann 1977 Decision Making. New York: Free Press.

Jervis, Robert 1976 Perceptions and Misperceptions in International Politics. Princeton, NJ: Princeton University Press.

Kahn, Herbert 1965 On Escalation: Metaphors and Scenarios. New York: Praeger.

Katz, Daniel, and Robert L. Kahn 1966 The Social Psychology of Organizations. New York: Wiley.

Kaufman, Herbert 1975 'The natural history of human organizations.' Administration and Society, 7: 131–149.

Kelley, Harold H. 1971 'Attribution in social interaction.' In E. E. Jones et al. (eds.), Attribution: Perceiving Causes of Behavior. Morristown, NJ: General Learning Press.

Kelley, Harold L., and John L. Michela 1980 'Attribution theory and research.' Annual Review of Psychology, 31: 457–501.

Kets de Vries, Manfred F.R. 1980 Organizational Paradoxes: Clinical Approaches to Management. London: Tavistock.

Kuhn, Alfred, and Robert D. Beam 1982 The Logic of Organization. San Francisco: Jossey-Bass.

Lawler, Edward E. 1976 'Control systems in organizations.' In M.D. Dunnette (ed.), Handbook of Industrial and Organizational Psychology: 1247–1291. Chicago: Rand McNally.

Lévi-Strauss, Claude 1977 *Antropologie structurale.* Paris: Plon.

Luhmann, Niklas 1972 *Rechtssoziologie.* Rheinbeck b. Hamburg: Rowohlt. 1982 The Differentiation of Society. New York: Columbia University Press.

March, James G., and Herbert A. Simon 1958 Organizations. New York: Wiley.

Masuch, Michael 1984 'The negative bureau hypothesis.' Working paper, Resource Policy Center, Dartmouth College.

Mazur, Marion 1978 'Cybernetic theorems on feedback in social processes.' In F. Geyer and J. v.d. Zouwen (eds.), Sociocybernetics, 2: 31–39. Leiden: Martinus Nijhoff.

Merton, Robert K. 1957 Social Theory and Social Structure. New York: Free Press.

Miller, Danny 1982 'Evolution and revolution: A quantum view of structural change in organizations.' Journal of Management Studies, 19: 131–151.

Miller, Danny, and Peter Friesen 1980 'Archetypes of organizational transition.' Administrative Science Quarterly, 25: 268–299.

Mintzberg, Henry 1973 The Nature of Managerial Work. New York: Harper & Row.

Mitnick, Barry M. 1980 The Political Economy of Regulation: Creating, Designing, and Removing Regulatory Forms. New York: Columbia University Press.

Neidhardt, Friedhelm 1983 '*Ueber Zufall, Eigendynamik, und Institutionalisierbarkeit absurder Prozesse.*' In Heiner v. Alemann and H.P. Thurn (eds.), *Festschrift fuer René König zum 75. Geburtstag:* 243–257. Opladen: Westdeutscher Verlag.

Neuberger, Egon, and W. J. Duffy 1976 Comparative Economic Systems. Boston: Allyn & Bacon.

Olson, Mancur 1982 The Rise and Decline of Nations. New Haven, CT: Yale University Press.

Parkinson, C. Northcote 1958 Parkinson's Law. Boston: Houghton Mifflin.

Parsons, Talcott 1937 The Structure of Social Action. Glencoe, IL: Free Press. 1956 'Suggestions for a sociological approach to the theory of organizations.' Administrative Science Quarterly, 1: 63–85, 225–239.

Perrow, Charles 1979 Complex Organizations: A Critical Essay. Glenview, IL: Scott, Foresman. 1984 Normal Accidents: Living with High-Risk Technology. New York: Basic Books.

Peters, Thomas J., and Robert H. Waterman, Jr. 1982 In Search of Excellence. New York: Harper & Row.

Pfeffer, Jeffrey, and Gerald R. Salancik 1978 The External Control of Organizations. New York: Harper & Row.

Platt, John 1973 'Social traps.' American Psychologist, 27: 641–651.

Rapoport, Anatol, and Melvin Guyer 1966 'A taxonomy of 2×2 games.' General Systems, 11: 203–214.

Reich, Robert B. 1981 'Regulation by confrontation or negotiation.' Harvard Business Review, 59(3): 82–93.

Richardson, George P. 1983 'The feedback concept in American social science, with implications for system dynamics.' Working paper D-3417. System Dynamics Group, MIT.

Salancik, Gerald R. 1982 'Attitude-behavior consistencies and social logics.' In M.P. Zanna et al. (eds.), Consistency in Social Behavior: The Ontario Symposium, 2: 21–51. Hillsdale, NJ: Lawrence Erlbaum.

Schelling, Thomas C. 1960 The Strategy of Conflict. Cambridge, MA: Harvard University Press. 1978 Micromotives and Macrobehavior. New York: Norton.

Schutz, Alfred 1967 The Phenomenology of the Social World. Evanston, IL: Northwestern University Press.

Schwartz, Joseph E., and Merle Sprinzen 1984 'Structures of Connectivity.' Social Networks, 6: 103–140.

Simon, Herbert A. 1979 'Information processing models of cognition.' Annual Review of Psychology, 30: 363–396.

Smart, Carolyne, and Ilan Vertinsky 1977 'Design for crisis decision units.' Administrative Science Quarterly, 22: 650–657.

Smith, Kenwyn K., and Valerie M. Simmons 1983 'A Rumpelstiltskin organization: Metaphors on metaphors in field research.' Administrative Science Quarterly, 28: 377–392.

Starbuck, William H. 1983 'Organizations as action generators.' American Sociological Review, 48: 91–102.

Staw, Barry M. 1975 'Attribution of the "causes" of performance: A general alternative interpretation of cross-sectional research in organizations.' Organizational Behavior and Human Performance, 13: 414–432. 1976 'Knee-deep in the Big Muddy: A study of escalating commitment to a chosen course of action.' Organizational Behavior and Human Performance, 16: 27–44.

Staw, Barry M., and Jerry Ross 1978 'Commitment to a policy decision: A multi-theoretical perspective.' Administrative Science Quarterly, 23: 40–64.

Staw, Barry M., Lance E. Sandelands, and Jane E. Dutton 1981 'Threat-rigidity effects in organizational behavior: A multilevel analysis.' Administrative Science Quarterly, 26: 501–524.

Stinchcombe, Arthur L. 1965 'Social structure and organizations.' In J. G. March (ed.), Handbook of Organizations: 142–193. Chicago: Rand McNally.

Thompson, James D. 1967 Organizations in Action. New York: McGraw-Hill.

Thompson, Victor A. 1961 Modern Organization. New York: Knopf.

Türk, Klaus 1975 *Grundlagen einer Pathologie der Organization.* Stuttgart: Enke.

Turner, Barry A. 1976 'The organizational and interorganizational development of disasters.' Administrative Science Quarterly, 21: 378–397.

Vickers, Sir Geoffrey 1968 Freedom in a Rocking Boat. Harmondsworth: Penguin.

Vroom, Cas W. 1980 *Bureaucratie: het veelzijdig instrument van de macht*. Alphen a/d Rijn: Samson.
Wahl, Rainer 1980 '*Die bürokratischen Kosten des Rechts- und Sozialstaats.*' *Die Verwaltung*, 13: 273–296.
Weber, Max 1947 The theory of social and economic organizations. A. M. Henderson, trans. and Talcott Parsons, ed. Glencoe, IL: Free Press.
Weick, Karl E. 1969 The Social Psychology of Organizing. Reading, MA: Addison-Wesley.
Whetten, David A. 1980 'Sources, responses, and effects of organizational decline.' In J. R. Kimberly and R. H. Miles (eds.), The Organizational Life Cycle: 342–374. San Francisco: Jossey-Bass.
Wildavsky, Aaron 1983 'Information as an organizational problem.' Journal of Management Studies, 20: 29–40.

Reprinted from Vicious Circles in Organization by Michael Masuch published in *Administrative Science Quarterly*, **30**, No. 1 by permission of *Administrative Science Quarterly*.

# Part Five

# Creating Programmes of Change

---

## Introduction

Many people often ask the author whether or not a total quality management programme is an example of what this book talks about. Similarly people refer to business process re-engineering. When I say yes they then ask me what is different about such programmes of change. To this I answer nothing except that the 'packaging' is different. Thus far in this book we have been concerned to analyse change and the problems of change. Through such analysis comes better understanding and thus we are able to handle change more effectively.

But is that enough? In the real world change must be defined and 'sold'. It must be controlled (at some level). It must be managed to achieve and sustain momentum. Managers need to attract attention. In this chapter therefore we are concerned with programmes of change. We shall examine some of the important design parameters facing those taking overall responsibility for a major change effort. Our concern will be on how to create a programme of change.

What we deal with here is relevant to generic organization-wide change and to multi-organizational change. Total quality management programmes and business process re-engineering programmes are currently good examples of how to achieve change. Joint venture programmes such as that involving Rover and Honda arrived at revitalizing Rover's product portfolio would be a classic multi-organizational example.

One of the problems we each of us experience when we attempt to relate models of change with our real-world experience of change is that formal models of change generally give an impression of change as a neat, orderly sequence of activities or stages. Conversely our experience is usually all together more 'messy'. Activities are often going on in parallel. We often recycle through different stages as we pilot a new organizational design on new marketing policy only to find that in some respects it does not work. As we shall see, our response is to see change as a spiral process and to view it as comprising three essential characteristics (each of which comprises many detailed ingredients, programme elements, etc. to make it up).

## Cycles of change

Three characteristics are necessary conditions for effective change. These conditions are awareness, capability and inclusion. For change to be successful those involved must understand the change, its objectives, their role and so on. More than understand it must be credible in their eyes. Only then will they feel confidence in the likelihood of success and only then is there the prospect of energizing them to act appropriately. Given that they must have or be helped to acquire the necessary capabilities to handle the new tasks and new work situations. People must feel that they can cope with the new situation. Finally they must feel 'included' in the change process. To be successful those involved need to feel that they value the new objectives (individual and/or corporate) and that they both chose and feel able to choose.

Judson (1990) sketches out an outline of five key issues each of which can be related to one of these three necessary conditions.

## Awareness

1 How thoroughly does everyone affected . . . understand the needs of customers, objectives, strategy and timetable, resources required and new behaviour, techniques, systems, etc.?
2 How systematic a process has been instituted for tracking implementation and for making corrections whilst change is in process?

## Capability

3 How completely have the resources required been identified and provided, including financial resources, skills and time?

## Inclusion

4 How strong is the commitment of relevant managers and employees to implementing the change including how credible do they view the change as being, to what extent do they 'own' the approach, how can commitment be sustained, etc.?
5 How consistent and credible is the climate of accountability for the implementation period, including to what extent will those involved live up to their commitments, what are the consequences of failure, will reward systems differentiate between success and failure and how visible and consistent is leadership behaviour?

Turning now to Figure 1 we can see how to put some 'flesh' on to these ideas. At its simplest the figure defines three stages of change as follows.

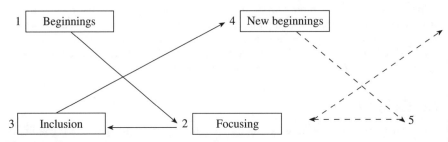

**Figure 1.** Change process

## Stage 1: Beginnings

Here the problems are recognized, awareness raising begins, diagnostic studies are undertaken, feasibility studies are begun and we look at the experience of other organizations. This begins to create a new perception of achievable performance in what may be rapidly changing markets, technologies and so on. The main focus of this stage therefore is that of creating awareness but, as we shall see, awareness building continues long into the next stage.

## Stage 2: Focusing

We show the first stage as including the establishment of a steering group taking responsibility for the 'problem' and even agreeing the basic approach. The next stage we call focusing. Here effort at building awareness continues but also people are moving toward decision and action. Task forces may be established. If new skills are needed then the first attempts to seek them or to attempt to create them internally will begin. Effort will be directed at building coalitions in support of the changes, both through work with opinion leaders and through other means. Pilot trials and experiments often will be undertaken. Visits will be organized to sites and organizations which have already implemented the changes. Early results will be used to further 'shape' and modify the change programme. Much attention will be devoted to 'selling' the new ideas and dealing with likely opposition.

**Table 1**   Cycles of management. From Juch (1983)

| | *Stage* | *Task/activity* | *Process* |
|---|---|---|---|
| 1. | Thinking | Objectives<br>Policies<br>Forecasts<br>Proposals<br>Projects | Preliminary discussion |
| 2. | Addressing | Budgets<br>Targets<br>Commitments<br>Organizing<br>Scheduling | Decision-making |
| 3. | Doing | Controlling<br>Training<br>Reporting<br>Progress chasing | Monitoring |
| 4. | Sensing | Analysis<br>Evaluation<br>Problem-solving | Evaluation |

## Stage 3: Inclusion

Now the focus of the change activity broadens. We both cascade and roll-out. Cascading is about creating and implementing a communication plan. Rolling out is about implementing the change throughout the organization as a whole. The two are often linked. Thus if two organizations are merged the initial announcement is often followed by a process of senior management appointments. This is followed by a process to decide the corporate structure for the merged entity. In turn this is followed by a series of lower level appointments. Then may follow detailed examination of work organization, information systems, procedures, etc., in which small task forces (for example) are charged with the task of picking the best ideas from the two original organizations to implement in the new. Here we see a process of decision and action both cascading down the organization, and at each level rolling out across the organization. This cyclical process is illustrated in Table 1.

## Learning and change

We have already noted that learning is a characteristic of effective organizational change possible best viewed as a consequence of change. This raises the question of whether we can identify any meaningful equivalence between individual learning and the processes of organizational change identified in the above. Juch (1983) has identified what has become a very influential model of learning which sees the learner at the centre possessing levels of sensory, cognitive, contactual (communication) and operational skills. The process of learning comprises a cycle of four stages namely thinking, addressing, doing and sensing with four barriers. He characterizes the four as follows:

1 '**Gate**' through which ideas are converted to intentions and declared to others.
2 '**Rubicon**' through which some proposals are considered as attracting commitment.
3 '**Window**' through which attention to certain outcomes is raised.
4 '**Skin**' through which new perceptions about, say possible performance, are accepted leading to a repeat of the cycle.

Clearly it is not difficult to relate these ideas to the processes of change which we have identified. Juch (1983) presents a 'cycle of management' which does. So the four stages being linked to typical management tasks or activities as shown in Table 1.

Derived from this revision of Juch's presentation and linking the change model with his learning model produces Table 2.

Thus the purpose of creating an effective design to a programme of change is to ensure the following:

1 that we establish the necessary conditions for effective change;
2 that we establish the appropriate programme management arrangements to achieve change;
3 that we maximize the ability for those involved in change to learn from the process of change;
4 that in particular learning demands thinking, focusing as well as the more familiar processes of including, cascading and roll. Of these least attention in the literature is devoted to the process of focusing, which is partly about the politics of change but partly about integrating people, support and resources to ensure *cohesion*.

As an example of these ideas applied in practice we might refer to the work of Argyris

**Table 2** Cycles of change

| 'Juch model' | Stage | Process | Task/activity | Programme management |
|---|---|---|---|---|
| | Change model | | | |
| 1. Thinking | Beginnings | Getting started | Diagnosis<br>Feasibility studies<br>Brain-storming<br>Communication of concerns<br>Problem recognition<br>Establish steering group | Establish targets, milestones, plans, scope, accountabilities, steering groups, etc.<br>Define an integrated programme |
| 2. Addressing | Focusing | Building capability | Task forces<br>Training<br>Buying in new skills<br>Building support<br>Building coalitions<br>'Pilot' trials | Establish taskforces, pilot trials, training and development, implementing communication plan |
| 3. Doing | Including cascading and roll out | Building and sustaining change | Creating change<br>Champions<br>Proposal for change<br>New structures and skills<br>Team-building<br>Rewards and recognition<br>Sell change<br>Publicize success | Execute projects and programme stages, completing, review trials modifying plans, identifying 'champions', establishing new structures and skills, rewards and recognition, communicate and diffuse success |

or the BA case study presented above. However Chapter 17 taken from Edgar Schein's seminal book on organizational culture reveals much about the dynamics of change programmes as well as about the dynamics of corporate culture.

Kolb explicitly includes an evaluation stage which we have omitted – largely because formal evaluation is rarely practised and also because the learning appears to take place throughout the process. There is an equivalence between our beginnings stage and Argyris' concept of action maps (Argyris, 1990). Argyris contends that, faced with contractions in behaviour, the process of mapping can lead to changes towards more effective behaviour, implying a much more natural process of learning than Kolb's model suggests – although in making this point I do not mean that Kolb adopted a static view of learning (i.e. that it did not take place until all thinking, addressing and doing were complete). The view offered here is that life, work and managing change were never so simple!

Again one can see how 'personal learning cycles', 'change coping cycles' and the organizational change cycle may fit together. Learning cycles may be 'nested' within the 'change coping cycle' which in turn is nested within the organization's change cycle. Add to that the concept of adoption of innovation which suggests that people vary in the pace of adoption of new ideas from innovators, early adopters to laggards and it is possible to suggest some interesting lines of thought both for the practice of organization change and for research.

For example can we pick out the most likely innovators? Rogers (1962) and many others subsequently suggest that they are venturesome and prepared to accept risks. Ket de Vries (1980) would probably add prepared to take calculated risks. Kirton (1988), and the originator of the Kirton Adoption-Innovation test or KAI, identifies various differences between innovators and adopters suggesting that both are essential to success. Amabile (1988) identifies components of individual creativity (e.g. product and technical skills and knowledge cognitive style, work styles, attitudes and motivation) which she sees as emerging from cognitive abilities, perceptual and motor skills, education, training, experience in developing new ideas, the ability to minimize extrinsic constraints which certainly suggest lines for further research but which *may* allow us to identify potential 'change champions' and 'change agents'. The champion may be the risk taker, strongly achievement oriented with the capability of ignoring or at least settling for one-side constraints until ideas are shaped through the process of early trials – Amabile (1983) suggests that the appropriate cognitive-perceptual style includes:

1 the ability to break the existing mind-set;
2 the ability to hold open options for a long time;
3 the ability to suspend judgement;
4 excellent memory;
5 the ability to break out of 'performance scripts'.

The links between these notions and the ideas articulated by Argyris in the reading we present (see Chapter 14) is clear enough.

Grundy (1994) adds important insight into strategic learning to the Juch model. For him strategic learning and strategic action are two linked cycles. Set out below is a modified version of his idea.

Thus strategic learning is a dual process of action and learning. Both loops operate simultaneously but are not often well synchronized. In much the same way the learning loop is often not completed and the learning maximized because formal evaluation is not encouraged. In effect Grundy supports our original view of that this does not require a separate stage but rather a linked process arrived at achieving the learning – not least this could be a management development programme used to both roll out and cascade major changes throughout an organization. Grundy also argues that a key feature of success is the ability to block out distractions (see our discussion of 'champions' above).

How do we block out distractions? Well as we have already implied this is partly an issue of cognitive style at the individual level. There are things we can do at the team and organizational levels however. Following Grundy (1994) these include:

1 manage personal and corporate agendas in order to meet the needs of either stake-holders, your board, other influential people along the way;
2 define some 'given' to stabilize the process;
3 flexible control to spread learning beyond the top team;
4 build learning into the organization through regular customer surveys, staff surveys, quality assurance, performance improvement, etc.
5 keep task forces, etc., involved until implementation is complete;
6 involve top managers at the centre of the process;
7 use communication as a vehicle for learning.

All of this has implications for what and how we manage which we have touched on at various points in this book.

## Programmes of change

Given that major strategic change creates tensions and conflicts, not least within an organization, *and* that many fairly rigidly structured organizations already experience such tensions, how can we at one and the same time encourage integration and learning? Set out below are a series of steps:

| | |
|---|---|
| 1 Building relationships | Company conferences, cross functional management development and functional training, job rotation, building *networks*. |
| 2 Creating project groups | Solving problems via project groups and task forces. Creating *centres of excellence* throughout the organization. |
| 3 Focused training and development | Total quality management programmes. Action/learning-based management development. Company tailored development. Business process re-engineering programmes. |
| 4 Career management | Defining and developing *managerial competence*. Performance appraisal. Career counselling and planning. |

Each of these steps is designed either/or to link or interface individuals in problem-oriented settings or to link the individual to the organization in an output-oriented way focusing upon achievement of objectives. Thus managing change appropriately can and should create and sustain both learning within the organization but also its integration.

There is another way of looking at these issues which takes as a starting point the idea of change as a natural process. Whilst our thinking about change tends to focus on change as a discrete activity, much of our attempts to achieve change comprise a series of adjustments to management style, the use of rewards/incentives, the use of information, etc., all aimed at securing changed patterns of behaviour. In Chapter 16, Prahalad and Doz set out how top managers in multinational corporations set about exercising strategic control in order to achieve 'strategic redirection'. The essence of their position is that a formalistic view of authority and structure is not sufficient to shape the views of key managers.

For these authors this change process comprises three broad stages:

1 Variety generation – with close involvement of subsidiary managers a process of questioning existing strategies and analysing alternatives is established.
2 Power shift – small, incremental shifts of power and resources are made to support the new strategy.
3 Refocusing – now more sweeping changes and more visible changes to corporate structure.

These stages require the use of conflict resolution to bring about (or make acceptable) the cognitive changes. Whilst, in a crisis, rapid change may be inevitable they argue 'In a multi-focal matrix organization managers may gradually introduce a sequence of changes rather than suddenly re-organizing. In designing such a sequence, managers have to pay attention to the set of management tools . . . the emergence of a new strategic consensus, and reallocation of power between product and rational executives.'

The similarity between these three stages and the models considered above is obvious enough. More importantly however these ideas lead us to note that programmes of change may be either explicit or implicit. For too long the focus of our thinking about change has been on single, explicit projects. It should surprise no-one that most managers have seen this as rather a partial view. Most change is implicit in the sense that whilst debated relatively openly change is moved forward through 'announcements' and 'task forces', promotions and so on. However, to the outside observer there may be no clearly identifiable starting point. Initially the ideas develop amongst key managers in a relatively closed way – subsequently the process 'cascades' both downwards and horizontally throughout the organization. Much fundamental change is effectively a natural process of evolution rather than 'step' change.

Be that as it may, fundamental changes often require a change to the culture of the organization. Thus it is that we conclude this book with a chapter by Schein in which he deals with how to structure a re-direction project taking account of the culture of the organization. In practice the corporate culture is a vital part of the context of change. Even if not easy to change it must at least be understood if changes are to be successful.

# References

Amabile, I. M. (1983) *The Social Psychology of Creativity*, Springer Verlag, New York.
Amabile, I. M. (1988) Creativity to organizational innovation in Gronhaus and Kaufman (eds), *Innovation: A cross-disciplinary perspective*, Norwegian University Press, Oslo.
Argyris, C. (1990) *Overcoming Organizational Defences*, Allyn and Bacon, Needham Hts, MA.
De Vries, K. (1980) *Organizational Paradoxes*. Tavistock Publications, London.
Grundy, T. (1994) *Strategic Learning in Acton*, McGraw-Hill, London.
Juch, B. (1993) *Personal Development*, John Wiley, Chichester.
Judson, A. (1996) *Making Strategy Happen*, Blackwell, London.
Kirton, M. J. (1988) Adaptors and innovators in Gronhaus and Kaufman (eds), *Innovation: A Cross-disciplinary Perspective*, Norwegian University Press, Oslo.
Rogers, F. M., (1962) *The Diffusion of Innovations* The Free Press, New York.

# 16 The multinational mission

## *C. K. Prahalad and Y. L. Doz*

### Managing strategic redirection

So far, in discussing strategic coordination and global integration, we identified the managerial task involved in implementing a specific strategy. We were concerned with *efficiency of implementation*. However, as we discussed in Chapter 2, the characteristics of a business can change as a result of changes in technology, competitive dynamics, changes in the competitive focus of customers, and actions by host governments. Top managers, in anticipation of those changes, and sometimes in response, have to change the strategy of the business. Strategic redirection of a business requires a change in the underlying relationships between headquarters and subsidiaries, which may have been cemented over a long period. In other words, efficiency of execution or desire for control over subsidiaries suggests the development of well-defined and well-understood roles for subsidiaries and headquarters, and a clear balance of power in resource allocation decisions. Redirection requires changing established relationships. The ability of a DMNC to redirect strategy in a given business is often impeded by the very efficiency with which the prior strategy was executed. Changing existing relationships can be extremely difficult.

Let us look at an example of strategic redirection to see the sort of changes needed in the underlying relationships between headquarters and subsidiaries. As we outlined in Chapter 2, the chemical industry was undergoing significant change during early 1970s. Prior to 1970, most ethylene oxide plants in Europe had capacities around 50 million to 60 million pounds. Technological changes and the investments made by a few firms, such as ICI, increased the most economic plant size from 50 million pounds per plant to between 120 million and 150 million pounds. MNCs competing in that business had to build large plants and gain the economies of scale or be shut out of the market by more cost-effective competitors. The change in the characteristics of the business is shown in the IR framework in Figure 1. What are the managerial and organizational implications of such a change?

In the DMNC we studied, the overseas subsidiaries, especially those in Europe, enjoyed a certain level of autonomy in operations consistent with the

**Table 1**　Control over subsidiary operations in a DMNC

| *Factors enhancing headquarters' capability to control subsidiaries* | *Factors impeding headquarters' capability to control subsidiaries* |
|---|---|
| Dependency of the subsidiary on resources of headquarters:<br>　technology, management, export markets,<br>　　finances | Historical evolution of headquarters – subsidiary relationship; extent of autonomy of subsidiary |
| Shared strategic vision and competitive strategy | Host government regulations |
| Systems that recognize contributions to global strategy | Presence of joint venture partners |
| Loyalty to the DMNC | Loyalty to country, host government policies |

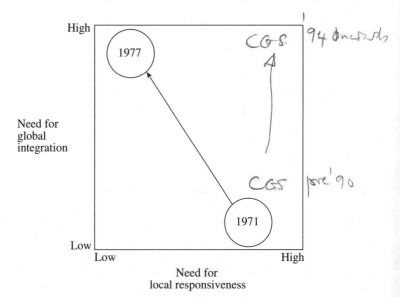

**Figure 1.** Changing competitive dynamics of the ethylene oxide business

strategy of the business during early 1970s. Each subsidiary was self-sufficient. Each subsidiary operated with a dedicated plant and its own marketing and sales force. Most subsidiaries, however, had a continuing dependence on headquarters for R&D and technology, even though their dependence varied. While headquarters still approved all capital budgets, especially budgets for plant and equipment, the decisions were primarily made by the subsidiaries. While subsidiaries were dependent on headquarters for aspects of their operations, the *relative balance of power* in decision-making rested with the subsidiaries. With the change in the nature of the business – due to technological changes and the investments made by competitors – that relationship had to change. For example, no single subsidiary could absorb the output of a new plant with 150 million pounds of capacity. The output had to be shared among two to five subsidiaries, which till then were quite autonomous. The need for central coordination of outputs, logistics, transfer prices, market forecasts, and raw material purchases meant that subsidiaries could not be autonomous and that they had to coordinate their decisions with other subsidiaries. Headquarters had to take on that role. More importantly, the capital costs of bringing a large plant on stream represented a different level of risk to the corporation, further reinforcing a stronger role for the headquarters staff. The change in the nature of the business, and as a consequence the change in strategy, forced a necessary change in the relationship between the headquarters (business group) and the subsidiary managers. Subsidiary managers had to give up their autonomy in a variety of decisions, and their roles had to change. The business manager and his staff at headquarters had to learn new ways of managing their relationships with subsidiaries.

Strategic redirection of the type described above would not take place unless the underlying organizational relationships between subsidiaries and headquarters were altered. The balance of power had to tilt from the subsidiaries to the business group.

## Managing for flexibility

While strategic redirection often involves the process of reorienting the relationships between headquarters and subsidiaries, flexibility requires the ability to *shift between orientations*, almost on a decision-by-decision basis.

The dilemma for DMNCs in a wide variety of businesses is clear. The desire to build and leverage global market positions and technology forces DMNCs to consolidate manufacturing and technical resources to obtain overall cost savings. A consistent direction and goals to guide the actions of subsidiaries is seen as a must. On the other hand, that ideal is constantly challenged by the persistent demands imposed on the business by host countries. The goals of a host country may be at variance with the goals of the DMNC, as we have seen in Chapter 4. Further, host country demands may never stand still. The public switching business is an obvious example. The technology-intensity of this business forces DMNCs like LM Ericson, Siemens, ITT, Northern Telecom, and AT&T to be globally integrated. On the other hand, in most of the world, PTT departments controlled by governments are the main customers for public switching equipment. Telecommunications is also a defense-sensitive business. As a result, in almost every country, governments seek to and do influence the choice of specifications, location of manufacturing, and pricing of such equipment. In order to sell switching equipment, subsidiaries must be seen to have a 'local face' and must be sensitive to the demands – both current and anticipated – of host governments. The perspective of subsidiary managers who constantly interface with host government officials is an important input to strategy making. On the other hand, the need to maintain a local face can lead to duplication of resources – duplicating manufacturing locations or building plants with a scale that is suboptimal, sourcing components from local vendors – and increases in costs. That often is the price for accessing markets such as telecommunications.

The inherent conflict between economic and political imperatives often turns the management process into an advocacy process, with the subsidiaries presenting and providing a country perspective and the business managers and the headquarter staff providing and defending a global perspective. The need for flexible, country-specific approaches must be balanced with maintaining a cost-competitive base of global operations. A constant dialog between managers, a process of internal negotiations, and flexibility become key. In a sense, managing businesses that occupy the 'High-High' position in the IR framework needs a different organizational capability from that of a global business. Organizations must allow both the country and the global perspectives to emerge and be visible. Decisions may favor one or the other perspective, and the slant toward either may depend on the nature of the problem. A very big order from China and India for public switching may force the DMNC to accommodate the interests of the host governments; on the other hand, a similar request from Kenya or Sri Lanka may be rejected. The strategic decision process must be flexible, suggesting that relationships between headquarters and subsidiaries must also be kept flexible.

## The managerial dilemma

Organizing for strategic control would itself be a large-scale managerial undertaking in a DMNC. If we add to that the need for anticipating and responding to strategic changes and skills for flexibly responding to opportunities, the complexity of the managerial task is compounded. The three tasks demand very different and often conflicting sets of managerial skills as shown in Table 2. It is obvious from the table that top managers cannot overemphasize any one of those tasks. If a business in a DMNC was well geared to 'control' – to implement a given strategy – then it may find itself hard pressed to anticipate and change strategic direction. Excellence in execution requires very clear delineation of roles between headquarters and subsidiaries and a clear balance of power between the two groups. However, strategic change requires undoing the existing relationships and establishing a new set of relationships – or establishing a new balance of power. Flexibility may require an inbuilt ambiguity of power relationships that allows for different groups – product managers,

**Table 2**   The variety of managerial tasks

| Managerial criteria | Control | Change | Flexibility |
| --- | --- | --- | --- |
| Purpose | To implement a given strategy | To modify a given strategy, develop a new strategy | To be opportunistic within the framework of an overall strategy |
| Task | Identify and implement a set of HQ–sub roles | Change the existing set of HQ–sub roles to meet the demands of new strategy | Create adequate room for continuous readjustment of HQ–sub roles based on the merits of the case |
| Measure of accomplishment | Efficiency of implementation | Ease of change | Extent of flexibility |

country managers, and functional managers – to take leadership in sponsoring different issues that affect the total business.

*Limits to formal structure*

Traditionally, managers confronted with the need to develop organizations capable of maintaining a delicate balance among strategic control, the ability to redirect strategy, and a capability for flexible response fall back upon formal structural solutions. Formal organization structures like the product or area organization forms represented in Figure 2 are used. In our experience, such traditional structures fall far short of the needs of managing a global business, save for a few very specific cases.

A product or an area organization imparts great clarity to the tasks that need to be performed as well as the roles and responsibilities of the headquarters and subsidiaries in getting them done. For example, a worldwide product structure focuses attention of managers on maintaining product and technological superiority and overall cost management. While it enables the management group to focus on worldwide operations, such a structure often induces a level of insensitivity among headquarters managers to local and national differences and host government demands. Managers tend to minimize or ignore the need for product adaptation and customized marketing approaches.

A traditional product organization, in its 'pure form,' is intended to leverage global integration opportunities at the cost of local responsiveness. It is an appropriate organizational form if managers can make a one-time choice on which factors to leverage (and which to ignore) for gaining and sustaining competitive advantage. This pure form is an efficient form of organization if the business is not too complex and permits those one-time choices to be

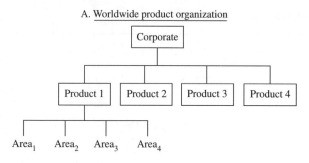

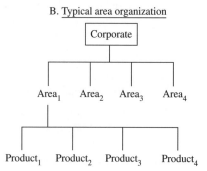

**Figure 2.** Formal organization structures

made. Further, we assume that if there are tradeoffs to be made between global integration and local responsiveness needs, they are few and far between. Given those simplifying assumptions, a unidimensional structure (one that leverages a single dimension in the IR grid) like the product organization is appropriate. The choice of such an organizational form also assumes that senior managers are willing to sacrifice strategic flexibility in favor of strategic control and efficiency of implementation of simple strategies. Such a choice also renders strategic redirection very traumatic, as significant structural changes will be needed before a new set of headquarters-subsidiary relationships, consistent with the new strategy, are built.

The choice of a pure area form of organization represents a similar unidimensional strategic choice on the part of management. While such a structure allows managers to become locally responsive, the ability to coordinate strategies (leveraging the global integration needs of the business) is sacrificed.

Such choices as worldwide product division structures or area structures – the unidimensional and pure forms shown in Figure 2 are extremely limiting in executing complex strategies. Even when the businesses are not very complex, they do not necessarily allow for strategic flexibility or ease of strategic redirection.

# Reorganization is not the answer

Often firms lose competitiveness in business because they cannot respond flexibly to problems and opportunities. For example, a business organized as a worldwide product organization is likely to miss opportunities in markets where product adaptation is a must or where a level of local manufacturing would help politically. Either action is unlikely, given the logic of low-cost, global standards, and uniform policies across markets, a hallmark of a pure product organization. Managers who perceive organizational choices in 'pure' form – either product or area – are likely to respond to the loss of competitiveness by reorganizing the business as an area organization. While that allows them to focus on local opportunities, over time it reduces the ability of the organization to coordinate strategies around the world. Further, such drastic shifts in structure are traumatic in terms of human cost. Conceiving organizational choices in pure structural terms, and as a binary choice – product or area organization – is often a self-inflicted restriction.

As the complexity of the businesses increases because of the nature of competition as well as the pressures imposed by customers and governments, managers have to learn to develop and implement complex strategies. At the same time, managers must explicitly examine the tradeoffs between local needs and global integration demands on an ongoing basis. Explicit considerations of the tradeoffs has become a necessity.

A variety of hybrid organizational arrangements is possible between the 'pure' form and a multifocal or a matrix organization, where the perspectives of both the area and the product are explicitly and continuously examined. We can discern at least three intermediate steps between a 'pure' form and a global matrix:[1]

1 When the businesses are not very complex or when the tradeoffs between area and global product management perspectives are not often an issue, senior management can take on the role of actively managing the substance of the decisions requiring such a tradeoff. For example, in a business operating with an area structure, senior managers could, on specific issues, request staff groups to present an alternative solution to those proposed by the area managers. Typically, issues like location of manufacturing, product launch strategies, structuring of marketing and sales forces, and choice of technology provide opportunities for substantive arbitration by top management. Essentially, the approach assumes that the organization will operate with the 'pure' form, with the provision that any time an important issue is identified and there is a disagreement among managers representing various interests, top managers will make the decision based on the presentations of the interested groups. That allows top managers to exercise control over critical issues. The mechanism is activated only on an 'exception' basis, when the interested groups cannot resolve the issue within the framework of the

organization. However, if not carefully managed, this can lead to top management overload. Further, top managers can become overly reliant on groups that are advocating fairly parochial views.

2 When the complexity of decisions or the frequency with which they have to be resolved increases, top managers can delegate the responsibility to trusted aides who are responsible for decision arbitration. Those trusted aides act as 'integrators' – sensitive to the needs and perspectives of the various groups and at the same time to the overall strategic vision of the firm and its businesses. Geographical units (area managers), product groups (headquarters), and functional groups (manufacturing, R&D) must depend on the arbitrators for some aspect of their operations if the arbitrators are to be effective. Further, a lot of the arbitrator's power comes from proximity to the top management of the firm. LM Ericsson, a Swedish manufacturer of telecommunications equipment, used that approach extensively. The company had operations in more than forty countries. The key product divisions – transmissions, switching, telephones, and accessories – were all located in Sweden, as was the R&D group. The area groups had no direct contact with the production division in Sweden, and vice versa. Contact was managed through the offices of the area marketing vice presidents, who controlled all the traffic of information between the various groups. Since each group, while autonomous, depended on the area marketing vice president for product and market access, he was able to arbitrate and establish priorities. He provided the first-level screening of all the critical issues for top management. LM Ericsson succeeded by using that approach, because it operated in a single industry environment where governments were the primary customers, resulting in a complex and relatively slow decision environment, and where product development cycles were long. The approach also is likely to suffer from an overload.

3 When the complexity of decisions and the frequency with which they have to be made increase, top managers have no choice but to withdraw from direct intervention and find other mechanisms, such as temporary coalition management. This approach is based on the assumption that the role of top managers in such situations can be only that of influencing the decision process rather than the decision itself, as in a 'substantive decision management' approach. Top managers can influence the decision processes by selectively including and excluding individuals in *ad hoc* teams organized to recommend specific key decisions. Task forces, committees, project teams, and working parties are but a few of the common variations of this approach. Firms like Brown Boveri, whose basic management structure was totally oriented to area management, used this approach frequently to focus the attention of the organization on issues that transcended area concerns. Decisions regarding product development priorities, design, and technology choices were subjects that lent themselves to the approach. Paradoxically, for this approach to work, the management systems and the focus of managers

must be broad. If the management systems overwhelmingly reinforce the area or the product perspective, task forces intended to resolve issues that require a careful balancing of both perspectives are unlikely to be successful. In other words, we have in effect moved away from a 'pure' organizational form at this stage.

When the businesses become extremely complex, and when the tradeoffs have to be made constantly, senior managers must ensure that the two perspectives of area and product are constantly and explicitly balanced. That leads to a matrix or a multifocal organization, meaning that the two focal points of gaining strategic advantage – local responsiveness and global integration – are explicitly examined and balanced.

Except in very simple businesses, a 'pure' organizational choice, be it area or product, is unlikely to be appropriate. In order to consider both local responsiveness and global integration needs, top managers can apply a series of 'Band-Aids' to the 'pure' form (as shown in Figure 3), moving from personal involvement in key decisions based on information provided by groups in contention over the issue (substantive decision mode), to delegating the job to a trusted aide and using that person as a screening device (substantive decision arbitration), to the use of *ad hoc* groups to study a specific issue (creating temporary coalitions). While the formal structure may remain the same, the decision-making process, with each one of these 'Band-Aids,' takes on a different color. The perspective in decision-making moves from one of leveraging a single perspective (unidimensional 'pure' organizations) to adding increasingly

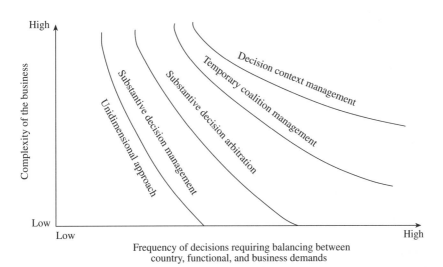

Frequency of decisions requiring balancing between
country, functional, and business demands

**Figure 3.** Evolution of Organizational Complexity. *Source:* Y. Doz, C. Bartlett, and C. K. Prahalad, 'Global Competitive Pressures and Host Country Demands: Managing Tensions in MNCs,' *California Management Review*, Spring 1981, Vol. XXIII, No. 3, pp. 63–74.

heavy doses of multiple and often conflicting perspectives. Further, these 'Band-Aids' provide increasingly sophisticated mechanisms for resolving those conflicts. As business complexity increases, managers have no choice but to move to a complex organizational arrangement, such as a global matrix.

## Managing in the global matrix

Most often, managers tend to resist the idea of moving into a global matrix organization, even if the nature of the business decisions – the complexity and frequency with which the tradeoffs between global and local issues have to be explicitly resolved – demand such an approach. Trained to think in terms of 'pure' organizational models – the area and the product forms – managers find it difficult to think of organizational forms where 'responsibilities are not clearly defined' or 'it is not clear who reports to whom or who is boss'. Managers often complain about the inefficiencies of the matrix such as delays in decision-making. However, if we evaluate the appropriateness of an organizational arrangement using the criteria we have developed in this chapter – a balance among ease of strategic control, efficiency of strategic redirection, and capacity for flexible response – no pure form of organization will meet the test.

## A concept of complex organizations

In our experience, most of the difficulty that managers face in coping with the demands of a complex organization like a global matrix stems from the fact that the concepts managers use to manage such organizations are derived from their experience of simpler forms. A new approach to organizations may be needed before we understand and exploit the opportunities provided by a global matrix.

It is interesting to listen to managers who have had little or no experience with complex organizational arrangements describe a global matrix. They tend to use language like this: 'I have a solid line relationship to the area manager and a dotted line relationship with the product manager.' Or 'I have responsibility for marketing decisions, but I have to consult with the product manager in deciding pricing levels.' If we carefully analyze the concepts that go into formulating such statements, they are derived from experiences in a 'pure line organization.' There is an inbuilt desire to 'fix' clearly the responsibilities and authority for decisions on a one-time basis.

A matrix is not a structure. It is a decision-making culture where multiple and often conflicting points of view are explicitly examined. Conflicts are resolved, ideally, through a process of analysis and on a basis of better problem definition. The relative roles and responsibilities of individuals and groups (e.g. area managers and product managers) may vary, depending on the problem at hand. The matrix is an attempt to track a 'moving competitive target.' Why, then, is there a significant discomfort with complex organizations among managers?

# 17 Corporate culture

## E. Schein

## Introduction

Here Ed Schein sets out the application of his approach to the study of corporate culture through a case study.

## Third year's work: assessing the redirection project

Most of my regular visits subsequent to the third annual meeting were devoted to working with John Lyons, the new director of management development. Stern had been asked to retire as part of the headquarters restructuring. Though I continued to meet with members of the executive committee on redirection matters, the priority shifted to helping Lyons think through his new role and reexamine how the entire process could be improved. Dr Stern was offered, as part of his retirement package, a consultantship with the company provided he developed a research project that could be jointly conducted with me.

We proposed a study of the careers of the top two hundred managers in the company, with the purpose of identifying critical success factors or problems in those careers. The project was approved by the executive committee on condition that I was to act as technical supervisor of the project, reminding me once again that my credibility as a consultant rested heavily on my scientific reputation and that scientific validity was the ultimate decision criterion for the company. The study involved a detailed reconstruction of the careers and revealed surprisingly little geographical, cross-functional, and cross-divisional movement as those careers progressed.

Stern presented these and other results to the executive committee, and this led to a major discussion of how future general managers should be developed. The committee reached a consensus that there should be more early geographical rotation and movement into and out of headquarters, but cross-functional and cross-divisional movement remained a controversial issue. The executive committee members also realized that rotational moves, if they were to be useful, had to occur early in one's career. They decided that such early movement would occur only if a very clear message about the importance of career development went out to the entire organization.

This decision led to the design of a half-day session on management development, which was inserted into the management seminars that are periodically given to the top five hundred managers of the company. A new policy on early rotation was mandated, and the data from the project were used to justify the new policy. Once senior management accepted a conclusion as valid, it was able to move decisively and to impose a proposed solution on the entire company. The message was communicated by having executive committee members at each seminar, but implementation was left to local management.

During this year Maier relinquished the job of chairman of the executive committee for reasons of health, providing a potential succession problem. However, the executive committee had anticipated the problem and had a new chairman and vice-chairman ready. The new chairman was a scientist, but the new vice-chairman was the chief financial officer who had shown great leadership skills during the redirection project. Both of them strongly reaffirmed the scientific and technical assumptions underlying the success of Multi, as if to say, 'We are making major changes, but we are the same kind of cultures as we were before.'

By the end of the third year, the financial results were much better, and the restructuring process in the unprofitable divisions was proceeding rapidly. Each unit learned how to manage early retirements, and a measure of interdivisional cooperation was achieved in the process of placing people who were redundant in one division into other divisions. Initial attitudes were negative, and I heard many complaints from managers that even their best people were not acceptable to other divisions; but this attitude was gradually eroded because the assumption that 'we don't throw people out without maximum effort to find jobs for them' eventually overrode the provincialism of the divisions. Managers who were too committed to the old strategy of running those divisions were gradually replaced with managers who were deemed to be more innovative in their approach. One of the managers of a division that needed to make major reductions and redesign its entire product line was deemed so successful in this project that he was promoted to the executive committee and is today its chairman.

Because the redirection project had fulfilled its functions, it was officially terminated at the end of the third year. Relevant change projects would now be handled by the executive committee, and I was asked to be 'on call' to line managers needing help. The new head of one of the previously unprofitable divisions, for example, wanted help in restoring the morale of those managers who remained after many of their colleagues were retired or transferred to other divisions. He sensed a level of fear and apathy that made it difficult to move forward positively. In true Multi fashion, he had tried to solve this problem on his own by bringing in an outside training program, but it had been unsuccessful. He then requested a meeting with me to seek alternative solutions. Given the Multi culture and this manager's own commitment, it was obvious that he should build his program internally and enlist the aid of the corporate training people, who would know how to design a program that would be culturally congruent. He had never considered using the corporate training group to help him, though he knew of it and liked some of the people in it. I found myself being the broker between two parts of the organization that could have been talking to each other directly. This individual followed up on my suggestion, and in the following year a successful in-house program was developed.

During the following two years my involvement at Multi declined gradually. The head of the redirection project on headquarters reduction has since become the chairman of the board and the former head of the division that needed the most down-sizing has become the chairman of the executive committee. Both of these managers showed their talent in the way they handled their projects. All of the changes were accomplished without any outsiders being brought into Multi. I continued to work with Lyons on management development issues and helped him implement some of his programs. I also worked with the US subsidiary on projects where my knowledge of the culture was considered an asset. Nevertheless, the assumption that one only uses consultants when one has serious problems prevailed. Since 1988 my involvement with Multi has been virtually zero.

# Summary and conclusions

Based on what I observed and have heard, Multi has successfully weathered a major organizational crisis involving many elements of its culture. Let us look at some specifics.

1 The financial trend toward nonprofitability was decisively reversed.
2 Two previously unprofitable divisions restructured themselves by drastically cutting products, facilities, and people and by reorganizing their production and marketing activities to fit the current market and economic realities. One of these divisions was considered a loser, but because of its successful restructuring under a dynamic manager, it is now considered the hero of the company.
3 The functions at corporate headquarters were reduced by 30 to 40 percent, and more line responsibility was delegated to the countries and divisions.
4 The functions in the divisions were also reassessed, and their role was changed in line with headquarters becoming more strategic.
5 The profitable divisions thoroughly reassessed themselves and initiated programs to become more competitive in their particular industries, particularly the pharmaceutical division.

6 Executive committee members restructured their own areas of accountability so that each division, country, and function now has a clear line boss
but one whose focus is strategic. In the previous system, these organizational units had felt accountable to the entire executive committee.

7 A major management succession occurred and was negotiated successfully
in that the new chairman and vice-chairman of the executive committee
were perceived by senior management as good choices, and the two have
been promoted further in recent years.

8 In the three-year change process, many managers who were considered less
effective were weeded out through early retirement, permitting key jobs to
be filled by managers considered more dynamic and effective.

9 Senior managers acquired insight into the ways in which their culture both
constrains and helps them.

10 A major cultural assumption about career stability, particularly at headquarters, was reassessed and abandoned. In that process another major
assumption about dealing with people on an individualized and humane
basis was reaffirmed.

11 Managerial career development was redefined in terms of required rotation
geographically and through headquarters.

12 The consumer goods acquisition that did not fit was reevaluated and the
decision was made to sell it. At the same time the corporate acquisition
policy was clarified to look only for companies based on technologies with
which Multi felt comfortable.

Most managers in Multi undoubtedly would say that they had undergone
some great changes and that many of their assumptions about the world and
the company have changed. However, when one looks closely, the cultural
paradigm of the company has not really changed at all. There is the same bias
toward scientific authority, the hierarchy functions as strongly as ever but with
redefined roles, the assumption that managers do their best job when left alone
to learn for themselves is still very strong, and lateral communication is still
considered mostly irrelevant. For example, there is still no regular meeting of
division heads except at the annual meeting, where they meet with everyone
else, and there are no functional meetings across countries or divisions.

Various projects – for example, to bring in MBAs on a trial basis and to hold
worldwide meetings of functional people, such as the management development coordinators from all the divisions and key countries – are being
advocated, but one senses that they are only tolerated in the culture, not
encouraged. On one of my visits, Lyons arranged for me to meet five of the
MBAs who had been hired into different parts of Multi to see how they were
reacting to their different situations. We had a productive and constructive
meeting. A week later Lyons was criticized by several MBAs' bosses for
organizing the meeting because he was stepping onto the turf of these other
managers, who would not have given permission for such a cross-departmental
group to meet.

I mention all this because when the redirection project began, we all talked of culture change. To label a change as cultural change enhances the drama of what is happening, so it may have some motivational value even if it is inaccurate. At the same time, it focuses people on the culture so that they can identify both the constraints and the enhancing features of the culture. The important thing to note, however, is that considerable change can take place in an organization's operations without the basic cultural paradigm changing at all. In fact, some of the assumptions could not have changed but for the even stronger action of deeper assumptions. Thus, some parts of the culture helped many of the changes to happen in other parts of the culture. In a study of major changes in large corporations, Donaldson and Lorsch (1983) report something very similar. The basic deep beliefs of management did not change but actually were used to fuel the changes that the organizations needed to make to become more adaptive and effective.

This insight leads to a further point. Many assumptions surrounding mission, goals, means, measurement systems, roles, and relationships can be superficial within the total structure of the cultural paradigm yet be very important to the organization's day-to-day functioning. The assumption that the headquarters functional groups had worldwide responsibility for tracking everything was not a very deep assumption within the whole Multi culture, but it was having a major impact on business performance and managerial morale in the country companies. Changing some of these superficial assumptions was crucial to Multi's effective adaptation. The deeper assumptions may drive the whole process but may not have to change.

It should also be noted that the deeper assumptions are not necessarily functional. Multi's commitment to science continued to be manifested in commitment to scientists, especially some of the older ones who had helped the company become successful. In one extreme case such a person was a country manager who was performing poorly in that role. A more skillful general manager had been groomed to take over in this country, but the decision to give him authority was held up for two full years in order to let the scientist retire at his originally scheduled time. It was felt that to force him into early retirement would not only be destructive to him but would send an incorrect signal to the rest of the organization.

What, then, really happened in the redirection project and why? Many in the company have also asked this question in order to understand the reasons for the success of the change effort. My own observation is that the effort was successful because the executive committee (1) sent a clear message that a change was needed, (2) involved itself fully in the change process, (3) tackled the impossible job of reducing headquarters staff as well as the power of the functional groups, and (4) thereby not only created involvement and ownership down the line in the country groups but made it clear that operational problems would increasingly be delegated downward. Even though lateral communication is still minimal, the vertical channels were opened wider.

Financial information was shared more than before, suggestions rising through the project structure were listened to, and proposals that were accepted were effectively implemented through the existing hierarchy as a result of clear top-down signals.

Two additional reasons why the redirection project was successful were that the project was designed with an externalized steering committee that created project groups with consultants and challenger managers and the design provided clear goals, timetables, and time off to work on the problem, reflecting skills embedded in the Multi culture. The organization knew very well how to design group projects and work in groups. In this sense Multi used its cultural strength to redirect itself more rapidly than might have been possible in a less structured organization or one less sensitive to group process issues.

On the original issue that Maier asked me to address, the stimulation of innovation, very little change has taken place from my point of view. However, the culture of Multi works, so one cannot readily assume that some other way would be better.

The driving force and many of the key insights behind this change effort came from Maier, who as mentioned before was the kind of leader who could step outside of his own culture and assess it realistically. The willingness of the chief financial officer and various division managers to step outside their own subcultures and learn some new approaches also played a key role. But in the end the culture changed only in peripheral ways by restructuring some key assumptions. Nevertheless, such peripheral culture change is often sufficient to solve major organizational problems.

# Reference

Donaldson, G. and Lorsch, J. W. (1983) *Decision Making at the Top*. Basic Books, New York.

Reproduced from Schein, E. H. (1992) *Organizational Culture and Leadership*. Jossey-Bass, Inc.

# Index

Notes: Figures (page numbers in **bold** type) and tables (page numbers in *italics*) are shown separately only when not included in page references to text. Subheadings in **bold** type indicate contributions to this volume